I dwell in Possibility —
A fairer House than Prose —
More numerous of Windows —
Superior — for Doors —

Emily Dickinson, "I Dwell in
Possibility" (Johnson, Poem #657)

Designs for Disciplines

An Introduction to Academic Writing

Edited by
**Steven C. Roe and
Pamela H. den Ouden**

Canadian Scholars' Press Inc.   Toronto

Designs for Disciplines: An Introduction to Academic Writing
edited by Steven C. Roe and Pamela H. den Ouden

First published in 2003 by
Canadian Scholars' Press Inc.
180 Bloor Street West, Suite 801
Toronto, Ontario
M5S 2V6

www.cspi.org

CSPI gratefully acknowledges financial support for our publishing activities from the Government of Canada through the Book Publishing Industry Development Program (BPIDP) and the Government of Ontario through the Ontario Book Initiative.

National Library of Canada Cataloguing in Publication Data

    Designs for disciplines : an introduction to academic writing / edited by Steven C. Roe and Pamela H. den Ouden.

Includes bibliographical references and index.
ISBN 978-1-55130-244-7

    1. English language—Rhetoric. 2. English language—Grammar. 3. Academic writing. I. Roe, Steven C. (Steven Charles), 1960- II. Den Ouden, Pamela H.

PE1408.R647 2003   808'.042   C2003-903673-1

Cover design by Drew Hawkins
Cover art: David James, "Interlace Mandala" from his book *Celtic Designs: An Arts and Crafts Source Book*, first published by Blandford Press, 1997; 4th printing Orion Books, 2001. Text design and layout by Brad Horning

Printed and bound in Canada

Canada

MIX
Paper from
responsible sources
FSC www.fsc.org **FSC® C004071**

We dedicate this book to our families:
thank you for your constant support and encouragement.

S. R. — For Jane, Paul, and Julia

P.D. — For Fred, Diana, Jadon, and Jordan

Table of Contents

Copyright
Acknowledgements

Baxter, Colleen. "Pete." Unpublished paper. Used by permission of the author.

Davies, Richard C. "'Thrice-Told Tales': The Exploration Writing of John Franklin." *The Canadian North: Essays in Culture and Literature*. The Nordic Association for Canadian Studies Text Series. Vol. 5. Eds., Jorn Carlsen and Bengt Streijffert. Lund: Lund UP, 1989. 15–26.

den Ouden, Pamela. "'My Uttermost Valleys': Patriarchal Fear of the Feminine in Robert Service's Poetry and Prose." *The Northern Review: A Multidisciplinary Journal of the Arts and Social Sciences of the North* 19 (Winter 1998): 113–121.

Didion, Joan. "At the Dam." *The White Album*. New York: Washington Square, 1979. 197–200.

Dressler, Laurie. "Harnessing the Peace: Environmental and Economic Themes Amid Public Responses to the Construction of the Bennett Dam, 1957–1968." Unpublished paper. Used by permission of the author.

Gallagher, Bernard. "Reading Between the Lines: Stephen King and Allegory." From *The Gothic World of Stephen King: Landscape of Nightmares*, by Gary Hoppenstand. Madison: U of Wisconsin P, 1987. 37–48.

Grant, Shelagh. "Myths of the North in the Canadian Ethos." *The Northern Review* 3–4 (1989): 15–41.

Hamer, David. "The Effect of Light Intensity, Heat, and Herbicide on Photosynthesis." Unpublished paper. Used by permission of the author.

Harper, Heather. "A 'Clumsy, Ugly, Goat-Skin Umbrella': Domestic Mercantilism in *Robinson Crusoe*. Unpublished paper. Used by permission of the author.

Herrero, Stephen, and Andrew Higgins. "Human Injuries Inflicted by Bears in British Columbia: 1960–97." *Ursus* 11 (1999): 209–218.

Keller, James R. "Masculinity and Marginality in *Rob Roy* and *Braveheart*." *The Journal of Popular Film and Television* 24 (1997): 146–151.

Langenau, Edward, Jr., et al. "Attitudes toward Oil and Gas Development among Forest Recreationists." *Journal of Leisure Research* 16.2: 161–177.

Mitchell, Jennifer. "Indian Princess #134: Cultural Assimilation at St. Joseph's Mission." Unpublished paper. Used by permission of the author.

Smyth, Heather. "'Lords of the World': Writing Gender and Imperialism on Northern Space in C.C. Vyvyan's *Arctic Adventure.*" *Studies in Canadian Literature* 23.1 (1998): 32–52.

Theberge, Nancy. "A Feminist Analysis of Responses to Sports Violence: Media Coverage of the 1987 World Junior Hockey Championship." *Sociology of Sport Journal* 6.3 (1989): 247–256.

Cover art

Thanks to David James for the cover art work, "Interlace Mandala," from his book *Celtic Designs: An Arts and Crafts Source Book*, first published by Blandford Press, 1997; 4th printing Orion Books, 2001.

Personal
Acknowledgements

Our work has been made possible by the extraordinary students we have learned with over the years. In addition, we are grateful to colleagues who generously shared their time and disciplinary experience. We would also like to express our appreciation for the help provided by the dedicated people at Canadian Scholars' Press.

Preface

> At the heart of all the curriculum changes is the attempt to be more
> explicit and concrete about precisely what students are learning.
> — Moira Farr, "The Brave New B.A.,"
> *University Affairs,* March 2000

Designs for Disciplines: An Introduction to Academic Writing is designed for composition courses that focus on academic writing. By and large, English composition courses have always professed to be about "academic writing," but that phrase has been defined loosely, to mean writing that demonstrates such qualities as critical thinking, intellectual curiosity, and a certain elegance or sophistication. Celebrating this general view of academic writing, Virginia Woolf, the great British author, referred to "the man or woman of thoroughbred intelligence who rides his mind at a gallop across the country in pursuit of an idea" (Enck, 1964, p. 2).

Envisioned on these grounds, academic writing embodies a relatively brief public performance that is intended to entertain or persuade. The writer is an intellectual aristocrat, a thoughtful individual who addresses and moves the masses. Broadly defined, academic writing can include anything from the witty observations of Woody Allen to the learned reflections of David Suzuki. Accordingly, students in English composition courses have been nurtured on a diet of popular journalism. Traditional anthologies such as *The Broadview Reader* (1987), *Canadian Content* (1996), *True North* (1999), and *Words in Common* (1999) tend to recycle an array of essays and authors that are grouped under broad "rhetorical modes" such as narration, description, division, comparison and contrast, process analysis, and so on. Students, in turn, have been asked to experiment with such modes in a series of short essays. Such assignments, which tend to have remedial undertones, demonstrate a general notion of literacy.

Here, we have tried to do something different. The material that follows takes a "more explicit and concrete" (Farr, 2000, p. 24) approach to academic writing by focusing on the writing that instructors and students actually engage in as members of academic disciplines ranging from anthropology to women's studies. Approached in this way, academic writing is a more specialized form of communication aimed at a more limited audience. Such writing reflects the voices and practices of scholarly communities that are dedicated to the pursuit of knowledge. Accordingly, this textbook, like a few others, raises the bar for expectations in composition courses. Discipline-based research articles take the place of popular journalism, and those basic rhetorical modes are situated amid other stylistic considerations that permit a finer, more nuanced analysis of "real" academic writing. Moreover, as the curriculum becomes narrower and deeper, remedial aims fall by the wayside. Students themselves are asked to think and work in an environment that can foster something other than short personal essays or four-week "term papers" on worn-out, general subjects. Indeed, first-year students are given the opportunity to engage in an original, sustained research project, which, upon completion, more closely resembles the kind of professional academic writing that is published in discipline-based books and journals.

This more focused approach to academic writing is rooted in the Writing Across the Curriculum movement of the 1970s. Bazerman and Russell (1994) trace the movement back to "the British classroom

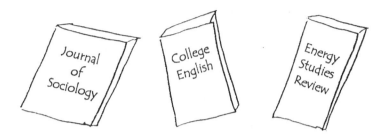

research" of James Britton and his colleagues at the London School of Education. Bazerman and Russell note that Britton's innovations included composition courses that introduced students to the kinds of writing done not only in English, but in other academic disciplines. These so-called *interdisciplinary* courses were taught by faculty or teaching assistants from English departments, but instructors from other disciplines were often invited to talk about writing in their area. Britton was guided by pragmatic objectives. His vision of academic writing involved neither remediation nor literary elegance. Instead, Britton wanted to teach the *real* writing of *real* students and professors in disciplinary settings (p. 5). Furthermore, Bazerman and Russell explain that, in the United States, the Writing Across the Curriculum movement was informally launched by Janet Emig's 1977 essay "Writing as a Mode of Learning," which claims that discipline-based knowledge is constructed through discipline-based ways of writing. From this perspective, "[s]tudents should not only learn to write but write to learn" (Bazerman & Russell, 1994, p. 5). Interest in writing across the curriculum has now developed to a point where interdisciplinary, non-remedial writing courses (supplemented by writing centres) are increasingly common at colleges and universities throughout North America.

Evidence of this curricular transformation is not hard to find. In "Why Johnny Can't Write, Even Though He Went to Princeton," an article that appeared in *The Chronicle of Higher Education*, Thomas Bartlett (2003, January 3) notes that major American universities have become increasingly dissatisfied with traditional approaches to composition courses. According to Bartlett, "professors cite a host of writing-related shortcomings among students, most often their inability to construct the sort of lengthy, sophisticated research papers required in upper-division courses" (p. A59). In response to the problem, a number of institutions now emphasize "writing in the disciplines, rather than a more general approach" (p. A39). Similar developments have recently occurred in Canada. The University of British Columbia (UBC), for example, offers a modified version of its traditional first-year composition course, English 112, presenting "an intensive focus on disciplinary discourse and academic writing. Twenty-eight instructors participated in the experiment and presented the new curriculum to about 1,600 first-year students" (Deer, 2000). The pilot project was successful, and the academically focused version of English 112 has found a place in UBC's curriculum.

The rise of discipline-based composition is underscored by a recent report entitled *A Review of the Proficiencies Required by Students Entering First Year Post-Secondary English Courses* (1999). This study identifies grammatical competence and a basic understanding of the essay as "a shaped piece of writing with a thesis and supporting evidence as necessary *prerequisites* [italics added] to successful performance in first-year English" (n.p.). The report goes on to state that "Students who make the transition between high school and post-secondary institutions engage, sometimes literally, but always metaphorically, in a journey: the academy is a domain of language use, and students come in as foreigners to the academy. . . . If one examines academic articles in any discipline, language differences become apparent: academic language consists largely of hypotheses, arguments, and evidence; of sources cited and evaluated; of standardized English; and of extensive vocabulary and jargon. It usually assumes an impersonal tone. New immigrants to the academy often grossly underestimate the time required to learn the language and the customs" (*Review*, 1999, p. 1). It is this transition—from a "deficit-driven" definition of writing competence based on grammar, spelling, and punctuation, to a "process-driven" redefinition of writing competence in terms of the knowledge-making practices within disciplines—that characterizes the changing face of composition.[1]

While our own work has been influenced by the innovative community of scholars who teach and research writing-in-the-disciplines, we owe a special debt to Janet Giltrow (2002, 3rd ed.; 1994, 2nd ed.), author of the highly acclaimed *Academic Writing: Writing and Reading in the Disciplines* and *Academic Writing: Writing and Reading Across the Disciplines*. Our book resembles hers in some fundamental ways, and we sometimes borrow terminology that Giltrow uses to identify the peculiar features of academic writing. Yet whereas Giltrow provides a theoretically sophisticated, socio-cognitive approach that highlights the experiential *process* of writing and reading scholarly prose, we have stressed what might be regarded as the "surface features of text" (Swales, 1990, p. 148). Thus, readers may detect a more pronounced structuralist orientation in that we place considerable emphasis on identifying and mapping the distribution of specific stylistic features throughout an academic article. Our effort to provide a classification of parts (that is, a taxonomy) incurs certain risks: most notably, perhaps, one might say that we have replaced the old rhetorical-modes formula with another kind of product-driven formula. However valid such an observation may be, we believe that the new formula is more challenging, more open to selective and flexible implementation than the old one. Moreover, like Giltrow, we believe that the "stylistic qualities which tax our capacities to name them are more than skin-deep. . . . That the 'originality' academic readers value *depends on style* — on the typical ways of speaking that produce certain kinds of knowledge of the world" (Giltrow, 2002, p. 9). Finally, our classroom experience has taught us that even the keenest students benefit from structural guidelines — that formal patterns can be enabling devices rather than hindrances.

Designs for Disciplines: An Introduction to Academic Writing is arranged as follows. Chapter 1 provides a theoretical foundation by exploring contemporary ideas about genre. Chapter 2 explores personal essays as a genre that most students are already familiar with. The rest of the book is devoted to a sustained inquiry into academic writing, dealing primarily with disciplines in the humanities and social sciences. By adopting this interdisciplinary perspective, we do not mean to underestimate significant differences between, say, the discourse of literary criticism and that of sociology. We do, however, feel that the humanities and social sciences have enough in common to permit shared treatment.[2] Chapters 3, 4, and 5 discuss preliminary matters such as research, note-taking, summarizing, and drafting a proposal. The epicentre of the book — Chapters 6, 7, and 8 — traces the development of scholarly papers through introductions, core paragraphs,[3] and conclusions. Chapter 9 briefly addresses writing in the sciences; Chapter 10 covers revision and proofreading.

Throughout, instructional commentary is accompanied by annotated passages that illustrate aspects of academic style. Moreover, virtually every chapter ends with an article or two that invite further stylistic analysis. Choosing the articles has not been an easy task. The selections here do not pursue a particular theme, although some readers may detect a bias toward topics that might be grouped under the heading of cultural studies. In any event, we have tried to select articles and excerpts, some of which have been written by students, that our audience will find challenging, intelligible, and engaging. At an instructor's discretion, our choices can be supplemented or replaced by others.

In sum, *Designs for Disciplines* will not ask readers to consider personal comparisons of snow boarding and skiing, or of Edmonton and Calgary, nor will it provide Peter Gzowski's own account of how to make his favourite stew. This text is fundamentally different from the multitude of texts that do just that. Instead, readers will undertake a careful examination of real academic writing on subjects ranging from bear attacks to the poetry of Robert Service. Such examples provide opportunities to learn about the value of focused inquiry and how it can accommodate abstraction and generalization, about explicit announcements of topic and thesis, about the careful acknowledgement of previous studies, about the role of theory and methods, about the attribution of detail through ongoing documentation, and about mixed attitudes toward the recognition of subjectivity in the construction of knowledge. Thus, what follows is founded on a belief that composition is not the poor cousin of literature, and that composition classes can be places for meaningful and exciting intellectual inquiry rather than mass holding tanks where students practise schoolroom exercises.

Granted, becoming an accomplished writer in any *one* discipline requires years of training, yet the interdisciplinary considerations presented in writing-across-the-curriculum classrooms provide relevant and viable starting points for students who arrive in composition classes with different educational goals (Faigley and Hansen, Freed and Broadhead; as cited in Swales, 1990, pp. 3–5, 23). In virtually every composition class, career plans will be as diverse as the people themselves, but for future engineers and teachers, accountants and social workers, scientists and foresters, for learners on the road to academic and professional specialization, this is a good place to begin.

Steve Roe
Pamela den Ouden
March 2003

NOTES

1. Graves (as cited in *Review of proficiencies*, pp. 5–7) notes that approaches to writing are often "deficit-driven" or "process-driven."

2. Treating the humanities and social sciences together may raise the prospect of an uneasy partnership, but there are certainly precedents for such treatment. Susan Peck MacDonald's *Professional and Academic Writing in the Humanities and Social Sciences* (1994) provides a recent example:

   > As arenas for knowledge making, disciplinary fields may be ranged roughly on a continuum from compact to diffuse in the ways they define, present, and attempt to solve problems. The terms here — "compact" and "diffuse" — are from Stephen Toulmin, but the distinction involved may be found in a variety of work on academic knowledge making. Kuhn has suggested that agreed-upon problems define the work of normal science, and Toulmin has suggested that there is a continuum from well-defined to diffusely defined problems. Toulmin sees compact fields as characterized by a "sufficiently agreed goal or ideal, in terms of which common outstanding problems can be identified." Diffuse and would-be disciplines, on the other hand, are the type found in the social sciences and humanities, characterized by their "absence of a clearly defined, generally agreed reservoir of disciplinary problems, so that conceptual innovations within them face no consistent critical tests and lack any continuing rational direction. (p. 22)

3. Our term marks a departure from the traditional language of composition, in which the "middle section" of essays or papers is often referred to as the "body," consisting of "body paragraphs." In our examination of the structural contours of texts, we prefer to use a less anatomical metaphor.

REFERENCES

Bartlett, T. (2003, January 2). Why Johnny can't write, even though he went to Princeton. *The Chronicle of Higher Education, 49*(17), A39.

Bazerman, C., & Russell, D.R. (Eds.). (1994). *Landmark essays on writing across the curriculum.* Davis, CA.: Hermagoras.

The Broadview reader (2nd ed.). (1987). H. Rosengarten, & J. Flick (Eds.). Peterborough: Broadview Press.

Canadian content. (1996). N. Waldman, & S. Norton (Eds.). Toronto: Harcourt Brace.

Deer, G. (2000, May). Report for the BC English articulation meeting. New Westminster, BC: Douglas College.

Enck, J. (1964). *Academic discourse.* New York: Appleton.

Farr, M. (2000, March). Brave new B.A. *University Affairs*, pp. 10–13; 24–25.

Giltrow, J. (2002). *Academic writing: Writing and reading in the disciplines* (3rd ed.). Peterborough: Broadview.

MacDonald, S.P. (1994). *Professional and academic writing in the humanities and social sciences*. Carbondale: Southern Illinois University Press.

Review of the proficiencies required by students entering first year post-secondary English courses. (1999, March). Prepared by Virginia Cooke, University College of the Fraser Valley, in collaboration with Ruth Derksen, Centre for Research in Professional and Academic Writing, Simon Fraser University.

Swales, J.M. (1990). *Genre analysis: English in academic and research settings*. Ann Arbor: University of Michigan.

True north: Canadian essays for composition. (1999). J. MacDonald (Ed.). Don Mills: Addison-Wesley.

Words in common: Essays on language, culture, and society. (1999). G. Thomas (Ed.). Halifax: Addison-Wesley.

The Concept of Genre

The strength of the genie comes of being confined in a bottle.
— Anonymous

The word "genre" is French in origin and means type, kind, or style. In English studies, the concept of genre has most often been used to differentiate literary forms. Poetry, for example, constitutes a genre of its own, and within this general category there are a variety of subgenres: epic, ode, dramatic monologue, sonnet, lyric, epigram, and so on. Historically, literary approaches to the concept of genre entail systems of classification. According to M.H. Abrams (1999), "through the Renaissance and much of the eighteenth century, the recognized genres . . . were widely thought to be fixed literary types, somewhat like species in the biological order" (p. 108). Furthermore, as Abrams notes, it was common to rank the various genres and subgenres in hierarchical order (pp. 108-109). The rigid dogma of this ranking system, which, for example, favoured the epic over the lyric, functioned as both a justification and as a disguise for politically based value judgements. Indeed, the supposed superiority of epics indirectly validated aristocratic authority, while the devaluation of the lyric assigned a lesser importance to the private emotions of ordinary citizens.

Today, however, the concept of genre has been revitalized by intellectuals who insist that all language, literary or not, must be evaluated within its social context. In turn, the content and form of diverse language behaviours are seen less as ends in themselves than as reflections of particular circumstances. Thus, contemporary genre theory tells us that forms of written and spoken communication are not higher or lower in any absolute sense, that one form is not intrinsically better than another, only different. It follows that each communicative act should be judged by the way it meets the demands of specific discursive situations. As Carolyn Miller (1984) explains, when we use language, most of the time, we engage in a "social action" that takes place in a "discourse community":

> What we learn when we learn a genre is not just a pattern of forms or even a method of achieving our own ends. We learn, more importantly, what ends we may have: we learn that we may eulogize, apologize, recommend one person to another, instruct customers on behalf of a manufacturer, take on an official role, account for progress in achieving goals. We learn to better understand the situations in which we find ourselves and the potentials for failure and success in acting together. As a recurrent, significant action, a genre embodies an aspect of cultural rationality. For the critic, genres serve as both an index to cultural patterns and as tools for exploring the achievements of particular speakers and writers; for the student, genres serve as keys to understanding how to participate in the actions of a community. (p. 165)

The contemporary concept of genre, therefore, situates notions of concision and grace within particular settings, turning style into both a relative and a pragmatic consideration.

 I like reading Alice Munro because her style is so clear. Why doesn't this rental agreement sound like that?

Such an approach liberates students from the tyranny of right and wrong, exchanging *a priori* rules for situation-based conventions that achieve desired effects. In lifting the burden of absolutism, genre theory also allows for stylistic flexibility: the forms of discursive effectiveness may change just as social conditions and expectations change. "The result," according to Carolyn Miller, "is that the set of genres is an open class, with new members evolving, old ones decaying" (p. 153). Style becomes a matter of choice rooted in social needs.

Composition handbooks frequently acknowledge the principles of genre theory by referring to the importance of "audience." Consider Barbara Fine Clouse's advice in *Patterns for a Purpose* (1995): "The writer of a successful essay will have a clear sense of audience—that is, a clear sense of who the reader is and what that reader is like. A sense of audience is important if the writer is going to fulfill his or her purpose. Suppose you want to write an essay about the pollution in a local river. If the essay were written for your biology class, it might include a great deal of technical information about specific chemical pollutants. However, if the essay were for a letter to your local newspaper, such technical information might overwhelm the average reader" (p. 4). We believe that genre theory intensifies this familiar regard for audience. In some sense, perhaps, the theoretical jargon— "communities of discourse," language as "social action," and so on—highlights context, encouraging a more extended analysis of the relationship between communication and situation. It is not enough, therefore, as a genre critic, to make a relatively simple distinction between technical and nontechnical information. Genre theory guides analysis to a deeper level by asking, for example, *how* technical information is conveyed and *why* it is conveyed in such a manner. Put simply, the contemporary concept of genre calls for a rigorous, sustained inquiry into the social rationale for virtually every aspect of style, reminding us that language is relentlessly situated.

Properly applied, then, genre theory requires a thoughtfulness on the part of instructors and students, a joint commitment to investigate content and form in relation to context. Such an investigation is challenging, to be sure, and it does not always yield certain answers. Yet the perspective that a genre-based approach offers—writing as a social activity rooted in a social context—can make composition more practical and more meaningful. Indeed, students who emerge from such a course should not be simply better writers, but writers who have gained a better awareness of the demands of particular discursive situations.

EXERCISE: LANGUAGE AND SITUATION

The following exercise has been adapted from Janet Giltrow's book *Academic Writing: Writing and Reading in the Disciplines* (2002, pp. 21–26). Read the following passages in light of the contemporary concept of genre. Your analysis should comprise three steps: (1) choose a term or phrase to describe the type of writing at issue; (2) note the social purposes that motivate the writing; (3) comment on how the form and content of each passage are related to the various social situations.

Example 1

*With a love and respect
for the completeness
we shall gain as a couple
and with the blessings of our parents
we will be joined in marriage
on Saturday, the second of August
nineteen hundred and ninety-seven
at two o'clock in the afternoon
Calvary Baptist Church
You are invited to share
This day of happy beginnings
Diana Grace den Ouden
and
Michael Mohninger*

Example 2[1]

Gentle Soul: You're tender-hearted, it's just your nature. In fact, everything you do or say hinges on it. The passionate proof, this dainty pair of dangles of the truest blue turquoise and most poignant purple sugilite. Two tiny hearts swing from ovals, to swirl and sway with your gentlest nods. Friendly reminders for everyone around you of what a sweetheart you are. Each setting, link and post is sterling silver. They measure about 7/8" long and are imported. Colors will vary from stone to stone. [H70540] $19.95 pr.

Example 3[2]

Final examinations will normally be held during the last two weeks of each semester. Examination period dates are outlined in the Academic Calendar of Events, and in the Course Timetable and Exam Schedule mailed each semester to students eligible to register. Students must check the exam schedule when planning course selections. Students are reminded that final examinations may be scheduled at any time during the examination period and that students should avoid making travel or employment arrangements for this period. The student is not allowed to register in courses with conflicting examination times.

Example 4[3]

The Alberta Bump & Grind
machinery constantly thrust pull thrusting
pumps perpetually pump pumping
oil from the earth
standing
forgotten
among fields yellow with wheat
or canola
endlessly reach reach reaching
to scrape metal fingers across the back
of the big blue sky above

and when winter comes
the pumps continue pump pumping
against the cold and the wind
stranded in frozen fields
like teenagers in the back of a truck
stuck in the ditch off a country road
trying
to keep warm

they move, keeping time,
as Alberta bumps and grinds
to the beat
is driven by the rhythm
of the rigs

6

DESIGNS FOR DISCIPLINES

Example 5

Romantic and creative SWF, young-looking, 42, 5'9", 130 lbs., long blonde hair and green eyes. I enjoy movies and music. Seeking a smart, funny, sensitive, and passionate SM, 21-45, N/S. Ad#:1791

Example 6[4]

Hero: He knew what he was doing to get into this safe.

Heroine: Did you try the numbers that Granville gave you?

Hero: Yeh. I tried those earlier. They worked perfectly.

Heroine: Well, you said it was an inside job, maybe they had the combination all the time.

Hero: Just trying to eliminate all the possibilities. Can you check this out for me? (*He gestures to his bow tie.*)

Heroine: Mm. Yes I can. (*He hugs her.*) Mm. Light fingers. Oh, Jonathan.

Hero: Just trying to keep my touch in shape.

Heroine: What about the keys to the door?

Hero: Those keys can't be duplicated because of the code numbers. You have to have the right machines.

Heroine: Well, that leaves the window.

Hero: The porthole.

Heroine: Oh yes. The porthole. I know they are supposed to be charming, but they always remind me of a laundromat.

Hero: I took a peek out of there a while ago. It's about all you can do. It's thirty feet up to the deck even if you could make it down to the window, porthole. You'd have to be a thin man to squeeze through.

Heroine: What do you think? (*She shows her jewelry.*) Enough honey to attract the bees?

Hero: Who knows? They may not be able to see the honey for the flowers.

Heroine: Oh, that's the cutest thing you've ever said to me, sugar. Well, shall we? (*Gestures toward the door.*)

Example 7

Spacious Condo

New West. 2BR, 2 ba, 1217 sf, with private entry, 9 ½ ft ceilings & a grt layout. Finished professionally for an exclusive atmosphere. Immaculate. Amens: swimming pool, sauna, jacuzzi, fitness room, U/G parking, near skytrain & schls. Safe neighbourhood.

Example 8[5]

Can so little success anywhere, on any field of play or in any walk of life, offer such rewards as a golf ball perfectly struck? Golfers know. And never mind the golfer's standard rueful lament. Asked after a round how he played, a golfer can quite rightly answer: "I didn't play my usual game today. Come to think of it, I never play my usual game."

But who needs "usual" games anyway? Golf, and especially late spring golf, when hope still is writ large in the golfer's mind, is about reaching for the unusual, the outer limits of what the golfer can do.

Example 9[6]

In 1954, Frederic Wertham characterized comic books as a *Seduction of the Innocent*. Their lurid sex and graphic violence, he argued, were symptoms of a popular culture that made all manner of delinquency attractive to young people. In particular, Wertham observed that "only someone ignorant of the fundamentals of psychiatry and of the psychopathology of sex can fail to realize a subtle atmosphere of homoeroticism which pervades the adventures of the mature "Batman" and his young friend "Robin." Among the seductive aberrations Wertham (1954) noted were that Bruce Wayne and Dick Grayson "live in sumptuous quarters, with beautiful flowers in large vases" and that "Batman is sometimes shown in a dressing gown," leading him to conclude that the comic "is like a wish dream of two homosexuals living together" (pp. 189–190). Fueled in part by Wertham's book, the United States Senate began investigations, hearings were held, books were burned, and "comic books, once the province of childhood fun and escapism, were being used as fodder for a censorship battle that emulated the self-serving smear tactics of Senator McCarthy" (Vaz, 1989, p. 44). To protect itself both from the bad press and the inevitable economic effects of this attack, the comic book industry developed a self-policing document called the "Comics Code of Authority," a set of moral standards by which the writers and artists would force their characters to live.[1]

1. The most thorough history of Wertham and the Comics Code of Authority is Amy Kiste Nyberg's *Seal of Approval* (1998). The Code is still in effect, and Nyberg includes in her appendix various versions of it.

IDEAS FOR FURTHER STUDY

1. In your own words, formulate a one-sentence, 25-words-or-less definition of genre theory.

2. Select a genre of discourse on your own and analyze how its rhetorical features fit a particular social situation.

CHAPTER NOTES

1. From *Coldwater Creek Catalogue: Signs of Spring* (1998).
2. From *Simon Fraser University Calendar, 2001–2002.* (2001), page 41.
3. From Sheldon Birnie (2002), *Adventures in Amateur Cartography*, page 6.
4. From John Fiske (1998), "Television Culture," pages 1087-8.
5. From Lorne Rubenstein (1996), "Passion Play," pages 32-3.
6. From Robert E. Terrill (2000), "Spectacular Repression: Sanitizing the Batman," page 493.

CHAPTER REFERENCES

Abrams, M.H. (1999). *A glossary of literary terms* (7th ed.). New York: Harcourt Brace College Publishers.

Birnie, S. (2002). *Adventures in amateur cartography*. Dawson Creek, BC: Small Change Press.

Clouse, B.F. (1995). *Patterns for a purpose*. New York: McGraw-Hill.

Coldwater Creek catalogue: Signs of spring. 1998.

Fiske, J. (1998). Television culture. In J. Rivkin & M. Ryan (Eds.), *Literary theory: An anthology* (pp. 1087–1098). Malden, MA: Blackwell.

Giltrow, J. (2002). *Academic writing: Writing and reading in the disciplines* (3rd ed.). Scarborough: Broadview.

Miller, C. (1984). Genre as social action. *Quarterly Journal of Speech, 70,* 151–167.

Rubenstein, L. (1996). Passion play. In N. Waldman & S. Norton (Eds.), *Canadian content* (3rd ed.) (pp. 32–33). Toronto: Harcourt Brace.

Simon Fraser University calendar, 2001–2002. (2001). Burnaby, BC: Simon Fraser University.

Terrill, R.E. (2000). Spectacular repression: Sanitizing the Batman. *Critical Studies in Mass Communication, 17*(4), 493–509.

Personal Essays

> I should not talk about myself if there were anybody else whom I knew as well. Unfortunately, I am confined to this theme by the narrowness of my experience. Moreover, I, on my side, require of every writer, first or last, a simple and sincere account of his own life.
>
> — Henry David Thoreau, *Walden Pond*

In personal essays, writers display their own temperament. Personal thoughts and feelings are front and centre, so that readers are introduced to the emotional texture of the writer's life. Personal essayists may turn inward and examine themselves. In these cases, the personal essay can be a very private, confessional document. Alternatively, personal essayists may look outward and choose to tell us how they feel about the world around them. In these instances, the personal essay is less confessional, but it is still rooted in the expression of individual feelings. Either way, the personal essay as a genre tends to presume a sympathetic relationship between writer and audience. The unguarded nature of such a relationship discourages the formal mannerisms that we associate with technical or academic writing, permitting personal essayists to engage in soul-sharing.

 I want to tell you something about myself. Are you ready to listen?

It's hard to give something like the personal essay a birth date. Some might say that personal essays have been around for as long as human beings have been recording their impressions of life—that prehistoric cave drawings are a version of the personal essay. However, it is possible to be more specific in the search for origins and to see the personal essay as a relatively late phenomenon that is peculiar to Western culture. Commenting on autobiography, a related genre, Georges Gusdorf (1972) claims that "the concern, which seems so natural to us, to turn back on one's own past, to recollect one's life in order to narrate it, is not at all universal. It asserts itself only in recent centuries and only on a small part of the map of the world. [Those] who [take] delight in thus drawing [their] own image [believe themselves] worthy of a special interest" (p. 19). According to Gusdorf, this interest in the personal, in the experience of individual lives, emerged during the European Renaissance, in countries such as France and Italy, from the fourteenth to the sixteenth century. If we were to entertain Gusdorf's thesis, the mysterious expression of Leonardo Da Vinci's *Mona Lisa* (1562) would provide a visual analogue for a new cultural interest in individual personalities. Or perhaps it would be even more fitting to find a later parallel in Rembrandt's obsession with *self*-portraiture (1631–1661).

What might have caused this purportedly new awareness of selfhood? The historical era at issue was typified by an extraordinary outpouring of scientific, geographical, artistic, and spiritual exploration. Indirectly, perhaps, this spirit of inquiry gave a new authority to individual perception. Renaissance physicians, for example, admired the accuracy of classical anatomists "but learned to rely on the evidence of their own eyes" (Jansen, 1977, p. 351). Similarly, the personal essayist is a writer who assumes that personal reality matters.

Looking for specific examples of the personal essay, we could turn to Julian of Norwich's *A Book of Showings* (1393), in which the author discusses her personal revelation about Christ. Among Renaissance writers, Michel de Montaigne (1533–1592), a French philosopher, is probably the most celebrated personal essayist. Around 1575, Montaigne published *The Essays*, a collection of relatively short, highly personal prose compositions in which he contemplates everything from his own sense of idleness to the education of children. In a preliminary note to the reader, Montaigne writes: "thou hast here an honest book . . . I have proposed to myself no other than a domestic and private end. . . . I have dedicated it to the particular commodity of my kinsfolk and friends, so . . . they may therein recover some traits of my conditions and humours, and by that means preserve more whole, and more life-like, the knowledge they had of me. . . . I desire therein to be viewed as I appear in mine own genuine, simple, and ordinary manner, without study or artifice: for it is myself I paint. . . . Thus, reader, [I] myself am the matter of my book" (p. 1).

Montaigne's precedent was followed by Jean-Jacques Rousseau, who published his *Confessions* (1781–1788). Shortly thereafter, Mary Wollstonecraft (1792) published *A Vindication of the Rights of Woman*, a personal essay on the position of women in society. In eighteenth-century England, Joseph Addison and Richard Steele became famous for publishing witty and widely read personal essays in coffeehouse journals. In America, the personal essay matured in the nineteenth-century work of writers such as Sarah Payson Willis (Fanny Fern), Ralph Waldo Emerson, and Henry David Thoreau. All of these writers passionately record their personal experience.

Today, amid the stresses of early twenty-first-century civilization, the personal essay is flourishing. According to Donald Hall (1995), we may, in fact, be living in the age of the personal essay (p. 1). For as technological, political, and cultural changes have progressed, altering our world at a dizzying pace and in sometimes troubling ways, the personal essay has gained popularity as a profoundly humanizing form of discourse. "When we read Stephen Hawking on physics or Vicki Hearne on animals or Alice Walker on her mother," Hall says, we span "gaps of knowledge and experience" (p. 4). In terms of contemporary genre theory, the content and form of personal essays serve a need that is prevalent in the overall context of our late-industrial society: personal essays build emotional bonds, promoting a sympathetic understanding of others. Given the importance of its function, the personal essay has been dignified by new names, and is sometimes described as "creative nonfiction" or "life writing."

For our purposes, it is important to note that the personal essay has also played an important role in the history of college and university composition. Placement exams that assess the skills of incoming students often have an essay component in which students are asked to elaborate on an assigned topic. Similar exercises are frequently reassigned in undergraduate English courses and presented through the framework of basic patterns such as description, narration, comparison, and so on. The presence of personal essays in composition classrooms can be attributed to a mix of idealistic and utilitarian considerations. On the one hand, as a genre that seems to pay homage to the uniqueness and value of individual lives, the personal essay is an attractive educational tool because it appears to typify the humanistic ideals of a liberal arts education in a democratic society. Thus, the personal essay can be valorized as a mode of expression that exemplifies and fosters imaginative creativity and critical thinking. On the other hand, however, the rhetorical situation of the classroom demands conformity. Educational institutions, after all, are at least partly designed to process and certify students, transforming them into productive members of society. Not coincidentally, the personal-essay-as-university-writing-task also contributes to this regulatory function.

The controlled nature of the personal essay in composition classes is evident in numerous handbooks for students. In terms of overall organization, for example, the *Harbrace Handbook for Canadians* (1999) tells students that all essays (personal or otherwise) must have a thesis—an overarching claim or position on the subject matter (p. 426).[1] The *Harbrace Handbook* adds that theses may be stated or implied, but asks for an explicitly stated thesis which shows that the student writer has firm control over his or her material (p. 427). Moreover, according to the *Harbrace Handbook*, some flexibility may be permitted in terms of thesis placement, but the preferred location for a thesis is at the end of the opening paragraph (p. 428). Standard compositional wisdom also says that the rest of the essay should work to validate the thesis (*Prose Models*, 1997). Thus, a neat beginning–middle–end structure emerges: an introductory paragraph with a thesis, core paragraphs with main points presented in guiding sentences that are augmented by supporting levels of detail, and a conclusion. Implicitly, that is, the carefully organized essay follows a scientific model of thesis and support (see Figure on page 15).

Another often-used rhetorical handbook, Strunk and White's *Elements of Style* (1979), provides advice on the finer points of essay writing, addressing matters of sentence-level style. The regulatory aims of William Strunk are manifest in a series of "Do-not rules": "Do not join independent clauses by a comma," "Do not break sentences in two," "Do not overwrite," "Do not overstate," and so on. For his part, E.B. White softens Strunk's commands and assures us that his mentor "was a friendly and funny man" (xiii). But despite White's

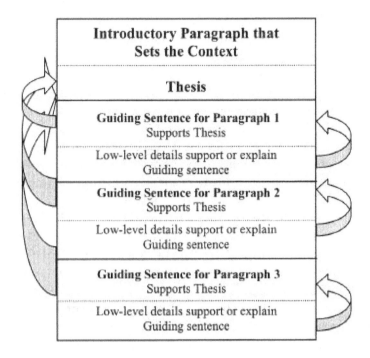

tempering influence, *Elements of Style* remains a very dictatorial book. Moreover, insofar as Strunk and White recommend a "common-sense" approach to sentence-level style, they blend regulation with remediation, implying that students are being taught nothing more than that which they should have already learned.

At a deeper level, one might even suggest that this edifice of rules is complicit with the materialist values of middle-class capitalism. As personal essayists, students are taught the virtues of obedience, economy, progress, and efficiency. Their work amounts to something — it is productive in the sense that it develops a clearly identified and predetermined goal. Perhaps well-ordered essays hold forth the promise of well-ordered lives, aligning the correction industry of composition with Western economies founded on growth and productivity. Accordingly, students who approach the personal essay in composition class may perceive a tension embedded in their writing task. While their writing should be original, unique, fresh, imaginative, and perceptive, it should also conform to a standardized array of stylistic conventions. Such tension is compounded by the fact that very few of the sample essays provided in anthologies pay much attention to the classroom rules. For example, the loose informality of Margaret Atwood's "True North" (1996) — which tells us that North Bay used to be "a bit of an armpit" (p. 96) — blatantly defies Strunk's rules about avoiding slang and one-sentence paragraphs, just as the bizarre diction of Aritha van Herk's "In Visible Ink" (1991) would surely make Strunk roll over in his grave: "Reader, this amulet of the first and most final of all crypto-frictions is that one can be disappeared and re-written in a language beyond one's own. Herein resides the ultimate illusion of text: you are not reading me but writing, not me but yourself; you are not reading writing but being read, a live text in a languaging world" (p. 11). And what of essays in which thesis claims are not readily evident? Given such incongruities, students confronted with the task of writing the so-called personal essay might justifiably throw up their hands in frustration while deriding the hypocrisy of educational institutions.

Nevertheless, it might be possible for students and instructors to work together in sorting through such difficulties. One approach is to see personal essays produced for composition classes as a peculiar *sub*genre whose various demands call for compromise. For example, if students effectively use a variety of sentence types, perhaps occasional sentence fragments, deliberately placed, become acceptable. Similarly, if an essay demonstrates an understanding of paragraph development, a one-sentence paragraph could be used for effect. As for the notorious thesis claim (you must argue something), William Zeiger (1985) points out that Montaigne's essays are exploratory trials or reflections, not linear proofs that develop rigid dogmas. Zeiger says that Montaigne "teases at an idea, like a cat playing with something. He presents ideas for their own sake, for their power to stimulate and broaden the mind" (p. 454). Zeiger concludes that "If we genuinely wish to promote freedom of thought . . . then we must establish the art of exploration as an equally acceptable and worthy pursuit [in the classroom]" (p. 459). Thus, in personal essays, thesis claims might express possibilities rather than certainties, problems rather than answers. Alternatively, questions may replace claims in introductions. And surely, in *personal* essays, the language of real experience should be embraced. Such possibilities suggest that students might find ways of moving quite freely within the harness of flexible expectations. Indeed, personal essays in composition classes can be reconceptualized as a form of creative nonfiction.[2]

CHAPTER NOTES

1. The *Harbrace Handbook for Canadians* (5th ed.) (1999) is not alone here. In an article on first-year composition, Keith Fort confirms the prevalence of the pattern: "In the essay it would seem that . . . [the] key rule is that there must be a thesis which the essay proves. The first question always asked about a prospective paper is whether the idea is 'workable' or can be 'handled' . . . [i.e.,] 'do you have a thesis that can be proved?' This formal requirement is a *sine qua non* for a paper" (p. 631).
2. See, for example, the *College English* special issue on creative nonfiction, edited by Douglas Hesse (2003, January).

CHAPTER REFERENCES

Atwood, M. (1996). True north. In L.H. Peterson (Ed.), *The Norton reader* (9th ed.) (pp. 94–105). New York: W.W. Norton.

Fort, K. (1971). Form, authority, and the critical essay. *College English, 32,* 629–639.

Gusdorf, G. (1972). Conditions and limits of autobiography. In J. Olney (Ed. & Trans.), *Autobiography: Essays theoretical and critical* (pp. 19–32). Princeton: Princeton University Press.

Hall, D. (1995). *The contemporary essay* (3rd ed.). Boston: Bedford.

Harbrace handbook for Canadians. (1999). J.C. Hodges, W.B. Horner, S.S. Webb, R.K. Miller, C. Werier, et al. (Eds.). Toronto: Harcourt Brace.

Hesse, D. (Ed.). (2003). Creative Nonfiction [Special issue]. *College English, 65*(3).

Jansen, H.W. (1977). *History of art: A survey of the major visual arts from the dawn of history to the present day* (2nd ed.). New York: Prentice-Hall.

Montaigne, M.E. de. (1952). *The essays.* Charles Cotton (Trans.). Chicago: Benton.

Prose models. (1997). G. Levin (Ed.). Toronto: Harcourt Brace.

Strunk, W., & White, E.B. (1979). *Elements of style* (3rd ed.). New York: MacMillan.

van Herk, A. (1991). In visible ink. In *In visible ink: Crypto-frictions* (pp. 1–11). Edmonton: NeWest.

Zeiger, W. (1985). The exploratory essay: Enfranchising the spirit of inquiry in college composition. *College English, 47,* 454–466.

INTRODUCTION TO THE READINGS

In a course on academic writing, personal essays might seem out of place. However, personal essays can be a good way of starting out: they tend to be shorter than research papers and call for a voice that is not quite so distant from the language of everyday life. Moreover, there may not be a hard and certain wall that divides personal essays from "academic" essays. Some would say that all writing is ultimately personal. More on this later.

The first essay centres on an individual's experience of place. Joan Didion is widely recognized as one of the best writers of nonfiction in America today. Didion's "The Dam" is taken from a collection of essays entitled *The White Album* (1979). The student essay is by Colleen Baxter, who writes about her relationship with her horse. Like the best writers of creative nonfiction, Baxter writes about what she knows.

JOAN DIDION

At the Dam

1   Since the afternoon in 1967 when I first saw Hoover Dam, its image has never been entirely absent from my inner eye. I will be talking to someone in Los Angeles, say, or New York, and suddenly the dam will materialize, its pristine concave face gleaming white against the harsh rusts and taupes and mauves of that rock canyon hundreds or thousands of miles from where I am. I will be driving down Sunset Boulevard, or about to enter a freeway, and abruptly those power transmission towers will appear before me, canted vertiginously over the tailrace. Sometimes I am confronted by the intakes and sometimes by the shadow of the heavy cable that spans the canyon and sometimes by the ominous outlets to unused spillways, black in the lunar clarity of the desert light. Quite often I hear the turbines. Frequently I wonder what is happening at the dam this instant, at this precise intersection of time and space, how much water is being released to fill downstream orders and what lights are flashing and which generators are in full use and which just spinning free.

2   I used to wonder what it was about the dam that made me think of it at times and in places where I once thought of the Mindanao Trench, or of the stars wheeling their courses, or of the words *As it was in the beginning, is now and ever shall be, world without end, amen.* Dams, after all, are commonplace: we have all seen one. This particular dam had existed as an idea in the world's mind for almost forty years before I saw it. Hoover Dam, showpiece of the Boulder Canyon project, the several million tons of concrete that made the Southwest plausible, the *fait accompli* that was to convey, in the innocent time of its construction, the notion that mankind's brightest promise lay in American engineering.

3   Of course the dam derives some of its emotional effect from precisely that aspect, that sense of being a monument to a faith since misplaced. "They died to make the desert bloom," reads a plaque dedicated to the 96 men who died building this first of the great high dams, and in context the worn phrase touches, suggests all of that trust in harnessing resources, in the meliorative power of the dynamo, so central to the early Thirties. Boulder City, built in 1931 as the construction town for the dam, retains the ambience of a model city, a new town, a toy triangular grid of green lawns and trim bungalows, all fanning out from the Reclamation building. The bronze sculptures at the dam itself evoke muscular citizens of a tomorrow that never came, sheaves of wheat clutched heavenward, thunderbolts defied. Winged Victories guard the flagpole. The flag whips in the canyon wind. An empty Pepsi-Cola can clatters across the terrazzo. The place is perfectly frozen in time.

4   But history does not explain it all, does not entirely suggest what makes the dam so affecting. Nor, even, does energy, the massive involvement with power and pressure and the transparent sexual overtones to that involvement. Once when I revisited the dam I walked through it with a man from the Bureau of Reclamation. For a while we trailed behind a guided tour, and then we went on, went into parts of the dam where visitors do not generally go. Once in a while he would explain something, usually in that recondite language having to do with "peaking power," with "outages" and "de-watering," but on the whole we spent the afternoon in a world so alien, so complete and so beautiful unto itself that it was scarcely necessary to speak at all. We saw almost no one. Cranes moved above us as if under their own volition. Generators roared. Transformers hummed. The gratings on which we stood vibrated. We watched a hundred-ton steel shaft plunging down to that place where the water was. And finally we got down to that place where the water was, where the water sucked out of Lake Mead roared through thirty-foot

penstocks and then into thirteen-foot penstocks and finally into the turbines themselves. "Touch it," the Reclamation man said, and I did, and for a long time I just stood there with my hands on the turbine. It was a peculiar moment, but so explicit as to suggest nothing beyond itself.

5   There was something beyond all that, something beyond energy, beyond history, something I could not fix in my mind. When I came up from the dam that day the wind was blowing harder, through the canyon and all across the Mojave. Later, toward Henderson and Las Vegas, there would be dust blowing, blowing past the Country-Western Casino FRI & SAT NITES and blowing past the Shrine of Our Lady of Safe Journey STOP & PRAY, but out at the dam there was no dust, only the rock and the dam and a little greasewood and a few garbage cans, their tops chained, banging against a fence. I walked across the marble star map that traces a sidereal revolution of the equinox and fixes forever, the Reclamation man had told me, for all time and for all people who can read the stars, the date the dam was dedicated. The star map was, he had said, for when we were all gone and the dam was left. I had not thought much of it when he said it, but I thought of it then, with the wind whining and the sun dropping behind a mesa with the finality of a sunset in space. Of course that was the image I had seen always, seen it without quite realizing what I saw, a dynamo finally free of man, splendid at last in its absolute isolation, transmitting power and releasing water to a world where no one is.

COLLEEN BAXTER

Pete
"There is no secret so close as that between a rider and his horse."
— Mr. Sponge's Sporting Tour

1   Since the beginning of my existence, I have been surrounded by a certain breed of animal with great athleticism and exquisiteness. When you look upon these animals, you can feel the force radiating from them. You are in awe of 1200 pounds of unrefined muscle and flesh, rippling beneath a dazzling coat of hair. American quarter horses have

been around since the late 1600s, and my lifelong dream has been to own one of these magnificent animals. On the third of October, 2001, my dream came true when I purchased a two-year-old, 15-hands-high, barely-halter-broke, bay gelding. His registered name is Justa Cool Zip, but I call him Pete. It was seven months later, in May, that I felt the thrill and trepidation of getting on my living powerhouse.

2   The day of the colt-starting clinic jumped up on me. I had been working with Pete at home, sacking him out, but that was nothing compared to what Ward Ferch, the colt-starting instructor, had set out for Pete and me. We completed various tasks such as leading Pete by his feet and lunging him around the round pen at the correct gaits and leads. Each powerful stride Pete took as he was traveling around the pen was a stride closer to the moment that I would get on him, a moment when my emotions would be at their peak.

3   After many exhausting hours of lunging and completing other tasks, it was time for a break, a break for Pete, that is. I had to go and collect all of my tack. I was using a saddle that my family uses only for colt-starting. It is rigged up with a back cinch and a breast collar so that the young horses get used to everything all at once. Such a device helps to avoid problems in the future because the horse is used to most tack. The saddle itself is not easy for me to carry, especially when I have my saddle pad and groom box. Nevertheless, I was too lazy to make more than one trip, as it would have taken more time, time that I did not have to waste. Leaving a trail of brushes and leg wraps, I made my way to the round pen. Pete peered through the rails, looking at me as if I were deranged. But then maybe I am deranged: who would be willing to get on 1200 pounds of steel that may or may not explode into striking hooves and flying dust? I proceeded into the round pen, dumping my tack in a chaotic pile on the ground, in the center. As I dropped my tack, I felt my excitement pool down into my stomach, knowing that the time was drawing nearer.

4   I worked Pete in the pen again after his break, tripping over my tack, perfecting the earlier tasks to prepare him for the final moment. Everything was deadly silent; I was concentrating on every muscle in Pete's body. The time was approaching. I piled my tack in the

appropriate order, saddle on the ground, first making sure that all the cinches and the breast collar were tied up, and then my saddle pad. I could feel my heart beating faster and faster as the time approached to tack him up. I placed the saddle pad gently on his back; he did not move a muscle. I felt my arm muscles straining to lift the saddle high enough, my whole body tense. I had to place the saddle gently on Pete's towering back. As I started to lift my saddle, it was as if Pete had grown a foot in the seconds that I had bent down to pick it up. It was a one-time chance, a memory that would be engraved in his mind forever. Everything had to go smoothly for Pete. With a deep sigh of relief, I managed to place the saddle smoothly on the tower of Pete. Yet it did not take long for the relief to be replaced by anxiety. The next step would tell me if I had something to worry about when I was getting on him.

5   I could feel Pete slowly tighten every muscle in his body, and this made every muscle in my body stiffen as well. I had to hurry and tighten the cinch and be careful not to startle him at the same time. I tightened the front cinch, notch by notch. Then I buckled up my breast collar, leaving the back cinch for last. If he was going to erupt, it would be now. As I was tightening the back cinch, I could feel vigilance creeping up the back of my throat, but it was slowly becoming overrun by the thrill of getting on! I finished fastening the back cinch and stepped back out of harm's way. Pete stood there, not even rippling his skin to remove the flies that had landed on him. He turned and looked at me. In his eyes I could see confusion and concern. I asked him to take a few strides forward, and soon he was starting to loosen up. His stride was lengthening and he was moving more freely through his shoulders. He looked impressive under that saddle. It was when I asked him to move up into a lope that the eruption occurred. The back cinch slipped back a little — and the volcano erupted. With hooves lashing out, he charged around the round pen like a mad man. If I thought I was worried earlier, it was nothing compared to what I was feeling now. Did I really want to get on a psycho horse? After he calmed down, I felt more confident in myself. I could feel a deep calm come over my body. It was time to get on.

6   I placed Pete in the center of the round pen, and then checked my cinches, making sure that they were tight enough so that the saddle

would not slip when I hauled myself up on his back. I had previously thought that Pete looked big when I was trying to place the saddle on his back. Now, however, he seemed a few storeys higher. I was going to have to get my short leg in my short stirrup, which did not even show below his belly. The time had come; I raised my left foot, to place it in the stirrup, but it just would not reach. This was another one of the things that had to go smoothly the first time. I tried again: nothing was going to stop me. As I raised my foot I could feel the muscles tearing in my hamstring, but I had made it! My foot was in the stirrup. Now, if only I could pull myself up and into the saddle. As I managed to pull myself up, the thrill hit me full force. The higher I pulled myself up, the stronger the feeling. My stomach was fluttery, not a good feeling, but not a bad one either. I had some strength come out of nowhere and a burst of energy helped push me up the last few inches into the saddle.

7   When I settled myself gently into the saddle, the thrill was still there, the thrill of being the first person on Pete's back. I felt like Christopher Columbus, sensing the exhilaration he might have felt being the first one to find America, or so he thought. Pete turned his head and tried to take a bite out of my foot, but I pulled his head back around so that he could not. It was time to ask him for our first stride together. Would this turn out to be a pleasant ride or one with striking hooves and flying dust? I gently rocked in the saddle, throwing him off balance, asking him to take that first stride. It was time consuming, but soon we were walking around the round pen with no problems at all. Pete and I slowly progressed into a jog and then to a lope, with only one small buck, nothing more. There are no words that I can use to explain the feeling of being on Pete, loping for the first time. His ground-eating stride made the round pen feel small, making me wish that I were in a larger space and not riding in a circle. All my energy was being put into him. I could not hear Ward or anything else, except the rush of excitement in my head. I was in a dream that I hoped I would never wake up from.

8   The thrill of riding Pete will never change. Every time I settle myself down in the saddle, the same emotions come over me. But I also feel at peace; whatever is out there in the world that may be bothering me is gone. The trepidation that I felt that first day is

replaced with trust and amazement at the bond that Pete and I have built. The knowledge that Pete and I have the ability to soar over the ground like an eagle soaring on the wind is like no other feeling: there is no one around to stop us; no one on this earth can touch us; we are free. Whether it is hunter-under-saddle, western pleasure, reining, or dressage, we will excel at our goals. No one can break our bond. Pete's my best friend.

Academic Research

Before you can do any research, you must set yourself a direction—
a general area to investigate. That direction can, and probably will,
change with time and knowledge—at least it will become more
specific and focused. But with the first step, as the cliché goes, begins
the journey.

—Charles Bazerman, *The Informed Writer:*
Using Sources in the Disciplines

English courses that focus on academic writing in the disciplines often
involve a research paper. English instructors who assign research
papers probably do so on the assumption that something important is
at stake. Evidently, this assumption is shared by other instructors in
other disciplines, for students are also asked to write research papers
in subjects such as anthropology, criminology, history, literature-based
English courses, sociology, and women's studies. The perceived
importance of such assignments is sometimes reflected in the percentage
of marks allotted to them: on occasion, research papers may comprise
30 percent or more of an overall grade for a course. Purely in terms of
marks, then, a research paper deserves to be taken seriously. Ideally,
however, marks should not be regarded as ends in themselves.

What is at stake (aside from marks) in college and university
courses that involve writing research papers? The answer to this
question lies in the discipline-based training and practices of instructors
themselves, many of whom have been writing research papers for
most of their professional lives. Instructors have been taught to regard
research papers (or articles published in academic journals) as a kind

of highly valued disciplinary currency, second in value only to full-length books.

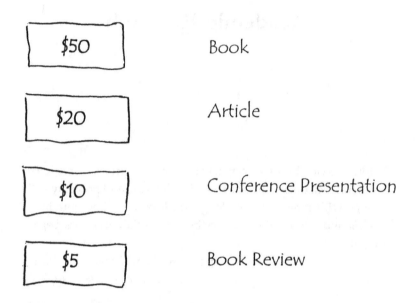

$50	Book
$20	Article
$10	Conference Presentation
$5	Book Review

Research papers have a high value in scholarly communities because they are the primary medium for presenting newly generated knowledge. As suggested earlier, we could regard research papers as the signature product of scholarly work. The resumés of senior academics often list page after page of research articles that represent a lifetime of academic achievement.

Accordingly, when students are faced with research papers in post-secondary academic courses, such assignments are steeped in cultural expectations. Whether they say so or not, most instructors probably have high hopes for student work and would like to see students produce the kind of paper that they themselves write. Indeed, while it would be too much to expect students in first-year courses to be writing for publication in scholarly journals, undergraduate papers may still share some of the characteristics of published research. In effect, students who are asked to write a research paper at the undergraduate level are being invited to join in scholarly conversations about the state of knowledge in a given area. Rather than a make-work project, such an exercise can be a meaningful initiation ritual, one that gives students the privilege of working on their own or in groups; one that closes the gap between student and professional responsibilities.

This chapter explores the process of getting started on a research project. It addresses the search for direction, how to construct a firm sense of topic, and how to find relevant sources. This business of searching, constructing, and finding is not always a neat, linear process. It often involves backtracking and uncertainty about how to proceed. Nevertheless, we encourage students to embrace the challenges of research with both determination and an open mind, for the difficulties of the process mark a passage beyond the impressionistic world of personal essays, into the domain of knowledge-making.

SEARCHING FOR DIRECTION

The ground rules for selecting a topic may vary from course to course. Some instructors may limit student choices to a list of prescribed topics. Other instructors might invite students to think of their own topics. Still other instructors might provide a list of suggestions and allow for innovation. Whatever approach is adopted in a given class, fundamental decisions about topic are vital to the success of a paper; yet such decisions can be among the hardest to make. Embarking on the research enterprise, writers may feel paralyzed—set adrift in an ocean of possibility, without a compass and with no shoreline in sight.

Whether the field of topics is open or limited, it might be helpful for the instructor to invoke some principles of selection. First, all writers intuitively understand that they should be engaged by their topic. Even at the undergraduate level, a research paper often involves a sustained commitment of time and energy over several months, and such prolonged endeavours tend to be easier to complete when the writer has an interest in the topic. However, the criterion of personal interest should be accompanied by a cautionary note: more so than a personal essay, which displays private convictions, the knowledge-making aims of a research paper call for a judicious logic that could be compromised by excessive emotional involvement. "If you are going through a divorce," advises Linda Deutschmann, a sociology instructor, "now is not the time to write on divorce" (*Writing Your "Self" into the Disciplines*, 1996). Second, most instructors have something to say about the importance of focus. Echoing advice that appears in the epigraph to this chapter, William Garrett-Petts, an English instructor, regards carefully focused writing as "emblematic" of the best writing in the disciplines (*Writing Your "Self"into the Disciplines*, 1996). Third, academic writers, unlike personal essayists, operate in a condition of dependency. The propositions that emerge in academic essays are buttressed by ongoing reference to external evidence. Thus, the search for a topic goes hand in hand with a search for sources. The issue of sources merits extended discussion a little later. In the meantime, a few other preliminary considerations are worth mentioning.

As student writers struggle to formulate topics, they should discuss their ideas with peers and instructors. Given their experience, instructors might be in a particularly good position to offer sound advice. Thus, student–instructor meetings, early in a term, can help to move ideas in a promising direction. Depending on the availability of instructors, ongoing meetings may also be a good idea.

Where the curriculum permits, opportunities to engage in original research can be enhanced when writers remain open to topics close to home, involving their local or regional surroundings. In the University of Northern British Columbia history program, for example, there is a "strong focus" on northern issues, and students are encouraged to work in local museums that house unique archival materials (Farr, 2000).

Looking further afield, one can sample the diversity and flavour of scholarly research by using the Internet to examine "calls for papers" in a variety of disciplines or subject areas. Let's say someone has an interest in writing on some aspect of popular culture. If that person were to employ a search engine and use "'calls for papers' AND 'popular culture'" as a search phrase, numerous Web sites would appear. Doing the exercise ourselves, we went to a site that deals with women in popular culture and found the following invitation:

Ally McBeal Essays

Contributions are sought for a collection of essays that critique the television show *Ally McBeal*. Essays should focus on issues of either [sic] gender, race, sexuality, class, psychology, or sociology. This critical anthology seeks to explore the pop culture television series through various approaches as well as the impact that the program has had in regards to social, cultural, and literary trends and traditions. Send 2-page abstracts.

We also found this one:

Fashion and Modernity

At least since Baudelaire identified the "heroism of modern life" and the "advent of the new" with contemporary fashion, the culture and literature of modernity has revealed its complex relationship with sartorial fashion. Despite a growing interest in the history and sociology of modernist cultural production, relatively little scholarly attention has been paid to fashion, which has tended to be dismissed as a frivolous footnote to the narrative(s) of modern experience. In a special issue on fashion and modernity, *Agora* invites submissions that discuss the histories, functions, and/or failures of fashion as a site of modern cultural production and/or academic study.

   Potential topics might address, but are not limited to, the following concerns:

* the function of fashion as a trope, theme, or mode in popular and canonical literature and motion picture
* the race, gender, and class politics of fashion (fashion as a potential instrument of socio-political oppression/expression/cohesion/resistance
* the history and politics of fashion production and manufacture.

And this one:

Mothering, Religion, and Spirituality

Historically and cross-culturally the world's religions and spiritualities have simultaneously restricted mothers' roles and activities while conversely giving mothers some agency and authority. This conference will explore, from a variety of perspectives and disciplines, the impact of religion and spirituality on the experience of mothering and of mothers on religion and spirituality. It will examine mothers' lived experience as well as representations of mothering–motherhood in religion. We welcome submissions from students, activists, scholars, artists, and others who work or research in this area. Cross-cultural, historical and comparative work is encouraged.

Topics can include, but are not limited to:

* Mothers in sacred texts and oral traditions
* Mother figures in religious history
* Mother deities/goddesses
* Religious feminisms.

Shifting subjects, we searched Google for "'call for papers' AND 'American history,'" and found the following invitation:

The Cultural Legacy of JFK

John Kennedy's brief administration occurred at the confluence of great events: there is hardly a need to enumerate the topics which were "on the boil" when he took office. But even the distance of time does not allow us to appraise his administration coolly on the merits of its handling of those issues, because the manner of his death has produced an ongoing, invisible sense of negation, a might-have-been in a world where we have carried on. It is nearly impossible to think of the Kennedy presidency without celebrating, criticizing, and mourning all at once. From such heady, dangerous times cultural renaissances and tragic perspectives emerge, and students of the humanities find themselves in a unique scholarly position.

We welcome original papers related to the following subjects:

---

* Analyses of the depiction of the life, times, and death of JFK in music, literature, film, and the plastic arts. Specifically relevant are papers dealing with the American creation and destruction of a heroic mythology around the president, and how such mythology relates to the spirit of the time.
* Examinations of the scholarly research for and against the possibility that there was a conspiracy to assassinate. Also specifically relevant are papers dealing with the "aura of conspiracy" which predominates in popular American culture on subjects wholly unrelated to JFK, and how such an atmosphere may derive from lingering doubts about the assassination.

Thus, calls for papers present a rich feast of possibilities drawn from the real world of academic research and can be used by students in search of their own topics.

CONSTRUCTING A TOPIC

Throughout the previous pages, the word "topic" has been used quite loosely, to indicate a general understanding of what a research paper is or could be about. From here on, however, our suggestion is to treat "topic" as a technical term that involves specific elements. Our approach can be used across the humanities and social sciences, in a variety of different courses. Indeed, even when instructors do not explicitly seek a more technical understanding of topic, students can successfully use the strategy on their own. And there are good reasons for doing so, since researchers do not really *have* a topic until it can be clearly and succinctly articulated.

 What is your paper about?

 Well, um, I'm sort of writing about relationships in Margaret Atwood's novels . . . I think . . .

In this text, we will begin to treat topic as a concept that involves *two* components: a **research site** and a **prestige abstraction**. Our use of these terms follows Janet Giltrow's lead (1995, pp. 370–2, 241–3; 2002, pp. 371–2, 119–122, 125, 380). We have built upon Giltrow's insights by developing them into a practical and sophisticated formula.

Topic

Research Site   Prestige Abstraction

Research Site

In everyday usage, *site* usually refers to a place where something occurs. In turn, a *research site* is a place chosen for scholarly activity. It is the thing under investigation, the phenomenon that is to be studied. Alternatively, a research site might be defined as the raw material upon which a paper is based. The phrase is commonly used in the social and natural sciences, where research often takes place in a specific physical setting. In archaeology, for example, a research site could consist of a carefully marked-off area in which archaeologists dig for artifacts.

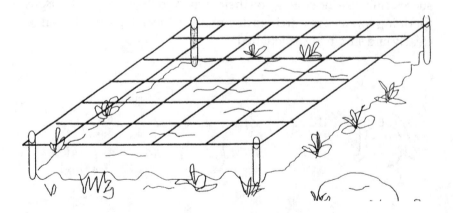

In these cases, research sites are very much "places," in the normal sense of the word. In other academic disciplines, however, the spatial reality of a research site might look a little different. In medical research, for example, biologists may investigate a single cell that can only be seen under a microscope. Alternatively, in English and history, research-site-as-place might be a textual "space" — Milton's *Paradise Lost* or old issues of newspapers. In sociology, on the other hand, a researcher may study the behaviour of children on an elementary school playground during recess periods.

> **Research sites** are the physical area, text, or event that is under consideration. Even though they can sometimes be hard to see, they have a concrete reality.

When you are at liberty to choose your own topic, you can consult your own life, your own field of interests for possible research sites. In any event, a focused topic often involves a carefully narrowed research site:

- Deafness in a Dene community
- The railway in Canadian poetry
- Quebec travellers in the Middle East at the end of the nineteenth century
- Age-related vision loss
- Indigenous education in Canadian universities since 1980
- Women in the post-NAFTA food system
- Writing instruction for kindergarten students with learning disabilities
- Full-service schools
- Mind mapping in elementary mathematics education
- Canadian mining in Costa Rica

Narrow research sites, such as these, help to create focused topics that permit in-depth analysis, one of the hallmarks of academic research. Unlike a one-hour newscast, which covers a range of stories, research articles frequently focus on one item — on one event, thing, or place. It is this careful scrutiny of one thing, rather than a cursory survey of many, that permits academics to make a contribution to knowledge.

Prestige Abstraction

If the research site is the carefully demarcated raw material on which a study is based, the prestige abstraction is an *idea* or *concept* that makes the research site meaningful in academic culture. Thus, while research sites have some physical reality, prestige abstractions cannot be touched or seen in and of themselves: their reality is mental rather than physical. For example, if children on a recess playground are a physical reality, concepts such as hope, freedom, power, authority, and change are ideas that we might use to interpret that physical reality.

In order to distinguish the two ingredients of topic, we could pay closer attention to the word "abstraction," breaking down its parts this way:

$$(AB) (STRACT ION)$$

The prefix "ab" means to lift away, remove, or take from. "Tract" means a stretch of territory — a place. Hence, "abstraction" involves a lifting away from concrete realities — a movement upward, if you will, into the airier realm of ideas. Thus, the verb "to abstract" means to remove or to take away. Put simply, abstractions are ideas that emerge from the raw material of life. They are the categories or mental boxes that we create for ourselves, in order to understand and interpret the world around us.

Abstractions are things we cannot touch. They have only mental existence.

Short Exercises

1. Working in small groups, come up with abstractions that could arise out of the situations or circumstances listed below:
   (a) Every lunch hour, thousands of children across North America line up in their school cafeteria, awaiting free lunches.
   (b) Teenagers in both small towns and large cities tend to be very aware of brand-name clothing.
   (c) Last summer, a record number of bear attacks occurred throughout North America.
   (d) Many people watch television sports on Sunday.
2. At home, make a collection of related items from one room in your house — you could, say, collect study materials from a desk area. Then arrange the items on a plate or some other flat surface. Bring the collection to class and ask people to think of an abstraction that applies to the collection as a whole.
3. For some movies you have seen, or novels you have read, think of one or more abstractions that express the theme of the work.

Once the basic concept of abstractions is clear, it is a short step to "prestige abstractions." Prestige abstractions are simply a select group of ideas or mental categories that enjoy a privileged existence in academic circles. Prestige abstractions are Big Issues that most academics immediately recognize as relevant to academic concerns. However, the appeal of prestige abstractions relates to shifting interests, so that prestige abstractions themselves are a reflection of currents in economic, political, and cultural thought. Right now, some of the most fashionable abstractions in the humanities and social sciences include the following:

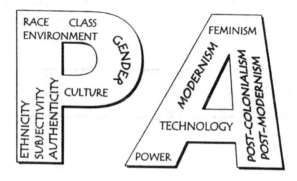

In any given discipline, at any given time, there is no fixed list or limited field of prestige abstractions. Nevertheless, some abstractions are noticeably "hot" insofar as they receive more attention than others. According to Janet Giltrow (1994), "It is hard now to foresee a time when *race* and *gender* will not be big issues, or when *community* will not give research rhetorical force, but there was a time when they did not have the prestige they have now" (p. 243).

You could try to identify the "hot" abstractions in your field, if you wanted, by perusing article titles in relevant journals. In all likelihood, you will find that certain abstractions recur more than others. Perhaps you will even find special issues devoted entirely to the development or exploration of a single abstraction. Similarly, calls for papers, such as those previously noted, are breeding grounds for abstraction. Sometimes a host of abstractions hovers around a single research site, such as that of John F. Kennedy (for example, heroic mythology, conspiracy, negation, cultural renaissance, tragedy). Prestige abstractions further refine or narrow topic, specifying ideas that can be brought to bear on research sites.

A **prestige abstraction** signals the scholarly importance of a research site by creating a partnership between the raw stuff of life and the concerns of the academic community. Prestige abstractions, therefore, are Big Issues that strategically position the research site in relation to academic culture.

To recap, a research site and a prestige abstraction fully articulate topic — the specific subject or "aboutness" of a paper. According to this formula, topic consists of something concrete (some raw material from life) and something abstract (some idea or mental category). For the sake of brevity, the formula can be expressed as a simple equation:

Research Site (RS) + Prestige Abstraction (PA) = Topic (Top)

When you apply the formula in an attempt to construct your own topic, you may discover that the prestige abstraction wants to push itself to the front of the lineup. As a Big Issue, it may press for first billing, so the formula might actually look like this:

Prestige Abstraction (PA) + Research Site (RS) = Topic (Top)

Moreover, we recommend that students use simple connecting words — coordinate conjunctions or prepositions — to unite prestige abstractions and research sites. Accordingly, the plus sign in the topic formula might be replaced by words such as "and," "for," "in," "among," "between," and so on. Consider the following example:

Community formation + the Williams Lake Museum
Community formation and the Williams Lake Museum

In cases like this, the topic formula can be used to clearly delineate the fundamental rhetorical building blocks of a university-level research paper. Indeed, the careful construction of topic, in the technical sense, will provide you with a clear idea of what your paper is about, while at the same time, signalling its relevance to the academic community. If you have a carefully defined topic, you have a centre of gravity for the paper as a whole, and you can be sure that your central focus will interest other scholars.

A Case Study
The Making of a University-Level Research Paper

Research Site
The flying career of Jimmy Anderson, bush pilot

Pondering Prestige Abstractions
{Jimmy Anderson's career as a bush pilot should be framed in a way
that makes him relevant to the scholarly community}

One might begin to think of Anderson in terms of concepts associated
with frontier areas, for example, individualism, heroic masculinity,
technology, environmental exploitation, and so on.

Potential Topic
Jimmy Anderson and frontier masculinity

The Emerging Paper

Flying High:
Jimmy Anderson and Frontier Masculinity
In both the Canadian North and the American West, culturally idealized
versions of frontier masculinity have been rooted in violence and
conquest. From Jesse James to Albert Johnson, North American frontier
heroes have embodied renegade individualism. However, Jimmy
Anderson, a bush pilot in northeastern British Columbia during the
post–World War II era, reconfigures the traditional ideology of the
frontier hero. Unlike his more celebrated counterparts, Anderson
represents communal and environmental values.

READING FOR TOPIC

The topic formula that we have discussed here is frequently evident
in published research, particularly within the humanities and social
sciences. In a paper on Feng Shui and village property development
in Hong Kong, for example, C.M. Tam, Tony Tso, and K.C. Lam (1999)

explicitly label their abstraction as an abstraction. "Feng Shui," the authors write, "is ancient Chinese geomancy. It is abstract, invisible, untouchable, and intangible — as the wind, hard to see, and as water, difficult to be grasped" (p. 152).

However, topic, as we have defined it, is not always readily visible. In some papers, for instance, one might be able to identify a research site, but the prestige abstraction could be harder to pinpoint. Indeed, on occasion, prestige abstractions may simply be implied rather than explicitly stated. This is perhaps the case in "Thrice-Told Tales: The Exploration Writing of John Franklin," Richard Davies' paper about Sir John Franklin's second overland expedition to the Canadian North.

When John Franklin journeyed across the North American continent to explore the shores of the Polar Sea on his second land expedition of 1825–1827, he kept — in accordance with British Admiralty convention — an official journal of his experience.[1] Later, perhaps during the lengthy Atlantic crossing on his return to England, Franklin prepared what appears to be a fair copy of this official journal. The fair copy encompasses roughly the same geographical and temporal scope as does the journal, but through selective editing, it condenses the account by half.[2] In 1828, John Murray published *Narrative of a Second Expedition to the Shores of the Polar Sea*.[3] This narrative, based on the original journal and the fair copy, was composed for a popular audience with an appetite for travel writing and an exotic interest in the far reaches of the Empire. We have, then, three accounts of the same experience, all told by the same author, or, as my title suggests, "thrice-told tales" — a journal, a fair copy, and a narrative.

A crucial assumption made in this paper is that the variations between these three accounts grow out of the author's sense of audience — of who reads the account and what they want to hear. The truth is that all three accounts bear a tedious similarity; Franklin's labouring imagination rarely capitalizes on the rich rhetorical possibilities offered by the different audiences he addresses. Perhaps encouraged by his military training, Franklin instead strived for an unattainable objectivity in his writing, resulting in a literary personality that is thin and obscure. Yet even though Franklin can hardly be said to take full advantage of the rhetorical situation, his accounts are not totally innocent of literary manipulation. His excessive self-effacement veils the process, but close scrutiny of the "tales" reveals an indisputable shaping of the narrative to meet the expectations of his audience. A full examination from this perspective must consider Franklin's perceptions of landscape, duty and leadership, native people, Canadians, and the experience in North America. This brief paper, however, focuses only on Franklin's portrayal of the Indians and Inuit.

Subtly but consistently, as one moves from journal through fair copy to narrative, one encounters an image of native people that grows gradually more disparaging and condemning. The narrative casts Indian and Inuit in the role of predatory antagonist to civilization and portrays them as the chaotic, irrational enemy of order, a disapprobation that is considerably intensified from what appears in the journal. I must emphasize that the differences are not extreme: Franklin's desire to avoid subjective evaluations prevents any dramatic alterations. Nevertheless, it seems fair to say that many of the indigenous North Americans who appear in the narrative are portrayed as savages opposed to such European virtues as industry, trust, and reason.

Although this is very much a paper about racism, racist discourse, and ethnocentrism, none of these high-powered words (or synonyms for them) appear in the introduction, or anywhere else in the paper.

On other occasions, general references to concrete phenomena seem to stand in for abstractions. This happens in Nancy Theberge's paper about media coverage of a hockey brawl (see Chapter 6). Here, Theberge situates her research site in relation to "sports violence," a Big Issue, to be sure, but not exactly an abstraction. In fact, to conceive of violence as an abstraction (as something intangible) is politically problematical. "Sports violence" certainly rises above specific reference, but its generality hovers somewhere *between* specific instances of violence and the concept of violence. In the case of Theberge's paper, then, we might again have to go searching for an abstraction, and that search might bring into view phrases like "masculinity" or the "social construction of masculinity." All of this suggests that the effort to identify topic in someone else's work might turn into a bit of a guessing game. Among a community of readers, there may be some disagreement over what constitutes the prestige abstraction or even the research site. Accordingly, all of us should be prepared to tolerate different versions of topic, although some versions may be more persuasive than others. We would like to suggest that what matters most is not having everyone agree on precisely the same phraseology, but that readers try to delineate topic according to the structural pattern described here.

As you encounter other people's research papers (and think about writing your own) there are certain places where topic is likely to appear. Frequently, for example, an announcement of topic will occur in the title of a paper, and topic will then be reaffirmed in a sentence somewhere within the introduction. Sentence-level announcements of topic often begin with subject-predicate patterns such as "This paper examines," "I will examine," "I investigate," "My paper focuses on," and "This paper describes." These constructions, which refer to the activity of the paper or author, represent highly self-conscious moments in the presentation of research. In passages such as this, readers encounter language about language or *meta*discourse, which can be envisioned as a flag that alerts readers to key moments in the development of knowledge. The following excerpts display the topic formula at work. Note that metadiscursive flags are underlined, research sites are in bold, and abstractions are in italics:

Cheryl Kirschner, "Desperate Measures": . . . this essay examines **the St. John's murders** (RS) in relation to the *commercial interests* (PA) of the Hudson's Bay Company .

James Ryan, "Experiencing Urban Schooling": The study outlined here describes *Native students' experience* (PA) of the circumstances associated with their participation in **an on-campus university program** (RS).

We suggest that the topic formula is also discernable in the next pair of examples. In these cases, however, topic is dispersed throughout long and involved sentences. In advising students, we would recommend simpler constructions:

Adele Perry, "Bachelors in the Backwoods": **In small towns, camps, and scattered cabins throughout the up-country, White men** (RS) developed a vibrant, *homosocial culture* (PA). It is *this rough culture*, forged out of *the disruption of customary gender organization* in **the British Columbia backwoods**, that this essay examines.

[or, more simply:]

This essay examines *homosocial culture* (PA) among **white men in up-country British Columbia** (RS).

I.S. MacLaren, "Retaining Captaincy of the Soul": This study of **the published writing and painting which record the first and dramatic overland trek from Hudson Bay to the Arctic Ocean (1819–1822)** (RS) will investigate the extent to which the great nineteenth-century Arctic explorer and his colleagues depended on *British conventions of landscape appreciation* (PA) for their comprehension and representation of Arctic terrain.

[or, more simply:]

This essay examines *British conventions of landscape appreciation* (PA) in **the published writing and painting from the first Franklin expedition** (RS).

FINDING SOURCES

Decisions about topic will be deeply influenced by the availability of sources. In fact, the success of academic papers written by students and professors depends in large part on their ability to find appropriate sources. Without appropriate sources, a good grade for the student or publication for the professor is very unlikely. Indeed, careful research is one way that scholarly writers indicate a respect for the knowledge-making practices of their discipline.

Primary Sources and Secondary Sources

We will begin with a distinction between primary sources and secondary sources. Primary sources "are written by people who have direct knowledge of the events or issues under discussion; they were participants in or observers of those events" (Rosen & Behrens, 1995, p. 570). Let's say that someone's research site involves the life of Monica Storrs, an early-twentieth-century missionary in the Peace River area of northeastern British Columbia. Although Storrs herself is now deceased, a number of primary sources from her era might be available. In this case, Storrs' own diary, for example, would count as a primary source (if the research site were redefined as the diary itself, Storrs' diary would do double duty, as both research site and primary source). Journals or diaries by people who knew Storrs or who lived in her time and place would also count as primary sources, as would historical documents such as old newspaper articles or photographs. Similarly, interviews with Storrs' surviving friends and family members would belong to the category of primary sources.

Secondary sources, on the other hand, have a "secondary" or more distant relationship to the research site — "authors of secondary sources have only *indirect* knowledge; they rely on primary or other secondary sources for their information" (Rosen & Behrens, 1995, p. 570). Following through on the prospect of a paper about Monica Storrs' life, scholarly discussions of Storrs or of matters that relate to her would count as secondary sources. Such sources, whether books or articles, may be extremely valuable, but they do not provide first-hand access to the subject; they are products of reflection and research. Put another way, secondary sources, which consist of someone else's research, involve a "re-seeing" or "re-envisioning" of someone or something.

> **Primary sources** provide first-hand observation or investigation. They are produced by people who have direct experience of the events or issues under discussion; **secondary sources** are created by people who have indirect or second-hand experience of the subject.

It may be tempting to assume that primary sources are inherently truer or more accurate than secondary sources, or, vice versa — that secondary sources are more accurate than primary sources. However, it would be unwise to generalize in this manner. Often in very obvious ways, diaries and journals, like personal essays, are coloured by the personalities of the people who wrote them. Such colouring can reveal all sorts of biases and distortions. Nor is the more distant reflection afforded by secondary sources any guarantee of truth. Primary and secondary sources are simply *constructed* in different ways, and the best papers often contain a mix of both.

In the case of secondary sources, it is important to make a further distinction between popular and academic material. Usually, the distinction is evident: for one thing, academic sources tend to *look* different from popular sources — the covers and texts of academic materials often have a more formal appearance. In any event, if the topic involves, say, the environmental politics of Grey Owl (otherwise known as Archie Belaney), an article in *Essays on Canadian Writing*, a peer-reviewed academic journal, will likely have more informational value than an article in *Maclean's* magazine. Instructors in college and university classes will be inclined to respond favourably to the former source, but may wonder about the relevance of the latter one. Accordingly, in relation to secondary sources, students should try to move beyond popular, journalistic fare and to access academic material. Scholarly research will likely make a greater contribution to the form and content that students should be attempting to cultivate in their own writing.

Computer-Based Research

Computers that provide access to the Internet are now a central aspect of scholarly research. The Internet can be used to conduct informal or formal searches. Informal research, in this context, involves relatively simple procedures such as entering a term or phrase in the search box of an Internet search engine. Formal research involves the use of more academic databases that are often linked to college and university library Web sites. If the popular term "surfing" describes the nature of informal searches, "digging" may be more apt for formal searches.

Informal Searches

Informal searches launch researchers onto the unmonitored information highway, where a lot of what is encountered may not have much scholarly value. Nevertheless, informal searches provide basic familiarity with a subject. Some of the most frequently used search engines are these:

- www.lycos.com
- www.infoseek.com
- www.altavista.com
- www.metacrawler.com
- www.google.ca

Metacrawler and Google are particularly powerful search engines. While conducting informal searches, it is a good idea to experiment with different search strategies and terms. Individual search engines often provide a "help" button that will advise users about how to refine their search. Putting terms or phrases in quotation marks, for example, normally results in an "exact phrase search" whereby the computer only selects items that contain the precise word(s) entered in the search box. Most search engines also allow for the use of Boolean operators involving "AND," "OR," and "NOT." Truncating search terms with an asterisk (*) is another option: "hunting" and "hunters," as search terms, will produce different results, whereas "hunt*" will yield combined results. Search engines have access to such a vast amount of material that they often produce too many results or "hits." Thus, users may get the best results when search terms are carefully narrowed.

The Internet can also be used to conduct other kinds of informal research. E-mail, for example, is an excellent means of communicating with people who may know about a topic. Rather than being aloof, the experts are usually willing to share their expertise. E-mail addresses can be tracked down in a variety of ways. One option is to join an electronic discussion group or "listserv" related to a subject area or research site and to watch for contributions by people who seem particularly well-informed. The addresses of listservs sometimes appear on search engines during the initial exploration of a topic.

Formal Searches

Formal searches are more selective and frequently involve two types of databases: university or college book indexes (also called catalogues) and article indexes (also called periodical indexes). On the whole, public libraries tend to contain books and periodicals that are less academic in nature, but it is wise, at an early stage in the research process, to check the book and periodical holdings at public libraries as well. However, the best place for scholarly researchers to start formal searches is at their own educational institution. Even if the institutional library is small and has a limited budget, researchers should know what it has to offer. First of all, use your own computer or a computer on campus to check the book catalogue and article indexes for the institution you attend.

The book indexes for other college and university libraries can be searched using on-line public access catalogues. Regardless of which book index you are using, you must choose search terms carefully. In a book catalogue, you will be able to search by author, title, subject, and key words. If you want to try a subject search, it's a good idea to consult the *Library of Congress Subject Headings* (*LCSH*), a multi-volume set of reference books that indicates what terms library cataloguers use to identify subjects. Hard-bound copies of the *LCSH* should be available in the reference section of your campus library. "Key word" searches are more inclusive and may produce better results.

Article indexes, which contain references to millions of articles published in academic journals, are maintained by private companies, but university and college libraries purchase the right to display these indexes on their home pages. For the academic researcher, article indexes are vital because they provide references to (or citations for) up-to-date articles recently published in academic journals. Indeed, since articles are shorter than books, and since most journals are published several times a year, they identify the frontiers of knowledge. The "newness" of information tends to be more important in the sciences than in the humanities, but even in the humanities there is considerable value placed on the most recent knowledge claims.

The indexes themselves vary in scope. Some, such as the Humanities and Social Sciences Index (HSSI) are "multidisciplinary," meaning that they cover many disciplines. Although the HSSI focuses almost exclusively on academic research, other multidisciplinary indexes range beyond academia, offering citations to articles that have appeared in popular magazines. In these cases, academic researchers should be selective about what they use. The more specialized article indexes, such as the MLA Bibliography for English Studies, focus on particular disciplines. These discipline-specific article indexes are probably the most valuable, but they are also the most expensive. Given their cost, small colleges cannot always afford them, and the universities often restrict access. If you happen to be a student at a small college, your campus librarian may have some suggestions about how to deal with such restrictions. In any event, as you search article indexes, either at your own institution or elsewhere, keep the following lists in mind:

Some Multidisciplinary Article Indexes
- Canadian Periodical Index
- Academic FullTEXT Premier
- Canadian MAS FullTEXT Elite
- The Humanities and Social Sciences Index (HSSI)
- Ingenta (direct access via www.ingenta.com)
- General Sciences Index
- Canadian Business and Current Affairs

Some Discipline-Specific Article Indexes
- Art: Art Index
- Art: Artists in Canada (direct access via www.chin.gc.ca)
- Anthropology: Anthropological Index
- Asian Studies: Bibliography of Asian Studies
- Education: ERIC; the Education Index
- Education: Educational Index
- English: the MLA Bibliography
- Sociology: Family Studies
- Sociology: Sociofile
- Sociology Abstracts
- Medicine: Med-Line
- Music: Canadian Music Periodical Index (direct access via www.nlc-bnc.ca/music/index-e.html)
- Leisure and Recreational Studies: National Recreational Data-Base (direct access at www.lin.ca/htdocs/findrs.cfm)
- Psychology: PsycINFO
- Wildlife Biology, Environmental Studies: Environmental Knowledgebase

Choose article indexes that sound appropriate for your field of study. Most indexes will allow you to experiment with exact phrase searching, Boolean combinations, and truncation. Search options may also involve author, title, subject, or key word(s).

Finally, it is worth remembering that book catalogues and article indexes do not exhaust the kinds of formal searching that you can do. There is a vast range of CD-ROM databases, for example, that can also be useful. These come in CD format and do not involve the Internet. The information on a CD-ROM disk is permanently stored on the disk itself. Familiarize yourself with the CD-ROM disks available at your campus library.

Inter-library Loans

If you are based at a small college, it is unlikely that your own library will house all of the books and articles that you discover. In fact, libraries at small colleges may have few if any of the books and journal articles that you want. This means that inter-library loans are often a necessity for people who are serious about their research. Individual libraries have their own inter-library-loan policies and procedures, so make sure that you are aware of the practices at your institution. Requesting an inter-library loan is a leap of faith: there is no guarantee that the material will arrive, and delivery times vary. To optimize your chances for success, you should begin the research process early. Some article indexes, such as the Humanities and Social Sciences Index, enable users to submit inter-library loan requests on-line. Finally, whenever possible, use article indexes that offer full-text options. This will help you to control the cost of inter-library loans.

IDEAS FOR FURTHER STUDY

1. Conduct formal searches for books and journal articles on one of two historical figures in twentieth-century Canadian culture: Grey Owl (Archie Belaney) or Emily Carr. Compile a bibliography that lists five books and five journal articles on the person you are researching. In looking for journal articles, distinguish between popular and academic sources, and choose the latter. Be prepared to explain elements of the topic formula (research site + abstraction) in some of the titles that you find.

2. The following passage is taken from the introduction to "Lords of the World," a research article by Heather Smyth. Smyth's article appeared in a special issue of *Studies in Canadian Literature*. Read through Smyth's essay and identify her articulation of topic. Is topic clearly stated? Can you differentiate topic (aboutness) from thesis (knowledge claim)?

A feeling persisted that I never should discover what I sought for unless I could travel in the wild, unpeopled parts of the world . . . (Vyvyan, *Roots and Stars* 131)

Women, too, have spirits which crave the adventure of the unknown and the silence of the northern wilderness. (Hoyle 117)

The adventurer is in flight from women. (Zweig 61)

The epigraphs that introduce this paper juxtapose a number of ideas about travel and travel writing: the traveller seeks to "discover" something in far-away or foreign places; these destinations are often scripted as "wild," "unpeopled," and "unknown"; women as well as men have the urge for travel and adventure; and, paradoxically, the persona of the traveller or adventurer has historically been masculine. This last point is the starting place for my reading of C.C. Vyvyan's *Arctic Adventure* (1961), a travel narrative of a journey through what is now northern Canada and Alaska, . . . taken in 1926 by C.C. Vyvyan, born Clara Coltman Rogers (1885–1976), and her friend Gwendolyn Dorrien-Smith.[1] The "adventure" portion of the trip involved the two English women and two Loucheux (now Gwich'in) guides named Lazarus Sittichinli and Jim Koe canoeing up the Rat River bridging the Yukon Territory and Alaska, and then the two women alone canoeing the 115 miles downriver from LaPierre House to Old Crow. Although *Arctic Adventure* has received little critical attention,[2] it is significant for being arguably the first travel narrative written about the Canadian Arctic by a white professional writer (MacLaren, "Land" 2); and Vyvyan and Dorrien-Smith are notable for being among the first recreational arctic travellers, so that Vyvyan's travel book marks a transition from centuries of arctic discovery and exploration narratives. *Arctic Adventure*, however, is also important for the ways in which Vyvyan manipulates her travelling and writing personae in a genre that has historically been masculine, and for the ways in which she both resists and reproduces the imperial baggage that accompanies travel writing. Vyvyan's representations of the northern space that she often calls "unpeopled" or "uncharted" are implicated in these negotiations.

I will therefore look at *Arctic Adventure* in terms of the intersections of gender and imperialism.[3] I will be starting from the premise that, although women have always travelled and often written about their travels, the activity of travelling and the genre of travel literature have historically been coded as masculine. This has meant that the conventions of travel writing have supported a reading of the adventurer or traveller as male. Travel writing has also often been accompanied by imperial interests. Earlier exploration ventures in what is now the Canadian Arctic were inspired by mercantile and imperial institutions,[4] and the interests of these institutions often inflect the resulting exploration narratives. In the same way, although Vyvyan travelled independent of any particular institution, her journey was largely facilitated by the institutions, transportation, and communications put in place by the gradual settlement and administration of the Canadian landscape. Her narrative also includes reflections on the legal and religious administration of the north and relations between Native, Inuit, and non-Native northerners.

[Thus,] although Vyvyan has inherited a genre that has historically interpellated the narrator and traveller as male and (to a greater or lesser degree) imperialist, she appears to be adjusting her personae to both fit and work against these confines.

3. Cruise a multidisciplinary index, such as the Humanities and Social Sciences Index, and compile a list of prestige abstractions. Do some abstractions seem discipline-specific? Do you notice densely recurring abstractions in certain disciplines?

4. Being mindful of your instructor's guidelines, begin thinking about a topic (research site + abstraction) for a paper of your own. On a single sheet of paper, present the topic formula accompanied by a list of potential sources from book and article indexes.

CHAPTER REFERENCES

Ally McBeal Essays. (2002, Apr. 11). Call for Papers. Women's Studies Database. Retrieved May 27, 2002, from www.inform.umd.edu/EdRes/Topic/WomensStudies/CallsforPapers

Bazerman, C. (1995). *The informed writer: Using sources in the disciplines* (5ᵗʰ ed.). Toronto: Houghton Mifflin.

The Cultural Legacy of JFK. (2000, Feb. 9). Call for Papers. Retrieved May 27, 2002, from www.english.upenn.edu/CFP/archive/1999-12/0067.html

Farr, M. (2000, March). Brave new B.A. *University Affairs.* 10–13; 24–25.

Fashion and Modernity. (2002, Apr. 11). Call for Papers. Women's Studies Database. Retrieved May 27, 2002, from www.inform.umd.edu/EdRes/Topic/WomensStudies/CallsforPapers

Giltrow, J. (1994). *Academic Writing: Writing and reading across the disciplines.* (2ⁿᵈ ed.). Peterborough: Broadview Press.

_____. (2002). *Academic writing: Writing and reading in the disciplines* (3ʳᵈ ed.). Peterborough: Broadview.

Kirschner, C. (1998). Desperate measures: The murders at St. John's Fort. Unpublished paper submitted for English 100, Northern Lights College.

MacLaren, I.S. (1984). Retaining captaincy of the soul: Responses to nature in the first Franklin expedition. *Essays on Canadian Writing, 28,* 57–92.

Mothering, religion, and spirituality. (2002, January 31). Call for Papers. Women's Studies Database. Retrieved May 27, 2002, from www.inform.umd.edu/EdRes/Topic/WomensStudies/CallsforPapers

Perry, A. (1998). Bachelors in the backwoods: White men and homosocial culture in up-country British Columbia, 1858–1871. In R. Sandwell (Ed.), *Beyond the city limits: Rural history in British Columbia* (pp. 180–194). Vancouver: UBC Press.

Rosen, L.J., & Behrens, L. (1995). *The Allyn and Bacon handbook* (2ⁿᵈ ed.). Toronto: Allyn and Bacon.

Ryan, J. (1995). Experiencing urban schooling: The adjustment of native students to the extra-curricular demands of a post-secondary education program. *The Canadian Journal of Native Studies, 15*(2), 211–229.

Smyth, H. (1998). "'Lords of the world': Writing gender and imperialism on Northern space in C.C. Vyvan's *Arctic Adventure.*" *Studies in Canadian Literature, 23* (1), 32–52.

Tam, C.M., Tso, T.Y., & Lam, K.C. (1999 December). Feng Shui and its impacts on land and property developments. *Journal of Urban Planning and Development, 125*(4), 152–163.

Writing your "self" into the disciplines. (1996). Video. Produced by William Garrett-Petts. Kamloops: UCC Media Production Services.

INTRODUCTION TO THE READING

Heather Harper is an English instructor at Northern Lights College. Her specialty is eighteenth-century British literature, and she has spent many years studying the culture and writing of that period. Despite this broad knowledge, she writes here on a carefully focused topic. Her research site, in particular, has been narrowed to the point where it involves a single object within *Robinson Crusoe*, a novel by Daniel Defoe. Can you spot the research site? This kind of focus is actually an enabling device that permits her to say something new about a work that literary critics have been examining for hundreds of years. Can you identify an abstraction that completes topic?

HEATHER HARPER

A "Clumsy, Ugly, Goat-Skin Umbrella": Domestic Mercantilism and the Umbrella in *Robinson Crusoe*

1   Critics looking at themes of British hegemony in *Robinson Crusoe* usually emphasize Daniel Defoe's vision of empire as it unfolds in colonial South America — understandably since few pages of text are dedicated to Crusoe touching base (but briefly) in England. Less emphasis has been placed on the extent to which Defoe's narrative concerns itself with internal political propaganda and England's internal economy. Accordingly, I wish to examine domestic mercantilism in relation to Robinson Crusoe's "clumsy ugly goat-skin umbrella." I will demonstrate that this umbrella is a site that enables Defoe to transform a foreign and "feminine" luxury item, a sign of decadence, into English and "masculine" mercantile initiative.

2   Towards the middle of the seventeenth century, the parasol, though not the more utilitarian folding umbrella, frequently appeared among the upper classes in France. It was usually delicate and pagoda shaped, with fringed edges. By the end of the century, two trends could be detected: French ladies began to carry their own parasols, which became increasingly lighter, smaller, and more elaborately decorated with fine fabrics and exquisite designs; and brightly-dressed servants, often children, began to carry their parasols for their mistresses. The umbrella was a luxury item, a sign of conspicuous consumption and of class distinction.

3 Some time in the period between 1685 and 1705, a new and more utilitarian waterproof umbrella made its way from France to England. In fact, at the time Defoe was writing *Robinson Crusoe*, this waterproof umbrella was used by women of all classes in England. Given the aristocratic significance of the French parasol, the waterproof umbrella may have seized the English popular imagination as a peculiar upper-class affectation. Two things are certain about the umbrella in Defoe's England: rain or shine, it was not a "masculine" accessory, nor was it a British manufacture. Contemporary journals mocked the few brave "masculine" souls who borrowed umbrellas to leave coffee shops for their carriages. The comic effect and English jingoism of a famous passage from John Gay's 1712 *Trivia* hinges on a popular perception of the umbrella as foreign, upper-class and "feminine." He contrasts the "Good housewives" and the "walking maid" of England with continental beauties. English gals brave the blasts of chastening British rain with the "umbrella's oily shed," while continental beauties bare their "umbrella's ribs" in attempts to screen heat—implicitly emanating from within as well as from without. Apparently, by the second decade of the eighteenth-century, the satiric potential of the umbrella was settled on a middle-class, masculinist, and xenophobic vision of a peculiar luxury object.

4 Why then is Robinson Crusoe, the prototype of virile, imperialist man-against-nature self-sufficiency, lugging an effeminate object of popular ridicule over the "Rocks," "Valleys" (61) and sands of his new "dominion"? I suggest the answer lies with Defoe's mercantilist stance in the second decade of the eighteenth century. Umbrellas were available in London when traders imported them from the continent, usually from France, whose manufacturers were involved in serious production of parasols at the turn of the century. And, as Gay's poem indicates, they were usually made of oiled cotton. Thus Defoe's opposition to the umbrella trade would have been twofold: the English were exporting unmanufactured goods, namely English fabrics, for the French to manufacture umbrellas and ship them back to England as manufactured commodities. Defoe is believed to have what economists term a "fear of goods." Such protectionist policies forbade certain imports in order to protect potential domestic industries, create a self-sufficient state, and gain from a foreign nation in the same manner as an individual merchant might gain from a competitor. Defoe particularly resented the importing of luxury items, feeling as he did that the East India Company was ruining England's domestic economy by paying for useless foreign items with precious bullion.

5   As Crusoe describes his construction of the umbrella, he emphasizes that he builds it because he "c[an] not bear the heat of the sun." In a sense this qualifies what must have seemed a peculiar endeavor to an English readership: he repeats, "I was indeed in great *want* of [an umbrella]" and "they are very *useful* in the great Heats [my emphasis]" (135). But Defoe also *needs* this sensationalism to capture the imagination of an English audience. By emphasizing that the umbrella is the "most necessary" (150) piece of Crusoe's equipment, Defoe yokes the trivial and the vital, the luxury item and the item of use value. Like the baskets, pots and tobacco pipe that Crusoe constructs on the island, the umbrella brings a degree of colonialist "civilization" to the island, but its actual value resides in its figurative marketability. For the reiteration that the umbrella is necessary in hot South American climates is also a reminder that the English merchant would find a potential market for such a manufacture. The umbrella is like lucrative English "Linnen" (134), which, as Crusoe points out, adapts to cold and warm climates, rain and sun.

6   Of course Defoe must engage in acts of fictional marketing to sell his belief in marketability to a male labouring and mercantilist audience. Virginia Woolf claims that Robinson Crusoe "comes in the end to make common actions dignified and common objects beautiful." But this is a dignity and a beauty of a strictly utilitarian cast: after all, Crusoe's motto is "That all the good Things of the World, are no farther good to us, than they are for our Use" (129). He touches on the irony of a man being enthralled with such "trivial" items as an umbrella, "Earthen Ware"(121) and baskets, claiming "No Joy at a Thing of so mean a Nature was ever equal to mine" (121). Just the same, he takes defiant pride in his homely creations. He makes a claim to a kind of creative sincerity by privileging the homely over the beautiful and, ultimately, the masculine over the feminine. The umbrella, signifying feminine loveliness and excess, becomes a "clumsy ugly" thing, ironically made of goat-skin, the goat, of course, a traditional figure for male sexual aggression. It is most often catalogued beside Crusoe's gun in his descriptions of island exploration, and the "dignity" of the construction and "use" of the

umbrella completely efface any "feminine" aesthetic value. There is conspicuous absence of satire of the umbrella's trivial "femininity," except, perhaps, what Defoe may have banked on as popular preconceptions. But woman is not even a potential consumer of luxury items in the text, for there is nothing beautiful for her to consume. She simply does not exist in this homosocial (business) transaction between male author and reader, except as reproductive potential for future colonists and future consumers of more utilitarian objects. The "feminine" must be absent from both the field of labour and the new domestic sphere if the business transaction between writer and reader is to be successful.

7   Who, then, is Defoe addressing by stressing the potential market for English goods in "the *Brasils*" (135) and future English colonies? As I've suggested, he sets out to convince English labourers, manufacturers, and traders of the happiness and pride found in labour. After all, he had previously secured the link between empire and industry with something like a missionary zeal in *History of Arts and Sciences,* claiming "no Man can do his Country greater Service than to open their Eyes, and encourage their Hands to Industry and Improvement." Defoe believed that with a little initiative the English could tap into, revive, and rework old inventions. But if he effaces the feminine with the ugliness of his umbrella, he appropriates rather than emulates its foreignness with his innovations, perfections and applications. For instance, when Crusoe describes taking "a great deal of Time and Pains" (135) to construct his umbrella, he reenacts a moral initiative and creativity that had actually already transpired on the continent. For the Parisian trader, Marius, had struggled to invent an umbrella that would fold and dismantle. Essentially Crusoe perfects Marius's imperfect collapsible invention. He claims,

> I took a world of Pains at it, and was a great while before I could
> make any thing likely to hold; nay, after I thought I had hit the Way,
> I spoil'd 2 or 3 before I made one to my Mind; but at last I made
> one that answer'd indifferently well: The main Difficulty I found
> was to make it to let down. I could not make it spread, but
> if it did not let down too, and draw in, it was not portable . . .
> However, at last, as I said, I made one to answer . . . and when
> I had no need of it, could close it and carry it under my Arm. (135)

As in all of Crusoe's "invention" passages, he writes to the moment in halting, repetitive, subordinate clauses, likely more motivating to the English reader than passages of straight moral didacticism. For the prose mirrors the frustration but also the enthrallment of intense labour and discovery.

8   Likewise it was intense labour and discovery that, in Defoe's opinion, linked social strata; the key to national wealth was the interdependence of the wealthy and the poor. In his economic writings Defoe demonstrates a Mandevillean acceptance of luxury items, insofar as he sees unnecessary commodities as necessary boosts to the economy. Before Crusoe makes his tour around the island in his boat, he places his "Umbrella ... in a Step at the Stern like a Mast, to stand over [his] Head, and keep the Heat and the Sun off [his head] like an Auning" (137). This is an obvious parody of the French royalty's *des parasols coudés en biais,* or royal umbrellas or "Aunings" as they are represented in contemporary portraits, protecting the nobility from the sun at ceremonies. For centuries the umbrella was the privilege of royals, nobles, or high church officials.

9   This parallel is particularly suggestive since Defoe is ceremonially touring his "little Kingdom" (137). Defoe believed that no gentleman or gentlewoman had the right to live in complete luxury and idleness, but his is a relatively untroubled aping of upper-class self-indulgence. Crusoe travels in his boat, the product of his own labour, which is packed with provisions he has laboriously supplied. This is an image of the man of "middle station" enjoying the fruits of his efforts with the well-deserved ceremonial pomp of a king.

10 So how did English readers react to Crusoe's remodelling the umbrella to make an English, masculine, middle-class convenience item? The most famous illustrations of Robinson Crusoe from the first English and French editions of the text are telling first reactions. Both engravings create enduring visual images of the passage in which Crusoe claims,

> But had any one in *England* been to meet such a Man as I was, it must either have frightened them, or rais'd a great deal of Laughter; and as I frequently stood still to look at my self, I could not but smile at the Notion of my travelling through *Yorkshire* with such an

> Equipage, and in such a Dress: Be pleas'd to take a Scetch of my
> Figure as follows. (149)

The 1720 French frontispiece portrait was influenced by the 1719 English engraving. Both show Crusoe standing beside the ocean in extraordinary dress of goat-skin jacket, breeches, and cap with his cave and "Fence or Fortress" (59) in the background.

11   The British engraving emphasizes his alienation from homeland: he has a wistful expression on his face, a merchant ship is leaving the island in treacherous waters, the land is desolate, and his fence is small and decrepit. His clothes are certainly peculiar, of shaggy and layered goat hair, but they are fitted and a fashionable length, and his beard is trim, despite Crusoe's textual detail, "I had trimm'd [my moustache] into a large Pair of *Mahometan* Whiskers, . . . they were the Length and Shape monstrous enough, and such as in *England* would have pass'd for frightful" (150). He looks like an adventurer or conqueror, carrying his "two pistols" (50) and a sword with his legs planted firmly astride. The umbrella is conspicuously absent from this first English engraving and would remain so until the nineteenth century, when the umbrella was no longer perceived as peculiar and effeminate.

12   *Robinson Crusoe* was more popular in France than England throughout the greater part of the eighteenth century. In the first and, perhaps, most famous French engraving, Crusoe not only looks more comfortable with his lush natural surroundings, but he looks more industrious, standing beside an elaborate fortress and carrying a pistol, a basket, some shot and a saw. His costume is more detailed and his appearance wild. But what first captures the eye is a magnificent and quite elegant umbrella; it takes up the upper third of the portrait, nearly eclipsing the sky. Oddly enough, its goat hair hangs over edges, forming fringe not unlike the stylish French parasol as it appears in many contemporary prints. Crusoe even holds his umbrella at a slant, as many fashionable French women did, to reveal its surprisingly delicate boning. Ironically enough, the umbrella was an increasingly elaborate accessory for Crusoe costumes at fashionable dress balls in France throughout the eighteenth century. And "Robinson" became a

popular name for the umbrella in France for two hundred years after
the publication of *Robinson Crusoe*.

WORKS CITED

Backsheider, Paula. "The Rise of Gender as Political Category." *Revising Women:
    Eighteenth Century 'Women's Fiction' and Social Engagement*. Baltimore: Johns
    Hopkins, 2000.
Bell, Ian. "King Crusoe: Locke's Political Theory in *Robinson Crusoe*." *English Studies:
    A Journal of English Language and Literature* 69.1 (1988): 27–36.
Blewett, Davis. *The Illustrations of Robinson Crusoe 1719–1720*. Gerrards Cross,
    England: C. Smythe, 1995.
Brown, Laura. "Amazon and Africans: Gender, Race and Empire in Daniel Defoe."
    Women, 'Race,' and Writing in the Early Modern Period. Ed. M. Hendricks and P.
    Parker. London: Routledge, 1994.
Crawford, T.S. *A History of the Umbrella*. New York: Taplinger, 1970.
Defoe, Daniel. *The Life and Adventures of Robinson Crusoe*. New York: Penguin,
    1985.
_____. *The Life and Strange Surprising Adventures of Robinson Crusoe of York, as related
    himself, with upwards of one hundred illustrations*. London: Cassell, Peters and
    Galpin, 1883.
_____. *Robinson Crusoe*. Ed. J. Donald Crowley. Oxford: Oxford UP, 1983.
_____. *Serious Reflections During the Life and Surprising Adventures of Robinson Crusoe:
    With His Vision of the Angelick World*. London: Taylor, 1720.
Downie, A. "Defoe, Imperialism, and the Travel Book Reconsidered." *Yearbook of
    English Studies* 13 (1983): 66–83.
Farrell, Jeremy. *Umbrellas and Parasols*. London: B.T. Batsford, 1985.
Flanders, W. Austin. *Structures of Experience: History, Society and Personal Life in the
    Eighteenth-Century British Novel*. Columbia: U of South Carolina P, 1984.
Kay, Carol. *Political Constructions: Defoe, Richardson, and Sterne in Relation to Hobbes,
    Hume and Burke*. Ithaca: Cornell UP, 1988.
Langer, Erick, ed. *Christian Encounters with the Other*. New York: New York UP,
    1998.
L'ombrell- le gant-le manchon. Illus. Paul Avril. Paris: A. Quantin, 1883.
Novak, Maximillian E. *Economics and the Fiction of Daniel Defoe*. Berkeley: U of
    California P, 1962.
Richetti, John J. *Daniel Defoe*. Boston: Twayne, 1987.
Ridley, Hugh. *Images of Imperial Rule*. London: Croom Helm, 1983.
Seidel, Michael. *Robinson Crusoe: Island Myths and the Novel*. Boston: Twayne, 1991.
Smith, Vanessa. "Crusoe in the South Seas: Beachcombers, Missionaries and the
    Myth of the Castaway." *Robinson Crusoe: Myths and Metamorphoses*. Eds. Lieve
    Spaas and Brian Stimpson. London: Macmillan, 1996.

Sorcini, Sara. "The Island as Social Experiment: A Reappraisal of Daniel Defoe's Political Discourses." *Robinson Crusoe and the Farther Adventures* 30 (1997): 11–43.

Still, Geoffrey. *Defoe and the Idea of Fiction, 1713–1719.* Newark: U of Delaware P, 1983.

Vickers, Ilse. *Defoe and the New Sciences.* Cambridge: Cambridge UP, 1996.

White, Michael. "Reading and Rewriting: the Production of an Economic *Robinson Crusoe.*" *Southern Review: Literary and Interdisciplinary Essays* 15.2 (1982): 115–142.

Woolf, Virginia. "Robinson Crusoe." *The Second Common Reader.* New York: Harcourt Brace Jovanovich, 1932.

Skimming, Note-Taking, and Summarizing

Knowledge never stands alone. It builds upon and plays against the knowledge of previous knowers and reporters, whom scholars call "sources." These are not, in scholarly papers, the source of your particular argument (you are), but rather persons or documents that help you arrive at and support your argument. They are sources of information that you interpret; of ideas that you support, criticize, or develop; of vivid language that you quote and analyze.
— Gordon Harvey, *Writing with Sources: A Guide for Students*

Since academic writers depend heavily on sources, they often have to wade through a lot of information. Indeed, writing a research paper may take weeks of preliminary research. Professors and graduate students sometimes spend longer periods — months, even years — doing research that precedes writing. Clearly, undergraduate students labour under more severe time constraints, but the ability to find texts, to extract and repackage information, and to record where the information came from remains crucial. Thus, good academic writers must develop special skills as readers.

SKIMMING AND NOTE-TAKING

To retrace steps from the previous chapter, imagine that you have a general research site in mind and that you have spoken to your instructor about it. You have also found related books and articles, some of which involve inter-library loans. You may be dismayed to see that a book received through inter-library loan is due back in one week, leaving only a few days to digest what's in there.

All due back
In one week?

You are taking three other courses—two of them also involve research papers—and you work part time. In situations like this, skimming and note-taking are vital to academic success.

Confronting the book that is due in one week, you are still trying to clarify your own sense of topic. Skimming the table of contents, introduction, and perhaps the index, you should be on the lookout for ways of narrowing the research site. It would also be a good idea to watch for recurring words or phrases that might eventually function as prestige abstractions. Remember:

Research Site + Prestige Abstraction = Topic

Let's say, for example, that a student has an interest in writing on some aspect of the western Canadian oil patch. Through inter-library loan, the student has requested and received *Oil and Ideology: The Cultural Creation of the American Petroleum Industry,* by Roger M. Olien and Diana Davids Olien (2000). The American focus is a bit off as far as the research site goes, but the book could still help to generate an abstraction. The title, for instance, refers to "ideology"—an intriguing yet ambiguous word.

The Table of Contents for *Oil and Ideology* doesn't appear terribly informative, but it does have suggestive chapter headings that sound like this: "Manhood against Money," "Hasting to Get Rich," "Numerous Offences against Common Morality," "Running Out of Oil," "Visions of Chaos," and so on. Accordingly, gender and/or masculinity, already familiar abstractions, again appear to be relevant. Concepts such as wealth, competition, ethics, resource sustainability, and industrial regulation may also be hovering in the background.

The Preface to the book is quite complex, leaving no doubt that this is a genuinely academic text (not coincidentally, the publisher is the University of North Carolina Press). In the Preface, we find out that this is very much a book about "discourse" — about the language and imagery used to describe the American petroleum industry. The authors say that they are going to investigate various "channels of discourse" (Olien & Olien, 2000, p. xiii) and that such channels involve the themes implicit in the Table of Contents.

Thus, *Oil and Ideology* suggests that a prestige abstraction for a ten-page paper could highlight a particular "channel of discourse" in the western Canadian petroleum industry. Skimming other sources as they become available, it would be a good idea to watch for overlapping concepts or issues. Ideally, clusters of related material will emerge. If, for example, other sources also have something to say about wealth, particularly the language and imagery of wealth, a viable abstraction might be on the horizon. Granted, a student wanting to write on the oil industry in western Canada may still have a lot of research to do. Such a student may, for example, feel a need to generate primary sources by conducting interviews with people involved in, say, northeastern British Columbia's oil patch. Students wishing to conduct personal interviews as part of their research should check their institution's research ethics guidelines before commencing their interviews.

As mentioned in the previous chapter, there is often no easy or linear route to finding a topic. Realistically, the process may involve agonizing indecision and a host of dead ends and frustrated hopes. It will almost certainly involve a mix of intuition and expedient decision-making, or maybe sheer stubbornness will prevail.

In any event, once you become reasonably confident about how your topic might be defined, it is time to begin making notes in earnest. Be a voracious, efficient reader. Go through as much material as you can, extracting information that you hope will be useful when you begin to draft the paper. The process of extraction can vary, and sometimes the differences are rooted in nothing more than personal habits or preferences. Some people like using note cards that can be easily shuffled, bound by an elastic band, or neatly packed inside plastic boxes. Some people have been writing on lined pages of loose-leaf since grade one and want to continue doing so. The relatively large amount of space on loose-leaf pages can accommodate a lot of notes and even provide room to photocopy and paste whole paragraphs or pages from sources. Other people feel most comfortable taking notes with a keyboard and putting pieces of information directly onto a computer screen. Choose a technique that works for you.

Whatever strategy you choose, your goal should be to create an intelligible, intermediate text that lies halfway between your raw source material and your first draft. In other words, you should be able to write the draft mostly from your notes rather than having to go back to the sources themselves. Charles Bazerman (1995) offers this advice on note-taking: "The most precise form of note is an exact quotation. Whenever you suspect that you may later wish to quote the writer's exact words, make sure you copy the quotation correctly. And whenever you decide to copy exact words down in your notes — even if only a passing phrase — make sure you enclose them in *quotation marks*. In this way you can avoid inadvertent plagiarism when you are working from your notes" (p. 305).

Although people's notes will have different characteristics, *everyone should carefully record where the extracted information came from*. In the days when scholars primarily relied on printed material, this information involved some basic bibliographical (or textual) data, such as author and/or editor, full title, publisher, date of publication, and page numbers. Today, if the full texts of some sources have been accessed through the Internet, the bibliographical fingerprint is more likely to involve author, title, access date, and Web address. Different scholarly disciplines have different and very elaborate, rule-governed procedures for presenting bibliographical information in finished papers. Be sure that you accurately copy down all the information you will need. This can be properly formatted later on.

Returning to the hypothetical paper on the discourse of wealth in the western Canadian oil industry, notes taken from the Preface of *Oil and Ideology* might look like this:

Roger M. Olien and Diana Davids Olien. (2000). *Oil and Ideology: The Cultural Creation of the American Petroleum Industry*. Chapel Hill: University of North Carolina Press.

Preface
- "College-level textbooks usually portray John D. Rockefeller, the archetypal oil man and CEO of Standard Oil, as a ruthless 'robber baron'" (x).

- "In short, Standard's predations and the anticompetitive and anticonsumer identity of the domestic oil industry are largely taken as 'given'" (x).
- "As we studied what has been said about the domestic petroleum industry, we came to recognize broad rhetorical categories, or, as we prefer to call them, channels of discourse. These are identified in terms of the subject area speakers addressed, the focus they took within that area, and the themes and rhetoric they used. Each channel has specific contextual information and characteristic perspectives along with broader elements of ideology" (xiii).
- One of the main channels of discourse is economic (xiii).
- "As we shall demonstrate, though there were differing ways of talking about oil, a great many of them were negative and tied the industry to problems such as the abuse of economic power or waste of natural resources. And, as we shall describe, such negative ideas, a staple in [the] discourse, had a powerful influence on the impulse to regulate the industry" (xv).

Given that chapters 1 and 2 in *Oil and Ideology* seem to pay special attention to the discourse of wealth, these chapters might also deserve carefully recorded notes. Such notes could be supplemented by pages photocopied from the source.

WRITING SUMMARIES

As mentioned, when you go through your sources, there's no telling what or how much you may want to lift out. In some cases, very short notes, like those above, will seem adequate: you may simply want to take a sentence here or there. In other cases, you may want to expand the note-taking process so that it encompasses larger amounts of material — paragraphs, say, or pages, perhaps even entire articles or books. This is where summary comes in.

When you summarize, you demonstrate your ability to condense and repackage extended blocks of information while preserving their "gist" or general meaning. The summary enables you to take charge of or manage your sources. It is a way for you to shape your paper (*to make your paper your own*) while at the same time relying on other voices. In a sense, summary writing points to a crucial principle of academic

Ten pages of stuff!
What do I really need?

writing. Summaries demonstrate that academic writing involves a kind of balancing act: on the one hand, academic writers tend to rely quite heavily on sources; on the other hand, such writers contribute something of their own. If a student paper consists of too many long passages pulled directly from sources, the balance is lost, resulting in what instructors derisively refer to as a "cut-and-paste job."

There is much more to say about the kind of contributions that academic writers make to their papers, but, for now, it is enough to acknowledge summarizing as an initial means of moving beyond passive copying. People who can write good summaries demonstrate that they can condense information by neatly packing it into usable bundles that can be sorted and arranged to enhance the development of a paper.

Summaries may turn up almost anywhere in a finished paper. For example, readers may encounter summary in an introduction, when the author of the paper (the primary writer) is describing previous research on his or her subject. Here, as the primary writer describes *a tradition of inquiry*, articles and books may be summarized in a sentence or two. At other times, however, in the middle of a core paragraph, say, the primary writer may be inclined to delve more deeply into the work of others, devoting more space to smaller amounts of material. In any event, summary writing is a practical skill that you will need as you put together your own research paper.

Summarizing a Portion of an Article

We'll begin modestly, by following an attempt to summarize a section of an article. Imagine that a student researcher (we'll call her Susan) has a general subject in mind: the Canadian north in Aboriginal cultures. While perusing the Humanities and Social Sciences Index, using "north AND Aboriginal people*" as a search formulation, Susan came across an article by Shelagh Grant (1989), entitled "Myths of the North in the Canadian Ethos." A section of this article deals with Aboriginal attitudes toward the Canadian north, and this is the section that Susan wants to preserve in her records. The section, in its entirety, reads as follows:

> Perhaps the oldest and most enduring perception of the north is one shared by the indigenous peoples long before Europeans set foot on the shores of the western hemisphere. There are many cultures and subcultures among the Indian and Inuit of northern Canada, but they share similar attitudes towards the land, derived in part from the long experience of survival in what many southerners consider a hostile environment. The image of the north as a "homeland" is essentially a southern expression for the intensely spiritual concept of land held by northern natives. To the Inuit, it is called *Nunassiaq*, meaning the beautiful land. Fred Bruemmer, who has lived and travelled extensively in the Arctic, describes the deeper meaning of *Nunassiaq:*

> > He (an Inuk) was a part of it; it brought him sorrow and it brought him joy, and he lived in harmony with it and its demands, accepting fatalistically, its hardships, exulting in its bounty and beauty.[11]

> Prior to European contact, everything within the Inuit's natural world had a spiritual connotation, a sanctity which must be respected. The infinite space and majestic grandeur of the Arctic "gave northern man a special awe for the might and mystery of the world, impressed upon him his own insignificance, and made him both mystically inclined and humble." This feeling of impotence was also the basis for the Inuit's belief in shamans to act as "intermediaries between the world of man and the world of the spirits." Any life form or inanimate object which had a sense of

permanency was thought to have had a spirit or soul, a belief which explains his profound respect for nature.[12] He was not a separate entity arriving on earth: he was always there, at one with, and a part of the natural world.

The Dene Indians of the Northwest Territories have similar beliefs, perhaps more estranged due to a more prolonged and intensive contact with western man. Significantly, there is no word for wilderness in the Athapaskan dialects. Wherever they travelled, it was simply "home." In the words of one Dene, the land represented "the very spirit of the Dene way of life. From the land came our religion . . . from the land came our life . . . from the land came our powerful medicine . . . from the land came our way of life."[13] There was also a strong mother image attached to the land and waters, which fed and protected them from adversity. To the Aborigines of the north, their land was never "owned" in the sense of western man. It was always there. Only with the intrusion of strangers who did not understand the bond between man and nature was there a disorientation in the symbiotic balance between humans, animals, plant life, and the earth. There was never an idea of frontier or imperial design. The land belonged to the Creator, and in the Dene expression, [was] only borrowed for their children's children.[14]

Because Susan is merely at the information-gathering stage, she could "note" or file this passage through a variety of shortcuts. One option would be to photocopy the passage, tape it onto a sheet of loose-leaf, and record the appropriate bibliographic data. Moreover, when it comes to drafting, Susan could again save time and effort by simply presenting Grant's information as one long *block quote.* However, Susan knows that too many block quotes create a cut-and-paste impression and that summary writing is worth the effort: it will enable her to take charge of Grant's material.

In this case, Susan has decided to aim for an 80-percent reduction of the original material. Since Grant's passage is approximately 500 words in length, this means that Susan will try to get it down to 100 words. She will adhere to the following guidelines that can be applied, with minor variations, to virtually every summary task:

Preparation: Carefully read through the material that you are going to summarize.

- **Step 1:** Reread the material, highlighting or underlining the major points in each paragraph. Be on the lookout for guiding sentences at the beginning of paragraphs. However, paragraph structure varies. Main points may be elaborated on at the end of paragraphs. Accordingly, each paragraph has to be individually analyzed.
  - Do not highlight examples or details.
  - Aim for gist. Remember, too, that this business of identifying main points is somewhat subjective. Instructor and students should tolerate some differences of opinion as to what constitutes a main point.
- **Step 2:** Copy the main points onto a separate sheet of paper.
- **Step 3:** Study and revise the list of main points: re-order the list where appropriate, and condense the list if you can. Is there needless repetition? Can some points be combined and condensed? Does the order of the points make sense — should you rearrange the points?
- **Step 4:** As much as possible, put the revised main points into your own words by paraphrasing them. Quote only where the exact words of the source are vital. Use transitions or logical connectives to ensure coherence.
- **Step 5:** Reformat the main points in a well-written paragraph. Begin by introducing the author and title. Then present the revised and paraphrased main points. Continually attribute these points to the author.

Below, Susan applies these five steps to Grant's passage. Study the application critically. See if you agree or disagree with the judgements made.

Step 1: Underlining main points

Perhaps the oldest and most enduring perception of the north is one shared by the indigenous peoples long before Europeans set foot on the shores of the western hemisphere. <u>There are many cultures and subcultures among the Indian and Inuit of northern Canada, but they share similar attitudes towards the land,</u> derived in part from

the long experience of survival in what many southerners consider
a hostile environment. The image of the north as a "homeland" is
essentially a southern expression for the intensely spiritual concept
of land held by northern natives. To the Inuit, it is called *Nunassiaq*,
meaning the beautiful land. Fred Bruemmer, who has lived and
travelled extensively in the Arctic, describes the deeper meaning of
Nunassiaq:

> He (an Inuk) was a part of it; it brought him sorrow and it
> brought him joy, and he lived in harmony with it and its
> demands, accepting fatalistically, its hardships, exulting
> in its bounty and beauty.[11]

Prior to European contact, everything within the Inuit's natural
world had a spiritual connotation, a sanctity which must be
respected. The infinite space and majestic grandeur of the Arctic
"gave northern man a special awe for the might and mystery of the
world, impressed upon him his own insignificance, and made him
both mystically inclined and humble." This feeling of impotence
was also the basis for the Inuit's belief in shamans to act as
"intermediaries between the world of man and the world of the
spirits." Any life form or inanimate object which had a sense of
permanency was thought to have had a spirit or soul, a belief which
explains his profound respect for nature.[12] He was not a separate
entity arriving on earth: he was always there, at one with, and a part
of the natural world.

The Dene Indians of the Northwest Territories have similar
beliefs, perhaps more estranged due to a more prolonged and
intensive contact with western man. Significantly, there is no word
for wilderness in the Athapaskan dialects. Wherever they travelled,
it was simply "home." In the words of one Dene, the land represented
"the very spirit of the Dene way of life. From the land came our
religion . . . from the land came our life . . . from the land came our
powerful medicine . . . from the land came our way of life."[13] There
was also a strong mother image attached to the land and waters,
which fed and protected them from adversity. To the Aborigines of
the north, their land was never "owned" in the sense of western
man. It was always there. Only with the intrusion of strangers who
did not understand the bond between man and nature was there a
disorientation in the symbiotic balance between humans, animals,

plant life, and the earth. <u>There was never an idea of frontier or imperial design. The land belonged to the Creator, and in the Dene expression, [was] only borrowed for their children's children.</u>[14]

Step 2: Copying out main points (note that superscript numerals are now omitted)

1. There are many cultures and subcultures among the Indian and Inuit of northern Canada, but they share similar attitudes towards the land . . .

2. Prior to European contact, everything within the Inuit's natural world had a spiritual connotation, a sanctity which must be respected.

3. Any life form or inanimate object which had a sense of permanency was thought to have had a spirit or soul, a belief which explains his profound respect for nature. He was not a separate entity arriving on earth: he was always there, at one with, and a part of the natural world.

4. The Dene Indians of the Northwest Territories have similar beliefs, perhaps more estranged due to a more prolonged and intensive contact with western man. Significantly, there is no word for wilderness in the Athapaskan dialects. Wherever they travelled, it was simply "home."

5. There was never an idea of frontier or imperial design. The land belonged to the Creator, and in the Dene expression, [was] only borrowed for their children's children.

Step 3: Re-ordering and/or condensing main points

1. There are many cultures and subcultures among the Indian and Inuit of northern Canada, but they share similar attitudes towards the land . . .

2. Prior to European contact, everything within the Inuit's natural world had a spiritual connotation, a sanctity which must be respected. ~~Any life form or inanimate object which had a sense of permanency was thought to have had a spirit or soul, a belief which explains his profound respect for nature.~~

3. He was not a separate entity arriving on earth: he was always there, at one with, and a part of the natural world.

4. The Dene Indians of the Northwest Territories have similar beliefs, perhaps more estranged due to a more prolonged and intensive

contact with western man. Significantly, there is no word for wilderness in the Athapaskan dialects. There was never an idea of frontier or imperial design.

5. Wherever they travelled, it was simply "home." The land belonged to the Creator, and in the Dene expression, [was] only borrowed for their children's children.

Step 4: Rewording the original (now that paraphrasing enters the process, quotation marks distinguish Grant's words from Susan's own)

1. Aboriginal peoples in northern Canada have different "cultures and subcultures," "but they share similar attitudes toward the land."

2. For the Inuit, virtually everything in their world has a soul that "must be respected."

3. Accordingly, the Inuit did not feel superior to or apart from nature: they were a part of it.

4. Given their "prolonged and intensive contact with western man," the Dene peoples of the Northwest Territories do not feel as close to nature, but they share Inuit values. Indeed, the Dene have "no word for 'wilderness,'" no sense of "frontier or imperial design."

5. For them, nature is "simply 'home'" — something that belongs to "the Creator" and is "borrowed" for future generations.

Step 5: The complete summary (attributive expressions have been placed in bold print, for emphasis)

In **"Myths of the North in the Canadian Ethos," Shelagh Grant contends** that Aboriginal peoples in northern Canada have different "cultures and subcultures," "but they share similar attitudes toward the land." **Grant notes** that, for the Inuit, virtually everything in the natural world has a soul that "must be respected." Accordingly, the Inuit do not feel superior to or apart from nature: they are a part of it. Given their "prolonged and intensive contact with western man," **Grant observes** that the Dene peoples of the Northwest Territories do not feel as close to nature, but they share Inuit values. Indeed, the Dene, **Grant says**, have "no word for 'wilderness,'" no sense of "frontier or imperial design." For them, nature is "simply 'home'" — something that belongs to "the Creator" and is "borrowed" for future generations.

Susan's summary sounds impressive, but it is a little long — around 130 words rather than 100. Given a little more work, Susan could probably reduce it to the intended word count. Remember, too, that another student might have been inclined to make some different decisions about what to highlight and what to leave, what to paraphrase and what to quote. Nevertheless, it is likely that other summaries would sound very similar to this one.

Summarizing a Complete Article

The length of article summaries varies. As noted, the summaries that are presented as part of a tradition of inquiry within research papers tend to be very short — a sentence or two. Here, in order to allow for more elaborate summaries, the scope will be set at 250–300 words. In effect, we are inviting what could otherwise be called "abstracts" — paragraph-length synopses of an entire paper. Given that a complete article is now at stake, the summary process could be reconfigured as follows:

Preparation: Read the entire article, then divide it into major structural divisions. Draw solid lines to separate the introduction, core, and conclusion. Draw dotted lines to separate major subdivisions within the core of the essay. In some essays, these subdivisions will be clearly denoted by subheadings.

- **Step One:** Reread the introduction, blocking its major rhetorical features (see Chapter 6 for more information). At a minimum, try to get the summary underway by formulating topic and thesis in a couple of sentences. Other introductory features, such as a theoretical framework, could also be included here.
- **Step Two:** Block or highlight guiding sentences (main points) in core paragraphs (see Chapter 7 for more information). Ultimately, each section or subsection within the core will have to be reduced to a few sentences.
- **Step Three:** Copy guiding sentences in the core onto a sheet of paper.
- **Step Four:** Study and revise the list of main points: re-order the list where appropriate, and condense the list if you can. Is there needless repetition? Can some points be

combined and condensed? Does the order of the points make sense — should you rearrange the points?

- **Step Five:** As much as possible, put the revised main points into your own words by paraphrasing them. Quote only where the exact words of the source are vital. Use transitions or logical connectives to ensure coherence.
- **Step Six:** Reformat the main points in a well-written paragraph that consistently employs attribution.
- **Step Seven:** Reread the conclusion, blocking its major rhetorical features (see Chapter 8). If a conclusion merely recaps a thesis or main points, it may not have to be included in the summary. However, if a conclusion contains other important rhetorical features, this material should be incorporated into the summary.

Writing Critical Summaries

Writing an accurate, comprehensive summary of an entire article is a noble achievement. Having successfully undertaken such a task, the summary writer makes something new. The academic community respects such efforts because it understands the importance of gathering and compacting knowledge. Indeed, prestigious academic journals frequently publish papers that are devoted to a "literature review" — a survey and synthesis of research on a given topic.

Frequently, however, journal editors and instructors expect something more: they may want the primary writer to move beyond synthesis to evaluation. For students who are newcomers to a given knowledge domain, evaluation can be a daunting task. Nevertheless, while it is wise to approach evaluation with some humility, novice scholars are entitled to judge the work of more senior people, just as students are entitled to judge or question the authority of instructors. In fact, such questioning fosters a free exchange of ideas that is vital to the health of the academic community. Moreover, "evaluation" does not necessarily put you in the position of a movie reviewer who gives a thumbs-up or thumbs-down, just as "criticism" does not consist solely of explicit praise or condemnation. Praise or condemn if you wish, but you are also free simply to comment on aspects of someone else's work. Here are some perspectives to consider as you try to develop a critical point of view:

- Inspect the connections in the argument: Are there weak connections? Are there gaps in reasoning or logical fallacies?
- Inspect the evidence: Is the evidence substantial or solid enough? Is it sufficient to support the writer's thesis? What kind of evidence is being presented? Is the evidence mainly anecdotal? Is it limited to one person's view? Is it circumstantial?
- What is the writer's relation to his or her own topic? Is the writer too emotionally involved in the material? Is there an unacknowledged personal bias in the paper? If so, how does this bias manifest itself?
- What is the other side of the argument? Are opposing views acknowledged and/or given fair treatment? What else can be said for the other view?
- Is there an underlying, Big Issue in the article, one that is not fully acknowledged? Do you see any prestige abstractions that may be buried in the paper? If so, bring these to the light of day. Introducing related ideas is another form of commentary.
- Does the author seem to be working from assumptions, unstated or stated, that you can call into question?

When writing a critical summary, criticism is usually appended to the topic, thesis, and main-point structure of straight summary. Remember that your comments are your own: say what you think is pertinent. What catches your attention?

IDEAS FOR FURTHER STUDY

1. In 100–120 words, summarize another section of Shelagh Grant's article:

[In the nineteenth century,] the *voyageurs* hired by the Nor'Westers gave further credence to established fur trade myths. These men toiled endlessly without complaint, proud of their strength and skill, joyous of their freedom and relative independence. Following the amalgamation of the two major rivals, the North West Company and the Hudson's Bay Company in 1821, the term "voyageur" was commonly used to describe most participants in the fur trade, portraying a romantic image similar to that of the *coureurs de bois*, "living lives of perilous adventure, gruelling labour and boisterous camaraderie." As a result, the *voyageur* and his canoe became fully integrated into both English and French versions of our cultural heritage and an integral part of the romantic image of the north.

Much of our present knowledge of the fur trade history has come by way of the day books and diaries of fur traders. Their attention to detail and the desire to relate their impressions and emotional experiences have provided succeeding generations of writers and scholars with an authentic mirror on the past. An almost magical connotation was attributed to the voyageurs by a former Hudson's Bay employee who described the thrill of hearing the "wild romantic song" and seeing a brigade of twenty or more canoes rounding a promontory, "half shrouded in the spray that flew from the bright vermilion paddles."[18]

Visual images of the northern fur trade have also been faithfully preserved in the dramatic paintings of John Halkett, Frances Hopkins, Arthur Fleming, and others. Similarly, many French-Canadian folktales focused on the tragedies or heroic feats encountered in the north. While the characters and details were original, many plots were adaptations of European fables. The tale of the "Chasse-Galerie" is a classic example, based on the threat of eternal damnation for having sold one's soul to the devil. One French-Canadian version describes a flying canoe as having transported lonely men from a remote northern lumber camp to their loved ones in Montreal. Alas, the canoe was sterned by none other than the devil himself, and its eager occupants paid dearly for their escape from the fearful isolation of the northern wilderness.[19] The *voyageur* songs, on the other hand, were quite original. Singing and chanting in time to the dip of the paddles was a means of keeping a steady pace and relieving the monotony of long stretches of lake travel. Yet the message would vary to fit the mood or occasion, sometimes reinforcing the paddlers' quest for freedom and adventure, while ridiculing the life left behind; on the return voyage there would more likely be nostalgic reminders of those back home. Among the favourites were "En Roulant ma Boule," "C'est L'Aviron," and "Youpe Youpe sur la Rivière."[20] Thus, in folktales, art, and music, an image of the northern wilderness has been indelibly linked to freedom, adventure, and challenge.

Ironically, however, in the early 1800s the *voyageur* legends had seemingly little effect on the better-educated French Canadians, who were perhaps too preoccupied with re-orienting their own society and politics to be overly concerned with images of the north. But they were kept alive in the near north — the Laurentians, Lac St. Jean, Rimouski, and the upper Ottawa valley — where isolated lumber camps offered employment to sons of the poorer habitants. Here, the tales and songs of the *coureur de bois* and *voyageur* were added to those of the *forestier* to help while away the long winter nights. The myths that emerged were neither elitist nor intellectual; they were simply perceptions of common folk, passed on in the oral tradition. French-Canadian literature, on the other hand, increasingly focused on the agrarian myth and the "civilizing mission," no doubt influenced by a growing sense of Quebec nationalism and the dominance of the Catholic Church.[21]

2. Write a summary of James Keller's "Masculinity and Marginality in *Rob Roy* and *Braveheart*," an essay that appears at the end of this chapter. Do you see distinct divisions between the introduction, core, and conclusion? Do you see topic and thesis in the introduction?

CHAPTER REFERENCES

Bazerman, C. (1995). *The informed writer: Using sources in the disciplines.* 5th ed. Boston: Houghton Mifflin.

Grant, S. (1989). Myths of the north in the Canadian ethos. *The Northern Review, 3–4,* 15–41.

Harvey, G. (1998). *Writing with sources: A guide for students.* Expository Writing Program, Harvard University. Cambridge: Hackett.

Olien, R.M. & Olien, D.D. (2000). *Oil and ideology: The cultural creation of the American petroleum industry.* Chapel Hill: University of North Carolina Press.

INTRODUCTION TO THE READINGS

James Keller, author of "Masculinity and Marginality in *Rob Roy* and *Braveheart*," teaches in the Humanities Division at the Mississippi University for Women, in Columbus, Ohio.

JAMES KELLER

Masculinity and Marginality in *Rob Roy* and *Braveheart*

1   The release and success of films such as *The Crying Game* (1992); *Philadelphia* (1994); *To Wong Foo; Thanks for Everything! Julie Newmar* (1995); and *The Birdcage* (1996) would seem to suggest that the mainstream movie industry has softened its anti-homosexual bias so well documented in Vito Russo's book *The Celluloid Closet*. However, Hollywood's portrayals of gay men as villains and buffoons are seldom far beneath the surface of even the most positive gay characterizations. Consider, for instance, that all four of the above-mentioned films include characters who are antagonistic toward the gay characters, thus reinforcing the cultural presumption that homophobia is instinctual: in *The Crying Game* the central character, played by Stephen Rea, actually vomits when he realizes that he has made love to a transsexual. In *Philadelphia*, Denzel Washington, who plays a legal advocate, must struggle to overcome his own revulsion toward the dying, gay protagonist (Tom Hanks). The drag queens in both *To Wong Foo* and *The Birdcage* are forced to run or hide from police officers and politicians, respectively, whenever they leave the narrow confines of the big city bar circuit.

2   Most public discussions of homosexuality are accompanied by alternative and often openly antagonistic perspectives. The American public has been conditioned to conceptualize the gay lifestyle as the inferior half of sociosexual binarism — heterosexual/homosexual. This polarity, in the public consciousness, duplicates and encompasses still more basic binary and hierarchical assumptions shared by much of our culture: natural/unnatural, normal/abnormal, health/sickness, and masculine/feminine. However, it is the last of these polarities that appears to be the current preoccupation within recent debates over the "place" of gays in U.S. society. In the popular mind, gay men and lesbians breach the neatly defined and strictly policed gender divisions within our culture. Recent scholars within the field of men's studies have defined gay men as the "symbolic repository of all that is excluded from hegemonic masculinity" (Connell 78). The opposition between gay male and straight male has been used within the conceptual framework of numerous writers and filmmakers. Films such as *Rob Roy* and *Braveheart* are structured on a dichotomy that codes homosexuality as the negation of traditional masculinity.

3   Michael Caton-Jones's *Rob Roy* (MGM, 1995) is one of the two recent films that depict the struggle of the Scottish for self-determination. However, the film's narrative is less about eighteenth-century Scotland than about American family values and traditional masculinity. Robert Roy MacGregor (Liam Neeson), his wife Mary (Jessica Lange), and their two children are an anachronism, an American bourgeois family living in the preindustrial Scottish Highlands. Their peace is disturbed by an effeminate British fop and swordsman, Archibald Cunningham (Tim Roth), who is in the employ of the Marquis of Montrose (John Hurt). Cunningham hounds Rob Roy virtually to death, and his removal becomes vital to the maintenance of the family and the MacGregor clan. The film juxtaposes two separate masculinities: that of the Scottish highlander and that of the British fop.

4   Archibald Cunningham's behavior sets him up as the antithesis of the MacGregor clan and its values of honor, fidelity, and fraternity; but mostly, Cunningham is contrasted with the brutish masculinity of Rob. The effeminacy of the eighteenth-century fop was notorious, and Tim Roth's "Archie" is no exception: he bows, smirks, lisps, and poses. Although Archie is heterosexual in his choice of partners, his appearance and behaviour are negative stereotypes of the twentieth-century gay man. In the eighteenth century, the fop was commonly associated with same-sex eroticism involving adolescent boys, despite his reputation as a womanizer (Sinfield 33–37). In *Rob Roy*, a substantial part of the dialogue and imagery is committed to maintaining the association between Archie and same-sex practices. When Archie first meets the Duke of Argyll, the duke playfully inquires whether he is a "buggerer of boys," to which Cunningham responds, "In my own defense, I thought him a girl at the moment of entry." The duke quips, reinforcing Archie's sexual ambiguity, "Archie could not tell ass from quim."

5   Archie's mannerisms do not at all correspond with the gender codes of twentieth-century America. Even when he defeats the duke's champion in a sword fight, he does so with dainty swordsmanship. Indeed, the contrast between the Scotsman Gutherie's broadsword and Archie's rapier forms a symbolic contrast between the film's competing masculinities. Gutherie wields his broadsword with

powerful and awkward strokes while Archie sweeps his lighter sword nimbly and artfully. The "gentler party is the surest winner," to the watching characters' surprise.

6   The audience's anxiety over Archie's sexuality is permitted to linger through one intervening scene in which Rob and his wife make love. The couple's sexual dalliance, coded as legitimate because they are married, is immediately followed by the sexual transgression of Archie, who deflowers the serving maid Betty. Later, when Archie is awakened by Montrose's agent Killern, he perpetuates the homoerotic imagery associated with him: "Do you think I want to wake up and see some bloody Scotsman staring down at me?" Later when Betty asks to become his permanent partner, Archie responds:

> You think me a gentleman because I have linen and can manage a lisp. I am but a bastard abroad, seeking my fortune and the favors of great men, as big a whore as my mother ever was.

He abandons Betty when she becomes pregnant, telling her to "root it out." He explains that "love is but a dung heap" and he "but a cock that crawls upon it to crow."

7   Archie's sexual marauding extends beyond the seduction and discarding of servant maids. When he is commissioned by Montrose to hunt down the insolent and rebellious Rob Roy, Archie uses the Scotsman's wife in the execution of his designs. He rapes Mary and burns their house, hoping that the crimes will inspire Rob to seek revenge. However, Mary recognizes Archie's intentions and refuses to tell her husband of the incident. Eve Kosofsky Sedgwick's theory of homosocial bonding, in which the aggression and desire between men is mediated through a female, helps to define the nature of Archie Cunningham's destructive gesture (21). Archie rapes Rob's wife to guarantee that the two men have a private encounter of their own — that they have the opportunity to work out their aggressions on each other. In the brief exchange between Mary and Archie after the rape, he uses sword/phallus imagery to describe the score that must be settled between the two men. He describes Rob:

> Such a man will need to see blood on his blade before honor is satisfied. Tell him Archie Cunningham is at his service.

"Blood on his blade" may be an image of phallic penetration — for the homosocial bonding has a homoerotic subtext. However, when Rob learns of the rape of Mary, he is already Archie's prisoner. In a verbal exchange between the two men, Rob calls the Englishman a "violator of women"; Archie responds, "I had hoped you'd have come to me much sooner on that score." To enrage Rob, Archie describes the rape in a parody of "kiss-and-tell" male bonding: "Your wife was far sweeter forced than many are willing . . . not all of her objected."

8   In contrast to Archie Cunningham, Rob Roy is constructed as the quintessential family man, who looks after not only his wife and children but also his clan. Archie's villainy is punctuated by Rob's fatherly advice to his two sons, "never mistreat a woman or malign a man." Of course, those pieces of wisdom, intended to help Rob's boys become men, are the antitheses of the crimes committed by Montrose and Archie. The former desires to enlist Rob's assistance in maligning the Duke of Argyll, and Archie's abuses of women are already documented. The communal values of the clan are also distinguished from the solitude and murderous selfishness of Archie. While the MacGregor clan celebrates the thousand-pound loan intended to propel them into the cattle marketing business, Archie pursues Allen McDonald (Eric Stolz) through the forest to rob and murder him. Moreover, Archie's refusal to take responsibility for the child he fathered is opposed to Rob's embracing of the child of rape. Whereas the fop encourages the abortion of his own child, Rob raises a bastard as legitimate.

9   Rob's position as the symbolic repudiation of subversive desire is reinforced by dialogue. As Rob prepares to abandon his family in anticipation of the arrival of Montrose's troops, Mary asks him if he will seek comfort from a sheep while hiding from the English. Rob retorts that he will pick one that "does not bleat so bitterly." Absent is the suggestion that he would seek the company of his clansmen, an idea unthinkable for a family man such as Rob. The couple would never joke about Rob having sex with a man. The negation of any homoeroticism associated with Rob is continued when Archie Cunningham arrives at the household and demands the "outlaw MacGregor." Mary defends her husband's masculinity: "If you think

he'd be lying in his bed waiting for you, you're more a fool than you look." Her statement can be seen as a negation of the idea that, symbolically, Archie could be Rob's bed partner and that Rob would allow himself to be the subject of Archie's violation.

10   Rob's honor is set against the deceit of the Englishmen, particularly Archie. He offers his word as collateral for the thousand-pound loan; the Englishman requires Rob's family land. The naive honesty of the Scotsman is intended to be a refreshing break from the corruption and cynicism of the courtly world. When brought before Montrose to answer for his insolence, Rob reveals the plot against him perpetrated by Archie and Killern. Montrose asks for evidence and Rob gives only his word. The suspicious marquis responds, "It will take more than that." Rob then offers Archie's "nature" as evidence against him: the sexual renegade is also the social outlaw. The refusal of the marquis to recognize the Scotsman's veracity is offered as a sign of the former's corruption. Archie is indeed deceitful and unprincipled, but Rob mistakes the extent to which Montrose and Archie are in league to take his land.

11   There are stronger visual images that reinforce the opposition between the two masculinities. Rob is a kilt-wearing Scotsman who is often dirty. (He is, however, domesticated, taking a bath in the loch before entering his wife's bed.) He is the ideal of athletic masculinity — large and powerful, capable of enduring much pain. Archie, as stated before, is by twentieth-century standards effeminate: he wears powdered wigs, makeup, and fancy clothes. His movements are slow, affected, and dainty, and he holds his hands erect but limp-wristed. When the men finally settle their score at the end of the film, masculine brawn prevails over gentility. Although Archie is clearly the better swordsman, bringing Rob to his knees, the latter has greater endurance. As Archie waits to strike the mortal blow, Rob grasps the blade of the Englishman's sword, and with his free arm, virtually chops Archie in half with a single stroke — one we are led to believe Archie could never muster.

12   The contest between brawn and effeminacy is settled in favor of brawn, but what does this mean in terms of gender politics? The prioritizing of Rob's lifestyle within the film is not deconstructed. Indeed, it is reconstructed. Whereas much of Archie's actions and successes seem to suggest that effeminacy and deceit can win out over honesty and sheer strength, the conclusion restores the traditional hierarchical opposition between the competing values, raising the communal over the individual, honor over deceit, monogamy over promiscuity, brawn over gentility and art, the provincial over the urban, the plebeian over the aristocratic, and the Scottish over the English. The technique employed in the vilification of the Englishmen includes feminizing them. One might argue that such behavior was commonplace among heterosexual men in the eighteenth century, so such a portrayal is not ultimately homophobic, but the eighteenth-century audience is not watching the film: a late-twentieth-century American audience is, an audience that recognizes the stereotypes of the gay male. Despite the images of Archie Cunningham sexually exploiting women, his language, his mannerisms, and his behavior identify him as homosexual and, in the context of the film, as the antithesis of masculinity, honor, family, and integrity. He is successful in winning out over the more masculine males through cunning, but eventually sheer strength and endurance prevail. Archie is constructed as a violent threat to the social peace, quick to anger and quick to kill.

13 Mel Gibson's *Braveheart* (Paramount, 1995) deals with some similar themes, particularly the juxtaposition of competing masculinities. I do not claim to be the first to recognize the potential homophobia of this film. In nine separate cities, the Gay and Lesbian Alliance against Defamation (GLADD) led protests against the film, protests prompted by the film's controversial portrayal of the English Prince Edward ("Bravehunt" 69). Although the prince seems to have a minor role within the film, he is symbolically central, acting as a contrast to the portrait of William Wallace (Mel Gibson), the Scottish rebel.

14 Seldom in recent films has there been a more stereotypical and negative portrayal of a gay man than that offered in *Braveheart*. Edward (Peter Hanly) is a throwback to the characters of earlier decades. He is constructed as vain, frivolous, and effeminate. While his father wages war and handles the serious business of the state, Edward frolics and poses with his courtly friends, ignoring his wife and infuriating his father. The king, Edward Longshanks (Patrick MacGoohan), must slap his son to make him respectful of authority and sensible long enough to address the Scottish rebellion seriously. In another scene, while his father and William Wallace are busy attending to the affairs of war, the prince is shown vainly posing and modeling his new clothes in front of a mirror, surrounded by an entourage of courtly butterflies, who all, shortly thereafter, swish down the hallway and out of sight. In the most damaging scene of the film, Edward's lover attempts to discuss the appropriate military strategy to put down rebellion and is tossed out of a window by the king to the laughter and occasional applause of the movie-going audience ("Bravehunt" 69). The implicit message here is that gays have no place in the serious affairs of men. Edward's lover is killed because he presumed to knowledge about war, because he presumed to participate in the decision-making process of the state. The most persistent criticism of Prince Edward is related to his marriage. He refuses to embrace and comfort his wife, and it is here that the link between the prince and William Wallace is made.

15   Gibson's William Wallace, like Rob Roy, is represented as the ideal of raw manhood. At the beginning of the film, what appears to be a brawl between Wallace and another arrogant young Scotsman is in actuality a meeting of old friends. Wallace playfully punches his buddy in the face to greet him after a long absence, a behavior that constitutes the antithesis of Edward's amorous preoccupation with his friends. Moreover, the image of Edward preening himself before a mirror is contrasted to the image of Wallace, covered in the blood of battle, shouting "Freedom!" As in *Rob Roy*, the Scotsman is shown to have more integrity than the usurping, effeminate Englishman. Whereas Wallace struggles for freedom, the English struggle to maintain domination and tyranny. Wallace's homosocial commitment to his men is set against Edward's seeming indifference, when his lover is killed by the king, thus invoking the heterosexual presumption that no real affection could exist between gay men. Wallace is subject to constant betrayal, while the two Edwards deceitfully exploit his betrayers. Wallace's single shortcoming is his trust of other men, a flaw that Edward Longshanks manipulates to his advantage by enlisting the loyalties of Robert the Bruce with a promise of a Scottish throne. It is through treachery and subversion that Wallace is given up to his enemies and executed.

16   Wallace's marriage is an important point of divergence between the two representations of masculinity. Wallace secretly woos his wife

(Catherine McCormack) in a romantic fashion. And contrary to Edward's matrimonial indifference, Wallace vows to make war on the English when they kill his wife. Contrary to Edward's vain preoccupations, Wallace almost single-handedly wipes out an entire regiment, driving the English from the province. The traditional man could never patiently brook his wife's violation, because the crime is as much against his honor as against her body. It is the structural device of the two wives in the film (Wallace's and Edward's) that produces some of the most important issues in the film. William Wallace is "evened" with them, "wife for wife." However, he does not kill the English princess (Sophie Marceau), since such an action would undermine his own masculine honor and remove his motivation for righteous indignation. He falls in love with her, meets her in secret, as he did his wife, with the implication that the English cannot satisfy their women — a compromising of their masculinity. It is here that the link between Edward's and Wallace's manhood becomes most plain. What entitles a man to be a leader of men is his willingness and capacity to satisfy a woman (Sedgwick 26). Prince Edward is symbolically excluded from this realm; Wallace's triumph is his emasculation of the English monarchy.

17 What then are the politics *of Braveheart's* homophobic portrayal of Prince Edward? The director constructs Edward as the symbolic antithesis of manhood, incapable and unworthy of a place within the affairs of war and government. By defining Wallace's manhood in contrast to Edward's, Gibson invites a comparison of their politics. If Wallace fights for honor, justice, trust, integrity, and freedom, then the future Edward II must signify the negation of all these concepts. The effect of this portrayal is to construct the male homosexual as a representation of all that is repugnant.

18 I contend that the values embraced by William Wallace and Rob MacGregor are clearly intended to refer to contemporary American politics; thus the implicit message of the films reinforces the conservative agendas of the past decade and perpetuates the current trend to scapegoat homosexuals. In Archibald Cunningham and Prince Edward we see the revival of the homosexual villains and buffoons that Vito Russo described in his book. The sexual marauding of Archie Cunningham reveals the potential for violence and social chaos inherent in those unwilling to conform to American sexual norms. The depictions of Edward suggest that gay men are too frivolous, ineffectual, and vain to be trusted with the serious affairs of heterosexual men. *Rob Roy* and *Braveheart* reveal our culture's subconscious fear of the feminized man. The films portray gay men as destructive of manhood and virtually as a threat to the solidarity of the family.

WORKS CITED

"Bravehunt." *The Advocate* 11 July 1995: 69–70.

Connell, R.W. *Masculinities*. Los Angeles: U of California P, 1995.

Russo, Vito. *The Celluloid Closet: Homosexuality in the Movies*. New York: Harper and Row, 1981.

Sedgwick, Eve Kosofsky. *Between Men: English Literature and Male Homosocial Desire*. New York: Columbia UP, 1985.

Sinfield, Alan. *The Wilde Century: Effeminacy, Oscar Wilde, and the Queer Moment*. New York: Columbia UP, 1994.

Proposals and the Formality of Scholarly Style

Before you start your research, do not neglect another important resource: your professor. Schedule a conference or visit your professor during office hours. You may have little or no idea about what kind of paper you would like to write, but during the course of the discussion, something may occur to your professor or to you that piques your curiosity, that becomes the equivalent of [a] "burning question." Your conference may turn into a kind of verbal freewriting session — with several unresolved questions remaining at the end of the session — one of which may become the focus of your paper.

— Leonard J. Rosen and Laurence Behrens,
The Allyn & Bacon Handbook. 2nd ed.

As researchers move through the process of collecting information and securing a topic, the completion of a written proposal, accompanied by an annotated list of references, provides an opportunity to formalize plans, assess sources, and get more advice. Accordingly, this chapter comments on proposals and on the annotated list of references often associated with them. It also discusses some stylistic matters that might be overlooked by writers who are not yet familiar with discipline-based habits of expression.

PROPOSALS

Proposals are a common feature in the various disciplinary cultures of academic writing. "Seeking a place on a conference program, or a spot in a collection of essays that will be published on a particular topic, scholars answer 'Calls for Papers' with a proposal" (Giltrow,

2002, p. 381). Giltrow invites us to think of proposals as "bids" (p. 382), as research offers that may be accepted or rejected by those who monitor the production of knowledge. In college and university classrooms, that monitor is usually the instructor.

It's time to get some thoughts down on paper.

Instructors, like conference chairs or editors, evaluate the submissions they receive by using some criteria we are already familiar with. Those in a position to receive proposals will, for example, watch for clearly articulated, viable **topics** that involve focused **research sites** and **prestige abstractions** or Big Issues. They will also want to see that the person submitting the proposal is aware of previous research relating to the topic. Such research forms what might be described as a **tradition of inquiry**. Depending on the discipline or disciplines, proposals also tend to include other rhetorical features that we have not yet discussed at any length, features such as a **two-part title**, a brief presentation of **context, theoretical framework, definition of key terms, knowledge deficit, forecasting**, a description of **methods**, a **research question, thesis**, and a **statement of relevance**. Some of these terms should be self-explanatory, but brief descriptions might be useful at this point:

Two-Part Title: consists of an allusive phrase that indirectly relates to topic and an explanatory phrase that directly conveys topic.

Context: background information.

Theoretical Framework: consciously adopted assumptions that can be imposed on topic and influence a thesis claim.

Tradition of Inquiry: previous studies relating to the topic.

Topic: Research Site + Abstraction = Topic; or, Abstraction + Research Site = Topic.

Definition of Key Terms: define important concepts (e.g., the prestige abstraction).

Knowledge Deficit: a statement about what has not yet been covered by previous research.

General Forecasting: a structural comment that provides a broad sense of direction.

Specific Forecasting: more detailed structural comments that outline sections of the paper.

Methods: a description of procedures undertaken to generate knowledge.

Research Question: a central question that the research will answer.

Thesis: an answer to the research question (i.e., a knowledge claim).

Statement of Relevance: a comment about how the topic and/or thesis relate to broad social concerns.

Just as no two papers are identical, no two proposals are exactly alike. While the rhetorical features described above can be compared to building blocks used in the construction of knowledge, these blocks can be combined in different ways or even exchanged for still others. Thus, the precise architectural details of proposals will vary, but informed designers understand that habitual, time-tested elements and patterns are at their disposal.

In a pragmatic way, it might actually be helpful to think of a proposal as a trial introduction for the paper itself. Proposals and introductions share basically the same rhetorical function, and, in turn, share many of the same rhetorical features. From this perspective, the proposal is not simply a make-work exercise: it constitutes a tentative beginning, one that can be adjusted on the basis of comments or recommendations. Given the overlap between proposals and introductions, it might be a good idea at this point to look ahead, and at least browse the more comprehensive description of introductory rhetorical features described in Chapter 6, without becoming overwhelmed. Presented with a range of options, academic writers need to make careful choices, choices that are rooted in their discipline and topic.

An annotated list of references does not always accompany a proposal, but your instructor may ask you to submit one as further evidence of the research that you have done thus far. We are using "list of references" as a generic term for an alphabetical list of sources, yet such lists assume different names, depending on the style of documentation that you are using (APA, MLA, Chicago, CBE, and so on). At this point, it would be worthwhile to take a preliminary look at the various styles of documentation and to consider which style is appropriate for your paper (see Chapter 7). You can refine your presentation of sources later in the term, but, even at this early stage in the writing process, you should have at least some idea of how to format your list. Your instructor may also ask you "to annotate" the items that you plan to use. In an annotated list of references, academic writers simply provide a brief summary of each source, after the details of publication.

The sample proposals that follow are accompanied by lists of references that demonstrate different styles of documentation (Samples B through D were written by students). Some of the lists are annotated; some are not. Rhetorical features in the first proposal have been highlighted so they are easy to identify. As you proceed through the rest of this chapter, block and label features that appear in the other proposals, and note the subtle differences in styles of documentation.

Sample A: MLA Style

Steve Roe

"The Poet of our Survival": Images of the Mad Trapper and Attitudes Toward Masculinity

Two-Part Title

In early January, 1931, in the Mackenzie Valley of the Northwest Territories, an unidentified white male shot and killed an RCMP officer. Throughout the remainder of January and most of February, this so-called "Mad Trapper" became the object of what remains the largest manhunt in Canadian history. On February 26, 1931, the Mounties finally got their man. The emaciated and frost-bitten figure whom they were chasing was riddled with bullets after he had crossed the Richardson Mountains on snowshoes and entered the Yukon. Although the Mad Trapper is sometimes referred to as Albert Johnson, the identity of the bullet-ridden corpse has never been confirmed, intensifying the mysterious quality of someone who has become a Canadian legend.

Context

This essay will present a sustained analysis of cultural responses to Canada's most famous criminal. In particular, I examine popular images of the Mad Trapper as an index of shifting attitudes toward masculinity.

General Forecasting Topic

My survey follows a two-part, chronological order. First, I will consider material from 1931 to 1957, emphasizing supposedly realistic depictions of Albert Johnson in journalistic and biographical-historical texts. Second, I will consider material from 1958 to the present, emphasizing overtly imaginative treatments of Johnson in poetry, fiction, and film.

Specific Forecasting

Investigations into cultural images of the Mad Trapper did not begin until the late 1970s. In 1978, Rudy Wiebe, who was then working on both a short story and a novel about the Mad Trapper, published an essay entitled "The Death and Life of Albert Johnson." Wiebe's essay considers previous accounts of the Mad Trapper and provides the basis for my own study. Rather than asking "Who was Albert Johnson?" Wiebe asks, "What has the imagination made of him?" Subsequent studies by Jennings (1987),

Tradition of Inquiry

Bailey (1985), and Howell (1984) reconsider Wiebe's sources and carry his study forward by considering Wiebe's own fictional accounts of Johnson. Building on this tradition of inquiry, I will argue that accounts of the Mad Trapper, since the 1930s, demonstrate changing conceptions of masculine ideals: whereas Johnson was originally vilified as an outlaw, his renegade status has increasingly become a badge of nobility. Indeed, today, the Mad Trapper is frequently represented as an embodiment of besieged selfhood.

Thesis

Works Cited [annotated]

Bailey, Nancy. "Imaginative and Historical Truth in Wiebe's *The Mad Trapper*." *Journal of Canadian Studies* 20.2 (Summer 1985): 70–79. Bailey argues that Wiebe romanticizes Albert Johnson by embellishing the factual record of the manhunt.

Callaghan, Morley. "Shoot-Out." *Edmonton Bulletin*. Feb. 16, 1931. Evening Edition. C1. Callaghan describes a meeting between the Mad Trapper and the RCMP as a confrontation between an evil outlaw and defenders of social order.

Carter, Wilf. "The Capture of Albert Johnson." Copyright Gordon V. Thompson, n.d. (See Wiebe, "The Death of Albert Johnson," 227–228). Carter's song again valorizes the Mounted Police.

Jennings, John. "The Mad Trapper in Literature and Film." *Journal of Canadian Studies* 5.2 (1987): 55–66. Jennings discusses the Mad Trapper film, manhunt, and two recent Mad Trapper novels by Rudy Wiebe and Thomas York respectively. Jennings argues that all three representations represent the Mad Trapper as a hero.

Howells, Coral-Ann. "Silence in Rudy Wiebe's *The Mad Trapper*." *World Literature Written in English* 24.2 (Autumn 1984): 304–312. Howells argues that Wiebe portrays the Mad Trapper as a strong, silent male who resists oppressive government authority.

Hutton, Doug. "Rat River Trapper." *Scarlet and Gold* [memorial album to celebrate the RCMP centennial in 1974]. Bulrush Music, 1974. This song reinscribes the Mad-Trapper-as-Villain position.

Kroetsch, Robert. "The Poem of Albert Johnson." *The Stone Hammer Poems.* Toronto: Oolichan Books, 1975. In one of the most romantic treatments of the Mad Trapper to date, Kroetsch sees Johnson as "the poet of our survival."

O'Hagan, Howard. "The Man Who Chose to Die." *Wilderness Men.* Toronto: Doubleday, 1958. O'Hagan celebrates Johnson as "a new figure of loneliness" in the Canadian imagination.

Wiebe, Rudy. "The Death and Life of Albert Johnson." *Figures in a Ground.* Ed., D. Bessai. Saskatoon: Prairie Books, 1978. Wiebe examines poetry and short stories on the Mad Trapper, ranging from the work of Wilf Carter to that of Robert Kroestch. Wiebe anticipates my preliminary thesis that the Mad Trapper has been transformed from villain to hero, but he offers little in the way of critical commentary upon this development.

_____. *The Mad Trapper.* Toronto: McClelland and Stewart, 1980. Although Wiebe's portrayal of Johnson is complex and somewhat ambivalent, Wiebe appears to regard Johnson as a hero.

Sample B: A Variation of CBE Style

Julie Nixon Vander Linden
The Extermination of the Fort Nelson Bears

In just two days in September 1997, in the small, northern B.C. town of Fort Nelson, sixty-five black bears were exterminated. They had been frequenting the local garbage dump and roaming through the town itself, in a quest for an easy meal. The bears had become habituated both to human food and to humans (BC Environment 1997). Indeed, these bears would approach vehicles that arrived at the dump, not even allowing the human occupants enough time to unload their garbage (Parker 1999). Concern about the Fort Nelson bears increased in August 1997, when two people were killed by a black bear approximately 300 kilometres to the northwest. After the August attack, the Fort Nelson bears were regarded as an immediate threat to public safety. These bears were eating human food, but they were still, after all, wild carnivorous animals, inspiring a combination of awe and fear.

This paper focuses on the 1997 extermination of the Fort Nelson bears. First, I will explore the problems of habituation. Second, I will examine how aversive conditioning can sometimes be used as a solution to the problem of habituation. Finally, I will apply these concepts to the circumstances in Fort Nelson, to determine if aversive conditioning would have been a viable alternative to extermination. Thus, my essay asks this question: was it necessary to kill the Fort Nelson bears? I suggest that the extermination of the Fort Nelson bears may, in fact, have been necessary because the possibility of aversive conditioning was negated by human error in the way the landfill was managed.

Managing bear behaviour through aversive conditioning is not a new concept. Studies dating back to the 1970s show that beekeepers have tried both foul-tasting and illness-inducing ingestives, and electric shock (Gilbert and Roy 1973), while bear-chasing hound-dogs have been employed in Minnesota (Donelly 1999). The national parks of both the USA and Canada have used ingestives as well as rubber bullets and buckshot (Herrero 1985; Leonard and others 1990). Nevertheless, knowledge of aversive conditioning among wildlife managers remains limited. It is my hope that the information on aversive conditioning provided here will help to promote future alternatives to extermination.

Since written information on habituation and aversive conditioning is hard to access, I conducted telephone interviews with conservation officers, biologists, and wildlife advocates. To maintain accuracy when using information from any of these interviews, I have contacted the person again to confirm that the quote or paraphrase is correct. I also have used a disproportionate amount of research on grizzly bears, rather than black bears, simply because most studies tend to focus on grizzly bears, given their threatened status.

References [not annotated]

[Anonymous] 1997 Sep 17. 30 bears shot at the dump on Saturday night. [letter to the editor]. Fort Nelson News.

Aumiller LD, Matt CA. 1994. Management of McNeil River State Game Sanctuary for viewing of brown bears. Int Conf on Bear Res and Manage 9(1):51–61.

Bear-people Conflict Prevention Plan. 1995. Prepared by Kent Jingfors for BC Parks.

BC Ministry of Environment, Lands and Parks. 1997 Sep 19. 1 page press release.

Ciarniello L. 1997 Mar 27. Reducing human-bear conflicts: Solutions through better management of non-natural foods. Victoria, BC Min of Env Lands and Parks.

Conover MR, Kessler KK. 1994. Diminished producer participation in an aversive conditioning program to reduce coyote predation on sheep. Wildl Soc Bull 2:233–241.

Donelly E. 1999 Mar 16. Bear Watch representative. Telephone interview.

Editor's note. 1997 Sep 17. Fort Nelson News.

Gilbert BK. 1989. Behavioural plasticity and bear-human conflicts. Bear-People Conflicts Proc of a Symposium on Management Strategies. Northwest Territories Dept of Renew Res:1–7.

Gilbert BK, Roy LD. 1977. Prevention of black bear damage to beeyards using aversive conditioning. Proc of the 1975 Predator Symposium, Mont For & Cons Exp Stn, Univ Mont, Missoula, MT:93–102.

Gunther KA. 1994. Bear management in Yellowstone National Park, 1960-93. Int Conf Bear Res and Manage 9(1):549–560.

Hart J. 1999 Apr 13. Conservation Officer, Fort Nelson, BC. Telephone interview.

Herrero S, Fleck S. 1990. Injury to people by black, grizzly or polar bears: Recent trends and new insights. Int Conf Bear Res and Manage 8:25–32.

Herrero S. 1985. Bear attacks: Their causes and avoidance. 287 p.

Human-Bear Conflict in British Columbia: Draft Discussion Paper. 1996 Apr. Prepared by Sean Sharpe, Carnivore Management Specialist for BC Min of Env, Lands and Parks.

Jope KL. 1985. Implications of grizzly bear habituation to hikers. Wildl Soc Bull 13:32–37.

Leonard RD, Breneman R, Frey R. 1990. A case history of grizzly bear management in the Slims River area, Kluane National Park Reserve, Yukon. Int Conf Bear Res and Manage 8:113–123.

Local businessman loses his life in heroic attempt to save mother and son from bear mauling. 1997 Aug 20. Fort Nelson News.

Mattson DJ, Blanchard BM, Knight RR. 1992. Yellowstone grizzly bear mortality, human habituation, and whitebark pine seed crops. J Wildl Manage 56:432–442.

McArthur KL. 1979a. The behaviour of grizzly bears in relation to people in Glacier National Park. National Park Service Progress Report, Glacier National Park.

McArthur KL. 1979b. Methods in the study of grizzly bear behaviour in relation to people in Glacier National Park. In: Second Conf on Scientific Res in the National Parks. 1979 Nov 26–30. San Francisco, California.

McCarthy TM, Seavoy RJ. 1994. Reducing nonsport losses attributable to food conditioning: Human and bear behavior modification in an urban environment. Int Conf Bear Res and Manage 9(1):75–84.

McCullough DR. 1982. Behavior, bears, and humans. Wildl Soc Bull 10:27–33.

My name was withheld for a reason. [letter to the editor] 1997 Oct 1. Fort Nelson News.

Paige C. 1998 Nov-Dec. Bear busters. Montana Outdoors:24–29.

Parker D. 1999 Mar 5. Senior Conservation Officer. Telephone interview.

Schmidt K. 1999 Mar 12. Conservation Officer for Swan Hills, Alberta. Telephone interview.

Schmidt K. 1999 Apr 15. Telephone interview.

Wind River Bear Institute. 1999 Mar 25. Faxed information letter. 2 p.

Wooldridge DR. 1980. Chemical aversion conditioning of polar and black bears. Fourth Int Conf on Bears:167–173.

Zukewich M. 1999 Apr 16. 1 page fax.

Zukewich M. 1999 Apr 13. Conservation Officer, formerly posted in Fort Nelson, BC. Telephone interview.

Sample C: APA Style

Kendra Hunter
"Box Office Poison": Misogyny in Luc Besson's
Portrayal of Joan of Arc in *The Messenger*

The basic biographical details of Joan of Arc's life comprise a generally accepted historical record. Joan of Arc was born in Domremy, France, in 1412, as a member of a peasant family. At the age of nineteen, she was successfully able to lead an entire army of men to victory. Joan claimed that she heard the voice of God, and that God had a personal mission for her: to save France. Initially, King Charles supported Joan by providing troops in the victorious battle to free Orleans. However, Joan's alliance with King Charles led to her betrayal and death. Eventually, she was sold to the English for 16,000 francs, charged with heresy and witchcraft, and burned at the stake. While the general outline of Joan's life is relatively clear, efforts to understand her character involve interpretation and speculation. Nevertheless, many assumptions have been made, and Joan has become a familiar icon in Western culture. Indeed, Joan's life has been the subject of numerous Hollywood films, including *The Messenger* (1999), directed by Luc Besson.

In an effort to explain my personal response to Besson's film, I have turned to Susan Faludi (1991), who claims that film-makers in the twentieth century are producing movies that denigrate independent women, making them appear weak or even psychotic (pp. 112–114). Faludi cites films such as *Fatal Attraction* (1987), which is about a married man who has an affair with a single woman. When the affair takes place, the man's wife is out of town. When the time comes that the man must return to his wife, the single woman suffers a mental breakdown and tries to commit suicide. Such behaviour shows that she is weak and unable to survive on her own. Drawing on Faludi's theoretical frame, this essay examines misogyny in Luc Besson's *The Messenger*. I will argue that Besson's film reveals a misogynistic backlash against twentieth-century feminism.

List of References [annotated]

Brunette, Peter. (1999). Review of *The Messenger: The Story of Joan of Arc*. Retrieved Feb. 14, 2002 from http://www.film.com/film-review. 1999. Brunette criticizes the historical inaccuracies in the film.

Faludi, Susan. (1991). *Backlash: The Undeclared War Against American Women*. New York: Doubleday. Faludi, as noted above, believes that twentieth-century film shows a backlash against feminism.

Maxwell, Ronald. (2000, Apr.). Review of *The Messenger: Joan of Arc. History Today*. pp. 52–53. Maxwell argues that Besson's portrayal "is founded on a lie": "a true story of love and sacrifice, of dedication and faith is turned to a false one of hatred, bitterness, fury, and revenge."

The Messenger: The Story of Joan of Arc. (1999). Directed by Luc Besson. Columbia Pictures. The movie provides Besson's creative interpretation of Joan's life and death.

Sample D: APA Style

Sarah Filmer

Two part title

Re-envisioning the "Three R's":
Teaching Strategies for Students with Dyslexia

context

Dyslexia is a neurologically based learning disability that hinders language acquisition and processing. This disorder is characterized by a difficulty learning to read, write, spell, and in some cases, problems in mathematics (Jordan, 1977, pp. 1–4; Sawicki, 1997, p. 1; Wadlington, 2000, p. 2). Dyslexia is not a result of insufficient motivation, sensory deficits, inadequate instructions, or a poor environment. Individuals coping with this disorder have a difficulty with language, not intelligence (Wadlington, 2000, p. 2). Robert Sheppard (1998) believes that dyslexia is the most common form of learning disorder, and may affect as many as 730,000 school-aged Canadians (p. 2). Nevertheless, Elizabeth Wadlington (2000) suggests that many teachers have not received the training necessary to meet the needs of these students. Thus, teachers are unsure of the definition and characteristics of dyslexia and may not even recognize the symptoms. Moreover, the manifestations of dyslexia vary from child to child, with symptoms ranging from mild to severe (p. 1). These factors make it difficult for the teachers to serve the needs of students with dyslexia while meeting the needs of all of the other pupils in the class.

Accordingly, this paper examines appropriate teaching strategies for students with dyslexia. First, I will explore the common effects and characteristics of dyslexia. Second, I will discuss types of instruction most appropriate for dyslexic students and the contributions that these teaching strategies may make to the academic success of dyslexic individuals. Finally, I will discuss my own personal struggle with dyslexia.

Dyslexia has prompted extensive scholarly interest and research. Numerous treatments and/or cures have been explored, involving disciplines ranging from computer science (Chenausky, 1997, p. 1) to neuropsychology (Robertson, 2000, p. 3). Despite such research, dyslexia remains a controversial issue. Today, experts may have an understanding of how dyslexia manifests itself, but there is still disagreement regarding effective treatment. In this paper, I will demonstrate that there is a range of potentially effective teaching strategies for students with dyslexia; however, the implementation of these strategies involves both a process of trial and error and a strong network for student support.

List of References [not annotated]

Chenausky, K. (1997, Aug.–Sept.). Training dyslexics first to hear, then to read. *MIT Technology Review*, 15–18.

Elbro, C., & Borstrom, I. (1998). Predicting dyslexia from kindergarten: The importance of distinctness of phonological representations of lexical items. *Reading Research Quarterly, 33,* 1, 36–74.

Jordan, D.R. (1977). Dyslexia in the classroom. Columbus, Ohio: Charles E. Merrill Publishing Company.

Miles, T.R., & Pavlidis, G. (1981). Dyslexia research and its applications to education. New York: John Wiley & Sons.

Riccio, N.M. (2000). Understanding dyslexia. *Current Health 2*, 30–31.

Robertson, J. (2000). Neuropsychological intervention in dyslexia: Two studies in British pupils. *Journal of Learning Disabilities, 33,* 2, 137–148.

Sawicki, S. (1997). Understanding dyslexia. *People,*149–153.

Sheppard, R. (1998). Why kids can't read. *Maclean's, 111*, 36, 40–48.

Skottun, B.C., & Parke, L.A. (1999). The possible relationship between visual deficits and dyslexia: Examination of a critical assumption. *Journal of Learning Disabilities, 32*, 2–5.

Tomatis, A.A. (1978). Education and dyslexia. Fribourg, Switzerland: AIAPP Publishers.

Tonnessen, F.E. (1999). Options and limitations of the cognitive psychological approach to the treatment of dyslexia. *Journal of Learning Disabilities, 32,* 5, 386–394.

Upbin, B. (1995). Rose-colored glasses. *Forbes,* 294–298.

Vellutino, F.R. (1980). Dyslexia: Theory and research. Cambridge: MIT Press.

Wadlington, E. (2000). Effective language arts instruction for students with dyslexia. *Preventing School Failure, 44,* 2, 61–65.

If you have been asked to prepare a proposal and working list of references for your own research project, consider the samples presented here as potential models.

THE FORMALITY OF SCHOLARLY STYLE

As we collectively move deeper into academic writing, it might be worthwhile to pause for a moment to consider the peculiar formality of scholarly discourse. Most of us would probably agree that the expressions we encounter in academic writing sound different from the expressions that we are used to in our everyday lives, as we converse with friends and family members. For this reason, academic writing often sounds unnatural. Confronted with a page of academic prose, we might feel as though we have suddenly parachuted into an alien country. The dialect, idiom, or accent is not quite what we are accustomed to.

Standard dictionaries attach different meanings to the word "formal." According to the *Oxford* paperback dictionary, "formal" can mean "prim," "stiff," or "perfunctory." It is associations like these that give academic formality a bad name. Reading published research articles, we might, for example, get the feeling that some authors take themselves and their subject too seriously.

On the other hand, there may be ways of justifying the formality of scholarly style. The *Oxford* dictionary also defines "formal" as "precise" and "explicit." Hence, when two people want to make sure that they understand each other, they might be inclined to write up a *formal* agreement. Academic writers, as people who deal with knowledge, share this desire for precision and explicitness. For academic writers, then, formality may actually foster clarity. Viewed in this more positive light, mannerisms that strike us as elevated may reflect the needs of knowledge-making communities. In sum, we should probably avoid blanket judgements about formality in academic writing. The style of an individual researcher needs to be judged on its own merits, based on how effectively it handles knowledge, the commodity of academic communities.

The subheadings that follow touch on some general aspects of style that academic instructors often comment on as they evaluate student writing. It is worth keeping these stylistic considerations in mind, from the proposal stage through to the final draft.

Grammatical Correctness

Most of your instructors will expect grammatical correctness. We are using the term "grammar" loosely, to include spelling, punctuation, subject–verb agreement, clear pronoun reference, effective transitions, and so on. While English instructors may pay special attention to grammatical correctness, it will also be a concern for instructors in other disciplines, even if they choose not to mark errors. There is, in fact, a cultural presumption that the ability to write grammatically correct prose is a prerequisite for university-level courses. Therefore, proposals and papers should be carefully checked.

Short Exercise

Identify grammatical problems in the following sentences. There may be more than one type of mistake in each sentence:

1. In the introduction to *Travels in Western North America*, Hopwood states that when he was two, Thompson's father passed away, leaving him, his mother, and his younger brother.
2. The intentions of the founders of the school, were to "educate poor children in the principals of piety and virtue and thereby lay a foundation for a sober and Christian life" (2).
3. This ominous doctrine gives the Kremlin the right to charge any reporter for conducting investigations. Except perhaps those who

only cover "the truth" as the government sees it, such as official anti-Chechen rhetoric.

4. In March of 1995; Silken Laumann and her Canadian teammates faced hardship when Pan-Am officials, in Argentina, stripped them of their gold medals.

5. Laumann states that Victoria Rowing Club physician Dr. Richard Backus had recommended the drug after coming down with the cold shortly before the Pan-Am games.

6. Women in most ancient civilizations were considered property and were used primarily to make babies to carry on the bloodline. The women of ancient Egypt were considered privileged because they had the same rights as men and were allowed to rule as men did.

7. To this day, the study of dreaming still remains a mystery as to what purpose dreams serve. Many studies have been done that reveal the daily lives of people reflect in their dreaming periods at night.

8. This illustrates the belief that people create their own reality in order to find purpose for their lives, Lois's purpose is to search for Lucy yet it is the loss of Lucy that gives her purpose.

9. A study by C.J. Carpenter (1983), is convinced that rules or guidelines in play, encourages long-term behaviour that is not creative, the child will always try to fit into someone else's idea of accepted behaviour (p. 142).

10. According to Bancroft and Hollyfield, (2002) the results were not surprising: when the company investigated it's own procedures no accounting errors were discovered (p. 111).

Colloquialisms

Informal speech is full of casual expressions and clichés, the meaning of which is readily understood in informal contexts (for example, "a bird in the hand is worth two in the bush"). In academic writing, however, your instructor might object to colloquialisms. In all likelihood, the instructor will understand your intended meaning, but that meaning may involve unexamined assumptions, figurative expressions, or word combinations that call for loose or inexact readings. Given the value placed on exactness in conducting and presenting research, such colloquialisms should be replaced by more precise or literal language.

Short Exercise

Identify colloquialisms in the following passages and explain how such constructions create ambiguity. Rewrite each passage in more precise language.

1. Since the dawn of time, human beings have sought metaphysical principles that would structure their lives.
2. Since the beginnings of Canadian history, Canada and the United States have had a relatively amicable relationship.
3. In 1975, the death penalty was banned completely on Canadian soil, even though many American states continued to dish it out.
4. For example, if Archie doesn't have enough money for two gifts, he will use all his money on a gift for Veronica, and he will claim that it is okay because Betty doesn't mind not getting anything (*Archie*, December 1999, pp. 3–5). However, the reader knows better. Guess you could say that even cartoon characters have their faults.
5. A great deal of Winston Churchill's life was directed by fate.
6. Along the same lines, I will argue that Tupac Shakur was not necessarily a great artist nor an artistic failure: he did make mistakes and struggled with pride, but, most importantly, Shakur had a good heart.
7. Even though Mary Rowlandson and her family made it to North America seemingly no worse for the wear, their travel was far from over.
8. Margaret Atwood's characters have a rocky relationship. Sure, Rob gives Lois everything she wants (116), but Lois is not genuinely happy.
9. One source of error was that the measuring scale could have been off.
10. The reason the data may be as they are is because of the fact that the crucible may have absorbed moisture during cooling.

Complex Terminology

Most writing handbooks discourage complex terminology, which often goes by the name of "jargon" or "technical language." The assumption seems to be that words or phrases readily understood by the general populace are almost always better than words or phrases that are not (the simpler, the better). Academic writers, in particular, are criticized for their use of "professional slang." Malcolm Cowley, an advocate of standard English, makes the case:

> . . . a vast majority [of academics] write in a language that has to be learned almost like Esperanto. It has a private vocabulary which, in addition to strictly [discipline-specific] terms, includes new words for the commonest actions, feelings, and circumstances. It has the beginnings of a new grammar and syntax, much inferior to English grammar in force and precision. So far as it has an effect on standard English, the effect is largely pernicious.
>
> Sometimes it misleads the [academics] themselves, by making them think they are profoundly scientific at points where they are merely being verbose. (as cited in *The Broadview Reader*, 1987, pp. 23–24)

From this perspective, complex terminology amounts to verbosity: academic writers use a "barbarous jargon" that "fuz[zes] up the obvious" (Cowley, as cited in *The Broadview Reader*, 1987, p. 23). Ironically, though, we suggest that Cowley's own prose demonstrates the pattern he's discussing. Esperanto? Pernicious? Verbose? Cowley himself is very much a part of an academic culture that uses language in peculiar ways. Nevertheless, the popular bias against what some view as academic snobbery is evident in a recent headline in the *Edmonton Journal*: "Professors who resort to jargon discredit society" (Simons, 1999, Jan. 10, p. A8).

Simple language, however, is not always the best solution in academic writing. Because academic writers often challenge our common sense, they may, at times, require uncommonly complex language that enables them to refine or revise our habitual understandings of the world. Accordingly, this text takes a more tolerant view of complex terminology. We believe that "big words" and even some discipline-specific jargon can be effective tools in academic writing, but we advise writers to use these tools responsibly, with careful definitions.

Needlessly Complex Wording

Reduce these phrases to something simpler without changing the meaning:

Observational data	food item
individual food item categories	abundantly found food constituent
given the fact that	in this day and age
for the purpose of	in spite of the fact that
was of the opinion that	as a result of

In the following sentence, highlight the simple subject and the two main verbs. In essence, the sentence is telling us that a "move" "brought" something and "marked" something. However, the subject–predicate pattern is packed with phrases and clauses that obscure meaning.

> The move from a structuralist account in which capital is understood to structure social relationships in relatively homologous ways to a view of hegemony in which power relations are subject to repetition, convergence, and rearticulation brought the question of temporality into the thinking of structure, and marked a shift from a form of Althusserian theory that takes structural totalities as theoretical objects to one in which the insights into the contingent possibility of structure inaugurate a renewed conception of hegemony as bound up with the contingent sites and strategies of the rearticulation of power. (as cited in Simons, 1999, p. A8)

Wording That Is Not Complex Enough

In the next example, complex terminology makes the statement more concise.

> This essay examines Ambrose Bierce's hatred toward people who were different from him.
>
> [or, more effectively:]
>
> This essay examines xenophobia in the writings of Ambrose Bierce.

Effectively Complex Wording That Occurs in a Larger Context of Definitions

First, I will explore the problems of habituation. Second, I will examine how aversive conditioning can sometimes be used as a solution to the problem of habituation. Finally, I will apply these concepts to the circumstances in Fort Nelson, to determine if aversive conditioning would have been a viable alternative to extermination.

Dyslexia is a neurologically based learning disability that hinders language acquisition and processing.

I will argue that Luc Besson's *The Messenger* reflects a misogynistic backlash against twentieth-century feminism.

In relation to Monica Storrs' descriptions of landscape, it is worth noting that the terms "sublime" and "picturesque" were used throughout the nineteenth-century British exploration of Canada.

The tendency toward complexity in scholarly wording can be explained at a grammatical level through a phenomenon called "nominalization" (Giltrow, 2002, pp. 213–218). When a sense of formality weighs heavily on us, we often encounter language that is packed with long noun phrases (see Chapter 9).

Objectivity

Delving more deeply into the formal qualities of research articles, we might take a preliminary look at the scholarly concern for patterns of communication that ensure reliability. Whereas personal essays and letters tend to convey *subjective impressions* (that which is true for one person), research articles tend to seek *objective knowledge* (that which is empirically verifiable). In academia, "knowledge" denotes a particular kind of truth: knowledge is founded on claims that can be validated on the basis of testing. It is important to remember that this academic turn of mind does not stem from some arbitrary devotion to certainty. To the contrary, insofar as universities are research institutions, they are in the knowledge-making business, and this means that knowledge itself is a valuable commodity, a product that bestows money and power on those who create it. In fact, advancements in the state of knowledge are intricately bound up with tenure, promotion, and research grants. Ideally, of course, universities generate knowledge for the well-being of society as a whole, but the relationship between knowledge and power means that the knowledge-making industry of academia also serves its own interests.

The distinct styles of the personal essay and the research article (which in turn point to apparent distinctions between subjectivity and objectivity, between impressions and knowledge) are evident in passages from two essays on related subjects. Both passages describe an aboriginal world-view, explaining how native people perceive nature and their relationship to it. In this sense, both passages essentially say the same thing or make the same point, yet they do so in very different ways.

The first passage is taken from a personal essay by Leah Idlout-Paulson, entitled "Wonderful Life" (1993):

> I can be a cloud ... way up in the sky where I can see you first, then everyone and go everywhere with all kinds of colors: hanging low or high, in the North, South, West, or East. ... But, when clouds are crying the people won't like it for me to cry for them; so I wish I was a big moon with a big, big, smiling face that everyone can see. But, the moon is always changing into different forms ... [and] I would only appear with a wide smiling face, so I wish I was a sun who is keeping warm and making everybody warm too at the same time. But, the people would always ask me to keep shining and keep them warm and when it is getting too hot for them, they would look for something to cover themselves from me or to hide from me where they can have more fun without me. So I wish I was a star, but I don't know which one. ... So I wish I was a tree, but trees don't move around at all to go with the others. So I wish I was an animal. ... (pp. 57–58)

Idlout-Paulson's essay was first published in *Inuit Today*, a monthly magazine devoted to Inuit culture.

The second passage, previously cited in the discussion of summarizing, is taken from a research article by Shelagh Grant (1987), entitled "Myths of the North in the Canadian Ethos":

There are many cultures and subcultures among the Indian and
Inuit of northern Canada, but they share similar attitudes toward
the land, derived in part from the long experience of survival in
what many southerners consider a hostile environment. The image
of the north as "homeland" is essentially a southern expression for
the intensely spiritual concept of land held by northern natives. . . .
Prior to European contact, everything within the Inuit's natural world
had a spiritual connotation, a sanctity which must be respected.
The infinite space and majestic grandeur of the Arctic gave northern
man a special awe for the might and majesty of the world, impressed
upon him his own insignificance, and made him both mystically-
inclined and humble . . . Any life form or inanimate object which
had a sense of permanency was thought to have a spirit or soul, a
belief which explains his profound respect for nature.[12] He was not
a separate entity arriving on earth; he was always there, at one with,
and a part of the natural world. (p. 122)

12. See *Northern Voices: Inuit Writing in English*, ed., Penny Petrone (Toronto:
University of Toronto Press, 1988) 202–203.

Shelagh Grant teaches history and Canadian Studies at Trent
University, and her article was published in *The Northern Review*, an
academic journal.

The authorial voice in the first piece describes personal *feelings*:
there is little or no distance between what is being written and the
writer herself. Accordingly, Idlout-Paulson gives free expression to
her emotions. As a personal essayist, she bares her soul, deriving
content from her own felt experience of the world. By contrast, the
authorial voice in the second piece is more detached and analytical. If
Idlout-Paulson wants to describe how life is for her, Grant wants to
describe how life is for other people. Thus, whereas Idlout-Paulson
uses "I" frequently, the first-person pronoun does not appear at all in
Grant's passage, which investigates phenomena external to the
authorial self. We do not mean to suggest that "I" *never* appears in
academic writing (see Self-Disclosure in Chapter 6), but the absence
of "I," in this case, contributes to the impersonal tone of Grant's
writing. Some readers might even characterize the Grant excerpt in
unfavourable terms, as comparatively cool or dispassionate.

Nevertheless, Grant's impersonal way of writing serves the knowledge-making values of her discourse community. As an academic, Grant is supposed to concern herself with objective truth, and her way of writing helps to satisfy this expectation. That is, Grant's style helps to create an impression of impartiality: she presents herself as an unbiased, logical expert, as someone who knows her subject through rigorous study. In addition, Grant inserts a superscript numeral (see the raised "[12]"), which, in context, refers the reader to an endnote, which in turn refers to an anthology entitled *Inuit Writing in English*. Grant cites this anthology to support the claims she is making, and it is probably safe to assume that several of the writing samples in the anthology bring us full circle, back to Idlout-Paulson's more personal approach. Curiously, Grant employs personal narratives such as Idlout-Paulson's as *evidence* for academic claims.

For aspiring academic writers, the distinction between subjectivity and objectivity may be a useful one, but it is also important to remember that this distinction is largely a matter of presentation. Indeed, although a professional academic writer like Shelagh Grant attempts to secure her claim to objective truth by heeding matters such as tone and evidence, her position is still very much a personal one. It is Grant herself, after all, who has decided what to focus on in her work, how to interpret the data before her, and how much to emphasize the significance of some data over the significance of others. Put another way, Grant's account of northern myths in the Canadian ethos cannot help but reveal something about Grant herself, even though she may not overtly refer to herself in her own work. Grant's description of the "homeland" myth, for example, may indirectly reveal an authorial disenchantment with Euro-Canadian attitudes toward nature. Thus, in describing native world views, Grant may be idealizing attitudes that provide a desirable alternative to her given reality. In this sense there may, in fact, be some hidden wish-fulfillment in Grant's piece, too. Ultimately, then, Grant's academic objectivity might be regarded as an illusion sustained by particular stylistic gestures.

In an effort to acknowledge the inherent subjectivity of all human perceptions, some academic writers have tried to put the writer back into the writing. "I," for example, frequently appears in academic articles from the humanities and social sciences. Some writers go a step further and embellish "I" by discussing their backgrounds and their relationships with their topics. Alice Carlick (1995), for example, in her essay on the importance of a girl's puberty rites in Tagish and Inland Tlingit society, briefly refers to her own personal investment in and experience of her research site: "As a First Nations person hearing and reading First Nations stories," Carlick writes, "I interpret such stories using both my personal experience and my academic training" (p. 34). In a follow-up comment, Carlick continues to situate herself in relation to her topic by elaborating on the nature of her academic training: "Because my studies at university have included literature as well as anthropology, I will combine both perspectives to discuss how Mrs. Sidney's story 'The Girl and the Grizzly' helps us understand social customs surrounding the training of young women" (p. 34). Paradoxically, then, for scholars such as Carlick, part of academic objectivity now seems to entail acknowledging one's subjectivity. Indeed, in other instances, the autobiographical impulse in academic writing results in more lengthy moments of self-disclosure (see Chapter 6).

While clear-cut distinctions between objectivity and subjectivity are ultimately hard to maintain, the *ideal* of objectivity still exerts a powerful force on academic writing. This is particularly evident when one examines the extent to which academic writers employ other voices. Academics use other voices whenever they invoke someone else's written or spoken words, yet this does not mean that academic writers must always agree with the voices they employ. In "American Crime Comics as Villains: An Incident from Northern Canada," Jon Swainger (1998) refers to post–World War II newspaper editorials with which he disagrees. In this instance, certain voices are employed only to be discredited. Nevertheless, by presenting other voices as foils, Swainger attempts, among other things, to situate his topic in a real historical world. The editorials, which happen to be colourful and flamboyant, press upon the reader with dramatic immediacy, becoming verified points of view if not reliable statements of fact. Thus, the presence of other voices is part of an empiricist style that *seems* to place checks on the personal perceptions of the author, guarding against what the academic community would regard as the danger of errant subjectivity. Hence, academic writers rely on supporting voices in an attempt to ground research articles in actual rather than imagined realms.

IDEAS FOR FURTHER STUDY

1. Block and label the rhetorical features in the following proposal:

Dallas Bartsch

"Survival of the Fittest": Gender Imagery in
Media Coverage of the Iditarod Sled Dog Race

In late January, 1925, a diphtheria epidemic broke out amongst the children of Nome, Alaska. Five lives were lost and the closest medicine was over 1,000 miles away, in Anchorage, Alaska. Although there were planes in Fairbanks, they had been dismantled for the winter. The only hope was to get the life-saving serum to the remaining victims by dogsled. A plan was made and with the help of twenty dog mushers who formed a relay from Nenana to Nome, the diphtheria medicine reached the stranded children in a record five days and seven hours. In 1973, Joe Redington founded the Iditarod Dog Sled Race in memory of the Alaskan dogs who ran the life-saving relay. This race covers 1,151 miles, by dog team, from Anchorage to Nome.

The Iditarod Sled Dog Race is one of the few sports where both men and women compete against each other. Accordingly, this essay examines gender imagery in media coverage of the Iditarod Sled Dog Race. First, I will consider media coverage of the race from 1985 to 1990, years of great success for female competitors. Second, I will look at how the media portrayed female racers from 1991 to 2001. My primary sources include promotional videos, Internet interviews, and newspaper articles. Gender stereotyping by the media is a familiar practice in the sports industry. Pamela Creedon (1999) states that the media denies sportswomen the power and prestige that should be theirs. In other studies, Alexander (1994), Miller and Levy (1996), and Koivula (1999) investigate gender conflicts and how the media depicts them. Building on these and other works, I will argue that the media has portrayed women in the Iditarod as having little if any value compared to the male competitors.

---

2. Check out the periodical shelves at your library or a periodical database that offers full-text articles. Read through an article or two for examples of scholarly wordings. Are such expressions used effectively?

CHAPTER REFERENCES

The Broadview reader. (1987). H. Rosengarten & J. Flick (Eds.). (pp. 23–29). Peterborough: Broadview.

Carlick, A. (1995). The girl and the grizzly: Bringing traditional narratives into Yukon classrooms. *The Northern Review: A Multi-Disciplinary Journal of the Arts and Sciences of the North, 14,* 34–47.

Giltrow, J. (2002). *Academic writing: Writing and reading in the disciplines.* 3rd ed. Peterborough: Broadview.

Grant, S. (1987). Myths of the north in the Canadian ethos. *The Northern Review, 3–4,* 15–41.

Idlout-Paulson, L. (1993). Wonderful life. In R. Gedaloff (Ed.), *Paper stays put: A collection of Inuit writing* (pp. 57–58). Edmonton: Hurtig.

Rosen, L.J., & Behrens, L. (1994). *The Allyn & Bacon handbook.* Toronto: Allyn & Bacon.

Simons, P. (1999, January 10). Top scholars scoop bad writing award. *Edmonton Journal,* p. A8.

Swainger, J. (1998). American crime comics as villains: An incident from northern Canada. *Legal Studies Forum, 22,* 215–231.

Front Matter and
Scholarly Introductions

Introductions are known to be troublesome, and nearly all academic
writers admit to having more difficulty with getting started on a
piece of academic writing than they have with its continuation. The
opening paragraphs somehow present the writer with an unnerving
wealth of options: decisions have to be made about the amount and
type of background knowledge to be included . . . about the
winsomeness of the appeal to the readership . . . and about the
directness of the approach.

> —John M. Swales, *Genre Analysis:*
> *English in Academic and Research Settings*

Our analysis of topic proposals has indicated that introductory material
in academic writing requires special handling. Our goal in this chapter
is to look more closely at introductions to research papers in the
humanities and social sciences and to elaborate on the patterns that
can be found in them. Many of these features are common across the
disciplines, but some (such as a Methods section) are reserved for
special kinds of disciplinary knowledge-making. At the outset of the
discussion, we need to make a distinction between the kind of
attention-getting introductions that we encounter in, say, personal
essays, and the more formal, knowledge-making introductions that
we encounter in academic writing. The introductions to personal essays
are **anecdotal** in the sense that they often tell a story, describe
something, provide a quotation, etc. Indeed, countless composition
handbooks provide student writers with a neat set of strategies for
beginning what are really pre-disciplinary essays. Such strategies are
supposed to function as "hooks" that engage readers. On the other

hand, the knowledge-making introductions of academic essays are
epistemic in the sense that they are concerned with the conditions
under which knowledge is produced. (The adjective "epistemic" comes
from "epistemology," a branch of philosophy that is "concerned with
the nature and scope of knowledge, its presuppositions and bas[es],
and the general reliability of claims to knowledge" [Edwards, 1967,
pp. 8–9].) Epistemic introductions tend to be more formal or serious
than anecdotal introductions because the shift from private belief to
disciplinary knowledge entails a host of very demanding expectations
involving issues of definition, procedure, metadiscourse, objectivity,
and evidence. Such demands tend to formalize academic writing (see
Chapter 5), and as John Swales (1990) observes in the epigraph above,
this formalization of the writing process is nowhere more apparent
than in scholarly introductions.

The bulk of discussion material in this chapter provides an
explanation of **rhetorical features** or **coherence structures**. Mindful of
Swales' (1990) observation that introductory "textual elements . . .
occur in suitably robust preferred orders" (p. 145), we have tried to
present these features in a logical order, but also wish to acknowledge
sequential variations. Moreover, few if any research papers contain
all of the coherence structures presented here. Accordingly, it would
be wise to regard the various elements as offering a set of possibilities
rather than prescriptive necessities. Indeed, while academic
introductions require a rigorous approach to knowledge-making,
academic writers are still faced with choices about how to present
their material. These choices may sometimes be influenced by personal
preference, but more often they are determined by topic and by
traditional disciplinary practices (Swales, 1990, pp. 137–166). After
reviewing the introductory features described below, we will observe
them at work by studying a group of full-length papers.

FRONT MATTER

The phrase "front matter" simply refers to the preliminary greetings
that researchers extend to their readers. The precise configuration of
front matter is usually determined by the different stylistic conventions
that prevail in different disciplines.

Hello,
Reader!

Two-Part Titles

Although the precise rhetorical configuration of two-part titles varies, a two-part format is common in academic writing across the disciplines, particularly in the humanities and social sciences. Loosely speaking, of course, *any* title with two parts is a two-part title. This text, however, recommends a specific structure consisting of an **allusive phrase** followed by an **explanatory phrase**. Allusive phrases indirectly refer to the topic at issue and may consist of a brief quotation, a pertinent noun phrase, some key words, and so on. Explanatory phrases, on the other hand, succinctly articulate **topic**, providing both the prestige abstraction and the research site.

Adele Perry

(Allusive Phrase)

Bachelors in the Backwoods:

(Explanatory Phrase)

{Homosocial Culture} and {White Men in Up-Country British Columbia}

(Prestige Abstraction)   (Research Site)

Tony Arruda

(Allusive Phrase)

"You Would Have Had Your Pick":

(Explanatory Phrase)

{Youth, Gender,} and {Jobs in Williams Lake, British Columbia, 1945–75}

(Prestige Abstractions)   (Research Site)

Heather Smyth
(Allusive Phrase)
"Lords of the World":
(Explanatory Phrase)
{Gender and Imperialism} in {C. C. Vyvyan's *Arctic Adventure*}
(Prestige Abstractions)   (Research Site)

George H. Lewis
(Allusive Phrase)
Lap Dancer or Hillbilly Deluxe?:
(Explanatory Phrase)
The Cultural Construction of Modern Country Music
(Prestige Abstraction)   (Research Site)

Elizabeth Jane Wall Hinds
(Allusive Phrase)
The Devil Sings the Blues:
(Explanatory Phrase)
Heavy Metal, Gothic Fiction, and "Postmodern" Discourse
(Research Site)   (Prestige Abstraction)

Dana L. Cloud
(Allusive Phrase)
Hegemony or Concordance?:
(Explanatory Phrase)
The Rhetoric of Tokenism in "Oprah" Winfrey's Rags-to-Riches Biography
(Prestige Abstraction)   (Research Site)

> **Richard Paul Knowles**
> (Allusive Phrase)
> Post-, "Grapes," Nuts and Flakes:
> (Explanatory Phrase)
> "Coach's Corner" as Post-Colonial Performance
> (Research Site)   (Prestige Abstraction)

In those cases where two-part titles depart from the pattern described above, any number of configurations may be present. On occasion, as in the example below, one will encounter a two-part title that "spreads" topic throughout the first and second parts, presenting the abstraction and then the research site.

> **Jeffrey S. Hopkins**
> (Research Site)
> West Edmonton Mall:
> (Prestige Abstractions)
> Landscape of Myths and Elsewhereness

Alternatively, as in the next example, one may encounter an allusive phrase followed by a partial articulation of topic in the explanatory phrase.

> **Kerry Abel**
> (Allusive Phrase)
> Of Two Minds:
> (Explanatory Phrase)
> Dene Response to the Mackenzie Missions, 1858–1902
> (Research Site only)

While practices vary, the precise configuration of an allusive phrase followed by an explanatory phrase offers an effective method of constructing scholarly titles in the humanities and social sciences. Indeed, the pattern we recommend is analogous to the larger patterns of clarification and discovery (or problem and solution) that characterize academic research: allusive phrases tend to present details or fragments of a larger whole ("The Devil Sings the Blues"), while explanatory phrases "process" such details through generalization and abstraction ("Heavy Metal, Gothic Fiction, and 'Postmodern' Discourse"). Accordingly, carefully configured two-part titles carry considerable rhetorical force.

In the natural sciences, and perhaps in some of the more empirical branches of the social sciences, there may be a preference for one-part titles that simply give topic (see Chapter Nine).

Title Pages

In disciplines belonging to the social sciences, which follow formatting guidelines established by the American Psychological Association (the APA Style), instructors will probably expect title pages. A sample APA title page follows, for a paper written by Shari Harrison (2001). This sample contains four things: (1) running head or abbreviated title accompanied by a page number; (2) announcement of the running head; (3) full title; and (4) byline and institutional affiliation.

Making the Grade   1

Running head: MAKING THE GRADE

Note the double-spacing. There are no extra spaces between the title, byline, school affiliation, and city.

Making the Grade: Creating a Successful Learning
Environment For Post Secondary Students with Learning
Disabilities
Shari Harrison
University of Northern British Columbia
Fort St. John, British Columbia, Canada

In disciplines such as English and Philosophy, which tend to follow formatting guidelines established by the Modern Language Association (the MLA Style), instructors will probably not expect a title page.

Abstracts

Abstracts (not to be confused with prestige abstractions) are another feature that appears more commonly in the sciences than in the humanities. Abstracts provide a brief summary of the ensuing research, highlighting key features such as topic, methods or theoretical frame (where applicable), thesis, and main points. Abstracts do not contain documentation, tables, and other supplementary features of the article. In APA style, abstracts appear on a separate page, after the title page and before the first page of text. The page on which the abstract is presented has a running head and is entitled "Abstract."

First Page of Text

In APA style, the first page of text follows a title page and an abstract. Note how the first page of the text of Harrison's article (2001) continues the running head and reiterates the full title:

Making the Grade   1

Running head: MAKING THE GRADE

Making the Grade: Creating a Successful Learning
Environment For Post Secondary Students with Learning
Disabilities
Shari Harrison
University of Northern British Columbia
Fort St. John, British Columbia, Canada

Making the Grade   2

Abstract

This article explores policies and practices that support the creation
of a successful learning environment for postsecondary students
with learning disabilities. I argue that instructors and institutions
can more effectively meet the needs of all students by re-evaluating
traditional instructional procedures. By using new pedagogical
knowledge and understanding, instructors can begin to focus on the
experience of learning from the student's perspective. The
philosophy of valuing the learner's experience of learning is
intertwined with the phenomenological approach to curriculum
theory, an approach which focuses on individual perceptions and
experiences of education and learning. Instructors undertaking this
paradigm shift toward learner-centred learning may diversify
learning assessment procedures without sacrificing assessment
standards. Moreover, learning-strategy instruction may also assist
students with learning disabilities. In sum, incorporating learner-
centred instruction and learning strategies into classrooms can help
make postsecondary education more responsive to social needs.

Making the Grade   3

Making the Grade: Creating a Successful Learning
Environment for Post Secondary Students
with Learning Disabilities
"Northern Lights College provides and promotes
opportunities for life long learning. Northern Lights College
will provide accessible, responsive and diverse learning
opportunities to enhance the quality of life for the community it
serves" (Northern Lights College Calendar, 2001, p. 3). So reads
the Northern Lights College Mission Statement, an educational
ideal that is echoed in colleges and universities across the
country. Creating an accessible and responsive environment for
all students, and especially those students with learning
disabilities, isn't as simple as it may sound though . . .

In MLA style, which does not call for a title page or abstract, the first page of text is what initially greets the reader. Here, author, instructor, course, and date are presented top left. A header, consisting of the author's last name and a page number, appears top right. The full title is centred, near the top of the page. See the example that follows:

Vokaty 1

Helen Vokaty

Professor Smith

English 105

3 Apr. 1999

"In Transaction with Nature:"

Into the Wild as Quest, Odyssey, and Ordeal

In "Canadian Exploration as Literature," T.D. MacLulich argues that exploration writing can fall into one of three categories: quest, odyssey, and/or ordeal. The various patterns are often guided by the narrator's shaping of the adventure, a concept that MacLulich refers to as "emplotment" (86). According to MacLulich, an adventure can be retold as a quest, in which the central theme is the successful attainment of a specific goal (87). An odyssey, on the other hand, places less emphasis on the attainment of a particular goal, and more on the "incidental details of the journey" (88). Finally, an ordeal entails great hardship and focuses on survival, often ending in tragedy (87). MacLulich states that "the three forms [of exploration writing] are not necessarily mutually exclusive, but may exist in combination" (88).

Note that the APA and MLA styles call for double-spacing throughout.

Epigraphs

Embellishing the text with an epigraph may contribute to the sophistication of your paper. Epigraphs are quotations that are usually placed immediately after the title and before the introduction. They are usually supplemented by an attributive noun phrase.

Robin Ridington
"When Poison Gas Come Down Like a Fog":
A Native Community's Response to Cultural Disaster

> Just like you blowing something, sounds like that.
>   And they knew it right away, something happened
>   down there.
>   And pretty soon, just like a fog come down.
>   Come down the hill.
>   —Angus Davis, Blueberry Band.

The Blueberry Reserve is a community of Cree and Beaver Indians about
72 kilometres north of Fort St. John, British Columbia. . . .

FEATURES THAT APPEAR IN INTRODUCTORY PARAGRAPHS

The following elements should be considered as you move beyond
the front matter. Try to make informed choices about which features
you will include, based on the requirements of individual topics and
disciplinary conventions. Ideally, the features that you incorporate
will be easy for readers to identify.

Establishing a Context

It is common for academic writers in the humanities and social
sciences to begin their papers by presenting background information
or illustrative material that establishes a context for topic. When
researchers provide context for their work, they "step back a pace or
two" (Northey, 1992, p. 72) and ease into topic. Context "sets the
stage" for knowledge-making activities.

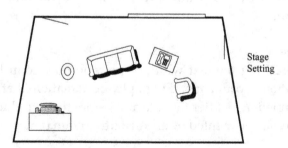

Stage
Setting

In pre-disciplinary composition classes, strategies for establishing a context are usually described as ways of "hooking" readers. Such classes emphasize catching the attention of a reader, as though readers are easily distracted people who must be enticed. The assumption is rooted in the competitive realities of popular journalism, where writers address a mass audience with a short attention span. The rationale for establishing a context in academic writing is somewhat different in that the social conditions of the genre involve a more limited audience with a professional interest in discipline-based topics. Accordingly, scholarly discourse probably exhibits openings that are somewhat less flamboyant or dramatic. Indeed, since academic writers assume that their readers are like-minded people who share an interest in disciplinary investigation, perhaps introductory contexts for research papers do not try quite as hard as those in journalism to engage the audience at an emotional level. To the uninitiated reader, the result might be uninviting, but academic readers are driven by interests that supersede entertainment value. The following excerpt simply begins with historical details:

Greg Gillespie
"I Was Well Pleased with Our Sport among the Buffalo":
Big-Game Hunters, Travel Writing, and Cultural Imperialism
in the British North American West, 1847–72

During the mid-nineteenth century, big-game hunters from Great Britain traveled to the British North American West and cast their imperial eyes across the landscape. These aristocratic men traveled thousands of miles for sport, exploration, and adventure, and recorded their experiences in their travel narratives. They used their books, arranged and reproduced for readerships in England, to inscribe cultural meaning on the little-known territory. Big-game hunters used their travel writings to construct the West as a familiar, resource-rich land that appeared ready-made for the encroaching imperial enterprise.

This next example of introductory context—which literally refers to a stage setting—does demonstrate a flair for the dramatic (not coincidentally, perhaps, the paper appears in a journal entitled *Modern Drama*):

Richard Paul Knowles
Post-, "Grapes," Nuts and Flakes: "Coach's Corner"
as Post-Colonial Performance

We're still trapped in Canada: we're the ventriloquist's dummy on the
British and American knee. When the voices come in from all these
other places, it's very hard to forge our own.
— Urjo Kareda

In "The Dummy," a short scene in the Rich Salutin/Theatre Passe Muraille
collective creation "1837: The Farmer's Revolt," two actors playing a
ventriloquist and his dummy address the crowd onstage and off in an
allegorical representation of post-colonial mimicry.[2] As the scene opens,
the (pre-)Canadian colonial dummy speaks only in the voice (literally)
of "John Bull—your imperial ventriloquist," mouths platitudes and
promises to cut trees and fight Yankees for England while being (literally)
manipulated and having his pockets picked by the imperial puppet master.
Towards the end of the scene, however, ignoring arguments that on his
own he will be helpless, "a pitiable colonial," he stands independently
and speaks in his own voice for the first time, rallying the crowd and
introducing William Lyon Mackenzie, the radical political reformer and
leader of the only class revolt in English Canada's history.

The scene is simple enough, except in its veiled critique (within the
context of a nationalist collective creation) of the power structures of the
traditional theatre in Canada, in which colonial actors, constructed as
workers, use British accents to mouth the words and mimic the manners
of British, or more recently, American playwrights and directors. I
introduce it here, however, as a starting point for the analysis of a different
kind of post-colonial performance, one that takes place not in the theatre,
but in the intermissions between the first and second periods of telecast
hockey games on the Canadian Broadcasting Corporation (CBC) . . .

In other cases, academic writers may omit background or
illustrative material entirely and demonstrate a more immediate focus
on the challenges presented by the topic (MacDonald, 1994, pp. 47–
48). As in the following examples, openings that get right down to
business may **define a key term**, provide an outright announcement

of **topic**, or present a **tradition of inquiry** (which identifies previous research related to the topic).

The first two papers begin with definitions:

C.M. Tam, et al.
Feng Shui and Its Impacts on Land and Property Developments

"Feng Shui," literally meaning "wind" and "water," is ancient Chinese geomancy. It is abstract, invisible, untouchable, and intangible—as the wind, hard to see, and as water, difficult to be grasped. Thus it is considered mysterious.

Scott MacAulay
The Smokestack Leaned Toward Capitalism:
An Examination of the Middle Way Program of the Antigonish Movement

The Antigonish Movement is the name given to a program of populist adult education and co-operative development that emerged in eastern Nova Scotia in the late 1920s. The intellectual and organizational center of the Movement was the Extension Department of St. Francis Xavier University in the town of Antigonish. The Movement represents the start of a long tradition of local development in this part of Canada that argues that people and communities in the region can and should take responsibility for local economic development.

The next paper begins with topic.

Pamela Hyde
Managing Bodies—Managing Relationships: The Popular Media
and the Social Construction of Women's Bodies and Social Roles
from the 1930's to the 1950's

This paper, based on a discourse analysis of the New Zealand *Woman's Weekly* from the 1930's to the 1950's, [examines] the ways in which women's bodies and social roles have been historically constructed and reconstructed in accordance with changing social circumstances and expectations during the prewar, wartime, and postwar period. It discusses the ways in which power operated as pleasurable and desirable codes of self-surveillance and improvement, and shows that these codes were inextricably linked with gender relations.

The next two examples present traditions of inquiry:

Tony Arruda
"You Would Have Had Your Pick": Youth, Gender, and Jobs in Williams Lake, British Columbia, 1945–1975

In 1990, Canadian historians Patricia Rooke and Rudy Schnell described the field of Canadian history of childhood and youth as a "truly marginal subspecialty" of Canadian historical scholarship dominated by studies of the child-saving movement, juvenile immigration, and juvenile delinquency, and offering up only a small volume of dissertations.[1] Not much has changed in the intervening years. In this paper I attempt to address two further observations of the field . . .

Joan Valery, et al.
The Nature and Amount of Support College-Age Adolescents Request and Receive from Parents

Many researchers have suggested that children are able to increase their capacity to deal with aversive stressors through the use of social support (Cause, Reed, Landesman, & Gonzales, 1990; Cutrona, 1990; Sandler, Miller, Short, & Wolchik, 1989; Thoits, 1986; Wills, Vaccaro, & McNamara, 1992).

Parenthesis

These blunter, down-to-business openings are particularly common in the sciences, where a greater emphasis is placed on brevity and where disciplinary processes can be compactly defined (see Chapter 9).

Acknowledging a Tradition of Inquiry

As researchers, academic writers are under an obligation to situate their own work in relation to other voices in the research community. Thus, early on in a paper, academics often refer to previous studies that bear some relationship to the current investigation (Swales, 1990, pp. 140–142). Janet Giltrow (1994) aptly describes this move as acknowledging "a tradition of inquiry" (p. 262). The closeness of the connection between the current study and previous studies may vary. Sometimes, for example, previous researchers may have anticipated the precise topic (both the research site and the prestige abstraction) under immediate investigation. In these cases, whether the current researcher wants to refute or build upon the previous studies, she must acknowledge her predecessors. On other occasions, a researcher will bring a new abstraction to a research site that has typically been studied from other perspectives. Even in situations like this, however, previous work should be acknowledged. Thus, traditions of inquiry "map" particular domains of knowledge (Giltrow, 1994, p. 286). John Swales (1990) draws an "ecological analogy," explaining that a writer's acknowledgement of previous studies situates her topic within an "ecosystem" of knowledge-making activities (p. 140–142).

Presenting a tradition of inquiry again calls on the summary skills of the primary writer. Once again, moreover, the primary writer will have choices to make. Indeed, previous studies can be summarized through what we have chosen to call **direct reference** or **indirect reference** (for a more comprehensive discussion of modes of reference, and for previous research relating to this distinction, see Chapter 7). In what we have called direct reference, previous researchers are named in an attributive expression before the citation. In indirect reference, the names of previous researchers appear in a citation only. See the examples below.

A Limited Tradition of Inquiry
Presented through Direct Reference

Pamela den Ouden
"My Uttermost Valleys": Patriarchal Fear of the Feminine in
Robert Service's Poetry and Prose

Margaret Atwood points out that Service "habitually personifies the North as a savage but fascinating female" (18).

A More Extensive Tradition of Inquiry
Presented through Direct Reference

Cheryl Kirschner
Desperate Measures: Corporate Designs and the Murders at St. John's Fort

Over the past decade, scholars have discussed the causes and effects of the murders at St. John's Fort. According to Robin Ridington, in "Changes of Mind: Dunne-za Resistance to Empire," the native people claim that the murders were "justified retaliation" for the mysterious death of a native hunter who had requested to leave the post in order to return to his band.[3] Conversely, in *Delayed Frontier: The Peace River Country to 1909*, David Leonard writes: "the perpetrators were reported to have been Beaver Indians who were angry at the pending closure of the post . . ."[4] In "Early Fur-Trade History in the Peace River District of British Columbia, 1794–1824," Finola Finlay focuses on the effect of the murders: "The murders at St. John's have been cited by all authorities as the cause of the closure of [the Peace River] forts."[5]

A Tradition of Inquiry Presented through Indirect Reference

David Hamer
Wildfire's influence on yellow hedysarum digging
habitat used by grizzly bears in Banff National Park, Alberta

Hedysarum roots are the primary food for grizzly bears in the Front Ranges of the Canadian Rocky Mountains. Hedysarum roots are dug from April through early June, before green vegetation is widely available; in August if buffaloberry fruits are slow to ripen; and from September through November after fruit-fall (Russell et al. 1979; Wielgus 1986; Hamer and Herrero 1987a; Hamer et al. 1991). In years of high fruit production, roots are dug infrequently by grizzly bears during autumn, but if the buffaloberry crop fails, roots can dominate the diet from August until hibernation in late October or November (Pearson 1975; Russell et al. 1979; Hamer and Herrero 1987a).

Describing a Knowledge Deficit

On occasion, academic writers discover a "new" research site (something that has received little if any scholarly attention); alternatively, they may discover that fresh abstractions reinvigorate "old" research sites. In these cases, researchers find unoccupied or relatively unpopulated niches for their own knowledge-making activities (Swales, 1990, p. 142; Giltrow, 1994, p. 286). These blank spaces present a special opportunity for researchers to make an original contribution to knowledge. Some of the most significant research often involves branching out into new territory. In order to affirm that a knowledge gap exists, researchers will sometimes sketch out *neighboring* knowledge domains. In circumstances like this, a tradition of inquiry is followed by the identification of what Janet Giltrow calls a "knowledge deficit" (Giltrow, 1994, pp. 286–287; Giltrow, 2002, pp. 262–269).

The Simple Articulation of a Knowledge Deficit

David Peterson del Mar
Pimping and Courtship: A 1940 Court Case
from Northern British Columbia

Historians of prostitution in North America have not much concerned themselves with small towns and rural areas. New York City has received the most attention. Prostitutes of western Canada and the western United States have also been the subjects of historical study, but only if they lived in urban areas like Calgary or Virginia City.[1] This is partly a matter of convenience. Large numbers of prostitutes lived in large cities. Big cities were also much more likely to spawn reform and police activities around prostitution. At the very least, cities offer the historian of prostitution voluminous arrest records and newspaper reports, materials that are either thin or non-existent for many towns and rural areas.

[1]Timothy Gilfoyle, *City of Eros: New York City, Prostitution, and the Commercialization of Sex, 1790–1920* (New York: W. W. Norton, 1992); Judy Bedford, "Prostitution in Calgary, 1905–1914," *Alberta History* 29 (Spring 1981): 1–11; etc.

The Articulation of a Knowledge Deficit
with an Extensive Supplementary Endnote

Heather Smyth
"Lords of the World": Gender and Imperialism
in C. C. Vyvyan's *Arctic Adventure*

Although *Arctic Adventure* has received little critical attention,[2] it is significant for being arguably the first travel narrative written about the Canadian Arctic by a white professional writer (MacLaren, "Land" 2).

[2] I have found only two published instances of critical treatment of *Arctic Adventure*: Gwyneth Hoyle summarizes the text and provides some critical commentary in "Women of Determination," and Judith Niemi and Barbara Wieser offer an excerpt from *Arctic Adventure* prefaced by a brief contextual description in *Rivers Running Free*. C.C. Vyvyan is noticeably absent from such valuable studies as Marni L. Stanley's "Traveler's Tales," and Jane Robinson's ambitious annotated bibliography, *Wayward Women*, both of which engage with many of Vyvyan's contemporaries and predecessors in Canadian wilderness travel. Future critical work on Vyvyan should be enabled by the forthcoming publication of I. S. MacLaren and Lisa N. LaFramboise's critical edition of *Arctic Adventure*, entitled *The Ladies, the Gwich'in, and the Rat: Travels on the Athabasca, Mackenzie, Rat, Porcupine, and Yukon Rivers in 1926*.

A Tradition of Inquiry in a Neighboring Knowledge Domain,
Followed by a Knowledge Deficit

James Ryan
Experiencing Urban Schooling:
The Adjustment of Native Students to the
Extracurricular Demands of Post-Secondary Education

While numerous studies have addressed the Native urban experience (Bud, 1986; Leibow, 1989; Shoemaker, 1988; Graves, 1970; Mucha, 1983, 1984; McCaskill, 1970, 1981; Clatworthy and Hull, 1983; Dosman, 1972; Moronis, 1982), the issue of temporary student migration to cities on the part of Native people seeking to expand their educational horizons, and the subsequent impact on their capacity to apply themselves to their studies, has received scant attention.

Topic

Readers of this text will now be familiar with a rigorous approach to articulating and identifying topic (see Chapter 3). As previously noted, we encourage students to think of topic as a rhetorical feature that consists of a research site (an *area* of investigation) plus a prestige abstraction (an *idea* or concept that is recognized as important in academic culture). Moreover, we have shown that academic proposals and introductions often explicitly announce (or flag) topic through metadiscursive verbs such as "examine," "explore," "focus on," and so on. Given the fundamental importance of topic, we have provided more examples of how it may surface in published research.

In the three excerpts below, the topic formula should be readily evident:

Lee Parpart

**Adapting Emotions: Notes on the Transformation of
Affect and Ideology from "We So Seldom Look on Love" to *Kissed***

This paper attempts to explore . . . shifts in affective and ideological meaning between Barbara Gowdy's short story "We So Seldom Look on Love" and Lynne Stopkewich's 1996 film adaptation *Kissed*.

Kyle D. Killian

**Dominant and Marginalized Discourses in Interracial
Couples' Narratives: Implications for Family Therapists**

Focusing on black-white couples, this exploratory study examines . . . dominant and marginalized discourses in interracial relationships . . .

David L. Share and Phil A. Silva

**Gender Bias in IQ-Discrepancy and
Post-Discrepancy Definitions of Reading Disability**

. . . we studied the extent to which the higher prevalence of specific reading disability among boys was an artifact of gender bias.

In the two passages that follow, the research site is easy to discern, but it might be harder to settle on an abstraction.

Annette Hill

Fearful and Safe: Audience Response to British Reality Programming

This article will focus on two BBC reality series, *999* and *Children's Hospital*, and will examine why these series are popular with British audiences, in particular, focusing on the "entertainment potential" (Kilborn, 1994, p. 425).

Karen R. Blaisure and Julie M. Koivunen

**Family Science Faculty Members' Experiences with
Teaching from a Feminist Perspective**

. . . the present study explored how feminist family science teachers conceptualize teaching, translate theory into classroom practice, and handle challenging situations.

It is also worth noting that the metadiscourse of topic can also be associated with nouns like "purpose," "aim," or "objective." Thus, when some instructors call for introductions that contain a "statement of purpose," they may simply be attaching a different label to topic. The samples that follow present this pattern in published research:

Arild Fetveit

Reality TV in the Digital Era: A Paradox in Visual Culture?

The aim in this article is to historicize and conceptualize [possible changes] in visual culture, and to suggest plausible explanations for the proliferation of reality TV in the digital era.

Joan Valery, et al.
The Nature and Amount of Support College-Age
Adolescents Request and Receive from Parents

The purpose of this study was to determine the nature and amount of
parental support older adolescents request and receive from parents.

C.M. Tam, et al.
Feng Shui and Its Impacts on Land and Property Developments

The objective of this paper is to explore whether Feng Shui would affect
property [developments].

In the above instances, topic sounds very much like the kind of
generalized structural forecast that is described below. Thus, in some
papers, topic may be rolled into a broad comment about structure,
but we advise student writers to make fine distinctions between topic
and structural forecasts.

Finally, since we are dealing with the various permutations of
topic, it is worth noting that there may be occasions where topic
(aboutness) and thesis (argument) appear interwoven within a single
sentence, as in the next example:

Dana L. Cloud
Hegemony or Concordance?: The Rhetoric of Tokenism in
"Oprah" Winfrey's Rags-to-Riches Biography

This article examines these narratives in order to understand how they
construct an "Oprah" persona whose life story as it is appropriated in
popular biographies resonates with and reinforces the ideology of the
American Dream, implying the accessibility of this dream to black
Americans despite the structural, economic, and political obstacles to
achievement and survival in a racist society.

Once again, however, we advise student researchers to make careful distinctions among introductory rhetorical features and to announce topic and thesis separately.

Structural Forecasts

Structural "forecasts" relate to matters of organization or arrangement (Giltrow, 2002, p. 236). That is, such statements anticipate the structure of a paper by providing advance notice about how material will be presented to readers. According to Giltrow (2002), "forecasts play an important role in helping readers manage the contents of their mental desktops. . . . [For example,] [t]hey guide readers in determining when one section is finished and another is beginning . . ." (p. 238). We wish to point out that such comments can be fairly general or quite specific. *General* **forecasting,** as we use the phrase, merely provides a broad sense of direction and may, as noted above, be virtually identical to topic. What we choose to call *specific* **forecasting,** on the other hand, is a more distinctive and perhaps more useful feature, functioning like a relatively detailed, step-by-step outline. Frequently, specific forecasting is accompanied by adverbs that designate chronology ("First," "Second," "Third," and so on).

General Forecasting

Shelagh Grant
Myths of the North in the Canadian Ethos

To fully understand [the overarching, national myth of the north], one must first identify the many lesser myths which gave special meaning to the north and eventually combined to form the vague but all-encompassing core myth.

Specific Forecasting

James Ryan

Experiencing Urban Schooling

My article is organized in the following manner. First, I describe the research setting and methods. Next, I recount students' experiences of city living and illustrate how they impede their ability to succeed in the program. Finally, I discuss the issue of urban adjustment and explore three possible solutions to the problems faced by Native students in cities.

Self-Disclosure

It is increasingly common in academic writing, particularly in the humanities and in some areas of the social sciences, for writers to situate themselves in relation to their topic. What we have in mind here are instances in which academic writers move beyond what Janet Giltrow (2002) refers to as the merely "discursive 'I'" (p. 233–236), which often appears in first-person metadiscursive announcements of such features as topic, thesis, and forecasting (for example, "I examine," "I argue," "First, I discuss). Even the modest appearance of "I" in constructions like these may surprise students, some of whom arrive at college and university with the sense that "I" should be avoided entirely in academic writing. Obviously, however, this is not a universally accepted rule.

In fact, in recent years, "I" or "We" — pronouns that designate authors — have made even bolder appearances in academic writing. In these cases, we begin to learn a little more about that "I" who examines, argues, or discusses. It is in these more intensely personal moments that readers encounter **self-disclosure**. Thus, self-disclosure is a personal gesture that acknowledges the "constructedness" of all knowledge. This tendency to reveal the self as the generator of knowledge has been associated with feminism, an intellectual perspective that has a political investment in disputing the notion of absolute objectivity. In this text, we suggest that it is possible to trace an ascending scale of self-disclosure, which charts increasingly bolder appearances of the writing self. We begin with the merely discursive

"I," then move toward a more autobiographical "I" that engages in the kind of self-disclosure that is associated with personal essays.

In the first sample, personal pronouns flag topic and thesis:

The Merely Discursive "I"

Franca Iacovetta
Gossip, Contest, and Power in the Making of
Suburban Bad Girls, Toronto, 1945–60

My exploration of the various forces that converged in the making of postwar suburban Toronto bad girls confirms the wisdom of Foucault's famous axiom, that knowledge is power, and the Gramscian concept of hegemony central to many Marxist and feminist analyses of moral regulation. *My* analysis has also obviously benefited enormously from the recent spate of excellent feminist works on female transgression and the courts, and on women and social-welfare systems more generally. . . . *I have tried to suggest* how parents, especially mothers, but also caseworkers, empowered themselves in battles to intimidate, supervise, control, or punish deviant teenage girls. [italics added]

In the next two samples, personal pronouns signal writing selves that have first-hand experience of the topic. Here, the "eyes" are witnesses to the research site.

The "I" as Witness: Sample One

Jacqueline Hookimaw-Witt
Any Changes Since Residential School?

The statement about Native people that "these people need education" is usually made when *our* situation in Canadian society is presented; and it is used as a suggestion as to how *our* problems should be solved. *I heard* this statement from the non-Native health director in *my community* of Attawapiskat when *I was there* to do research for my master's thesis. *I also worked in the Safe House*, which is the home to which solvent abusers were brought as an alternative to a jail cell. The form of solvent abuse in Attawapiskat is sniffing gasoline, and it has infested a large portion of our youth. . . . the health director set the stage for how to solve the problem, namely, by the education of youths. [italics added]

The "I" as Witness: Sample Two

David W. Friesen and Jeff Orr
New Paths, Old Ways: Exploring the Places of Influence on the Role Identity

We are both non-Aboriginal and former faculty members with the Aboriginal teacher education program from which the participants graduated. Long after joining southern teacher education institutions, *we continued* to hear stories about our former students and their influence as Aboriginal educators on northern education. *We began* to propose ways to document their influences without evaluating them or comparing them with non-Aboriginal teachers. *We wondered* what it was about their teacher identity that enabled them to influence positively students, schools, and communities. *We wished* to find out what Aboriginality means for their teaching by gaining insight into the notion of Aboriginal teacher role identity. *Our initial contact with the graduates* to propose this project was greeted with overwhelming support. [italics added]

In the next example, the writers express an even more intimate relationship with their research site, acknowledging their own emotional engagement:

The "I" as Emotionally Engaged Researcher

Susanna Egan and Gabriele Helms
The Many Tongues of Mothertalk:
Life Stories of Mary Kiyoshi Kiyooka

We ourselves come to Mary Kiyooka's life stories as outsiders, but undoubtedly read them for their resonance with *our own experiences. As women of two generations, and as immigrants from England and Germany respectively, we respond* to Mary Kiyooka's experience of immigration from Japan to Canada. *We respond* to Kiyooka's involvement with his mother's text, recognizing its power to explain his identity as both Canadian and Japanese. *We respond* to the challenges of translation and the grounding of Kiyooka's sensibilities in two languages. *We respond* to Marlatt's editorial involvement derived from her sense of responsibility to Mary and Roy Kiyooka and part of her longstanding commitment to oral and community histories. *We also read Mothertalk* in light of very significant help from those whose readings have preceded our own. [italics added]

In our final examples, the writers blur traditional genre distinctions by presenting autobiographical details in academic articles:

The Autobiographical "I"

Lorraine York
What It Took and Took/To Be a Man: Teaching
Timothy Findley and the Construction of Masculinities

Now,
it is their brokenness
you long to touch, the parts
they left behind or lost
as they learned too soon
too many years ago
what it took and took
to be a man.

This essay will be a journey through *my own thinking* about this complex
field of study: masculinities, social institutions (such as, in *my* case, the

---

university) and power, a journey that began with *my teaching* of a course on Timothy Findley and the construction of masculinities. Beginning *my narrative* of this journey with Crozier's lines [a reference to the epigraph] is *important to me*, I sense, because they present a woman in the act of speaking about masculinities — *a role that I have had to assume in the classroom and, to a lesser extent, with my teaching colleagues.* [italics added]

The Autobiographical "I": Sample Two

Robyn R. Warhol and Diane Price Herndl
Feminisms: An Anthology of Literary Criticism and Theory

"We" are Robyn and Diane; we speak as white, middle-class heterosexual American feminist academics in our early thirties (to cover a number of the categories feminist criticism has lately been emphasizing as significant to one's reading and speaking position: race, class, sexual orientation, nationality, political positioning, education-level, and age). Colleagues at the University of Vermont since 1989, we too have found that we share passionate interests in fiction, feminism and quiltmaking.

While self-disclosure represents an important new trend in academic writing, it would be misleading to say that the use of "I" has been sanctioned by all academics. To the contrary, the "avoid I" advice that students sometimes bring to post-secondary studies reflects real tensions in academic culture. Clearly, "I" is more acceptable in the humanities than in the natural sciences, leaving the social sciences as a kind of ambivalent middle ground. Here is what Margot Northey (2001) has to say about "I" in *Making Sense in Geography and Environmental Sciences: A Student's Guide to Research and Writing*: "A formal essay is not a personal outpouring, as in a personal letter to someone close to you. Therefore you should keep it from becoming I-centred. It's acceptable to use the occasional first-person pronoun if the assignment calls for your opinions — as long as they are backed by evidence. But you should avoid the *I think* or *in my view* approach when the fact or argument speaks for itself. Still, if the choice is between using *I* and creating a tangle of passive constructions, it is almost always better to choose *I*. (A hint: when you do use *I*, it will be less noticeable if you place it in the middle of the sentence rather than the beginning" (pp. 7–8).

In sum, "I" has "HANDLE WITH CARE" stamped all over it. Accordingly, it would probably be wise for students in college and university classes to consult with individual instructors about the use of "I."

Methods

Since we have already divided the narrative structure of humanities and social sciences articles into an introduction, core, and conclusion, we think it is logical at this point to treat "methods" as an introductory rhetorical feature.

In the humanities and social sciences, a Methods section may be advisable when scholars take special steps to generate original research. Thus, Methods sections may describe special instruments or procedures used in a study, or they may describe additional details that are relevant to the data-gathering process. If researchers in the social sciences rely on a questionnaire, for example, information about the questionnaire would likely be provided in a Methods section. Alternatively, if a historian consults museum archives, a Methods section might provide information about the archival material. Thus, Methods sections are generally advisable when researchers adopt distinctive knowledge-making strategies.

The traditional rationale for including a Methods section is that this feature enables a disciplinary audience to evaluate the reliability of knowledge claims. Hypothetically, at least, by setting out their methods, scholars hold their activities up for inspection, permitting colleagues to evaluate whatever claims or findings are being presented. Accordingly, we advise students to think of a Methods section as commenting on basic questions about who or what was studied, where and when the study was conducted, how it was conducted, and why certain choices were made. The length of Methods sections varies, from a paragraph (or part of a paragraph) to several paragraphs. From this perspective, Methods sections in the humanities and social sciences might be regarded as a fairly brief yet comprehensive story about how knowledge was made, and perhaps this thoroughness is something that students should aspire to (see Chapter 9).

Despite their story-like function, however, Methods sections often defy standard notions of good writing, tending to present what Swales (1990) describes as "bald" narratives characterized by choppy sentences, heavy doses of statistical information, and agentless or passive-voice constructions. These tendencies are more pronounced in the natural sciences, but it is possible to catch glimpses of them in the so-called "softer" disciplines.

Our first sample presents excerpts from a Methods section for a paper entitled "Attitudes toward Oil and Gas Development among Forest Recreationists." Note the use of subheadings within the section and how "Procedures" provides details about a questionnaire:

Edward E. Langenau, Jr., et al.
Methods

Study Area
Research on the attitudes of forest visitors toward oil and gas development was done on the Pigeon River Country State Forest (PRCSF). At the time of the study, the forest comprised about 83,000 acres of public land in Otsego, Cheboygan, and Montmorency counties of Michigan, about 200 miles northeast of Lansing.

....

Subjects

A sample of recreationists visiting the forest between March 1, 1981 and February 28, 1982 were participants in this study. About 38 percent of all people visiting the PRCSF during the year were included in the sample. Individuals that were cutting firewood for noncommercial use were included, although this may not always have been recreation. Individuals working for an oil or logging company in the forest were included only if contacted while recreating on their own time.

Procedures

A recreational use survey was conducted on 152 sample days between March 1, 1981 and February 28, 1982 (Ryel et al., 1982). Field workers left 1,569 postcards with vehicle occupants or on vehicle windshields on sample days. These pre-paid and pre-addressed postcards asked for names and addresses of all people in the vehicle. About 62 percent of the postcards were returned. A sample of 596 vehicles was drawn from those contacted during recreational surveys. Names and addresses of individuals in sample vehicles were taken from postcards. Telephone calls were then made to registered vehicle owners if a postcard had not been received. Names and addresses of all vehicle occupants were requested.

A mail questionnaire was developed to measure attitudes toward oil and gas development in the forest. This was pre-tested and modified after interviews in the field. Questionnaires were mailed to two sets of visitors (those contacted between March 1, 1981 and August 31, 1981, and those contacted between September 1, 1981 and February 28, 1982). Two follow-up forms were mailed to visitors who did not initially respond. The cover letters specified that children under 12 years of age need not return forms.

Questionnaire items were written and data analyzed according to the model previously discussed to include visitor characteristics, recreational behaviour, values, beliefs, and attitudes. Relationships were tested at an alpha level of 0.01.

In this next sample, taken from an article entitled "The Nature and Amount of Support College-Age Adolescents Request and Receive from Parents," the Methods section again involves subheadings and a questionnaire:

Joan Valery, et al.

Methods

Instruments

Perceived parental support was assessed using a 15-item, Mother/Father-Adolescent Interaction Inventory measuring the adolescent's perception of emotional and instrumental support (Wills, Vaccaro, & McNamara, 1992). Items tapping into emotional support inquire about communication and sharing, whereas items tapping into instrumental support inquire about the availability of assistance and advice (see Table 1 for domains). The perceived support inventory uses a 4-point Likert scale with "always" and "never" as anchor points. Two separate inventories were used to measure perceived support from the father and from the mother. Students having contact with only one parent ($n = 19$) were asked to complete the inventory in reference to that parent only, leaving the other inventory blank. Wills, Vaccaro, and McNamara (1992) have used factorial analyses to confirm a two-dimensional structure with items on the instrumental and emotional scales loading on different factors. The correlation between the two scales in the study was .57 (Wills, Vaccaro, & McNamara, 1992).

Procedure

After IRB approval was obtained, the behaviour science departments of five two-year colleges in upstate New York were contacted, and permission to solicit students to participate in the study was granted from all the schools. Eight professors were then contacted and arrangements made for the first author to attend 18 introductory psychology and sociology classes to solicit student participation.

Questionnaires were assembled into packets that were identical except that half had the Mother-Adolescent Interaction questionnaires first, and the other had the Father-Adolescent Interaction questionnaires first.

The first author met with students during class time to inform them of the study. Students were told that the study concerned the ways in which adolescents and their parents interact, and were asked to volunteer to complete the packet of five questionnaires. A letter from the first author to each student was also included in the packet. General instructions and informed consent were included in this letter. To ensure anonymity, all questionnaires were identified by code numbers.

The next Methods section, from an article entitled "Images of Society in Klondike Gold Rush Narratives," refers to oral interviews and archival documents. In this case, however, the account of procedures is not very detailed. Moreover, the statement of Methods was incorporated into an introductory paragraph that was not preceded by a Methods subheading:

Julie Cruikshank

The oral accounts come from two native women with whom I have been recording life histories for a number of years: Mrs. Kitty Smith, born about 1890, and Mrs. Angela Sidney, born in 1902. Each incorporates references to the gold rush into her life story (Cruikshank et al. 1990).[3] Parallel accounts have been recorded with native elders who are no longer living (see Skookum Jim Friendship Centre),[4] but I refer here specifically to Mrs. Sidney's and Mrs. Smith's accounts because we have discussed them so fully. The written accounts come from books and from archival documents — private and published journals, lawyers' records, newspapers — located while I was trying to put the oral narratives into some broader historical context.

The final sample is from a student paper that appears later in this book (see Chapter 8). Here, the use of archival material is described in greater detail:

Laurie Dressler

Methods

The information gathered to describe public responses to the building of the Bennett Dam is taken from articles and editorial comments in the *Alaska Highway News*, 1957–1968. The North Peace Museum maintains a catalogued archive of newspapers from March 16, 1944, to December 24, 1975. Articles pertaining to the dam are recorded in the catalogue; however, editorial comments and Letters to the Editor are not. Thus, in order to ensure the thoroughness of my own research, it was necessary to review each of the *Alaska Highway News* weekly publications, page by page, between 1957 and 1968. The back issues of the newspapers have been kept in very good condition in cardboard boxes, one year per box, and shelved according to the year of publication. Further responses by local residents are taken from *This Was Our Valley*, written by Shirlee Smith Matheson and Earl K. Pollon. I will also be drawing information from the Fort Chipewyan Way of Life Study, which addresses the impact on economic and environmental issues downstream of the dam on the Peace-Athabasca Delta, once the waterflow of the Peace River was reduced.

Theoretical Framework

In the humanities and social sciences, methods are sometimes implied and so do not call for formal declaration. In these cases, a theoretical framework may take the place of methods (Giltrow, 2002, p. 279), although the two features are not mutually exclusive. To those unfamiliar with the features of academic writing, the notion of a theoretical framework may sound daunting. However, such frames simply offer a scaffolding that enables scholars to construct knowledge in new and sometimes surprising ways. Indeed, theory, as an intellectual support system, often fosters a departure from common habits of construction (that is, from *common sense*), and it is this element of departure that makes theory in academic writing so controversial and so potentially valuable.

Theoretical frames, then, are portable, ready-made structures that provide a way of building upon a research site and prestige abstraction. Such frames, in this sense, are different from **traditions of inquiry** because they tend to exist independently of **topics**. In fact, one of the tell-tale characteristics of theoretical frameworks is that they involve systems of ideas that can be shuffled around and applied to different areas of investigation. Because of this, although theory is maligned in some quarters, it has also been celebrated as a genuinely interdisciplinary force in academic writing.

In presenting theoretical frames, academic writers frequently borrow ideas from other people, often from famous scholars who have become shining stars in the halls of academia. However, not all theoretical frameworks are flagged by big names. On occasion, theory is introduced simply as a consciously adopted assumption. In either case, though, the inclusion of a theoretical framework is not generally something that a researcher must justify. Instead, the value of theory is tacitly understood, so disciplinary audiences tend to accept announcement and imposition as rhetorical strategies, unless, perhaps, a particular set of theoretical ideas is out of vogue.

Notice, then, that there is also an important distinction to be made between theoretical frameworks and **thesis claims**. Whereas thesis claims must be justified or demonstrated through argument and evidence, theory helps *to shape* argument and evidence. Thus, a theoretical framework is a thought-apparatus that will influence **thesis**; it should not be confused with the thesis itself, the specific knowledge claim that the primary writer makes in his or her own words.

While we incur the risk of mixing our metaphors, we suggest that another way of thinking about theory is to regard it as a lens through which a researcher *views* her work. If nothing else, this definition is loyal to the semantic roots of "theory" — a Greek word that means "to see." In effect, therefore, academic writers who adopt theoretical frames choose to see the world through someone else's eyes. This opportunity to see differently holds a special appeal in the humanities and social sciences, where the serious business of knowledge-making may sometimes appear to be a little too subjective. Indeed, theoretical frames seem to come between the researcher and her work, thereby placing an apparent check on uncontrolled subjectivity. Such a check may, however, be more apparent than real, for there is clearly a good deal of individual discretion involved in the choice and application of theoretical frames.

Finally, it is worth noting that theory is often a rhetorical feature that recurs *throughout* research articles: typically, readers will encounter a sustained imposition and explanation of theory in an introduction; lighter returns to theory throughout core paragraphs; and a heavy reinstatement of theory in a conclusion. Alternatively, the presentation of theoretical concepts may be delayed, so that theory does not make an appearance until relatively late in a paper.

In the example that follows, notice how theory is associated with some big names:

> **Robert M. Seiler and Tamara P. Seiler**
> **The Social Construction of the Canadian Cowboy:**
> **Calgary Exhibition and Stampede Posters, 1952–1972**
>
> The approach we have taken builds on the work of socio-semiotics theorists, including Roland Barthes, Stuart Hall, Mikhail Bakhtin, Pierre Bourdieu and Michel de Certeau. It sees popular culture as a site of struggle, focusing on the popular tactics used to evade or subvert the

forces of dominance (Fiske 20). Analysts who take this approach argue that ordinary people use the resources the elites (who control the cultural industries) provide to produce popular culture. In contrast to the mass cultural model, which conceptualizes artifacts in terms of unified meaning, the popular cultural model conceptualizes cultural artifacts as polysemic, open to a variety of quite different, even contradictory, readings. Some support the ideological meanings of cultural elites; others clearly oppose them . . .

In the next example, watch for thesis (argument or knowledge-claim) emerging from theory:

D.A. West
Re-searching the North in Canada:
An Introduction to the Canadian Northern Discourse

The geographical region known commonly as the North in Canada has been, and continues to be, produced by a discourse of power which emanates from the strategic deployment of a grid of knowledge. In other words, the North in Canada is more than simply a geophysical region. It is also and concurrently a region of the mind. In this sense, it appears to be very much like Edward Said's Orient.

In his much-discussed study of Orientalism, Said argues that the Orient was constituted as an "other" to the West. Through the deployment of the strategies of power/knowledge by the Orientalist, the Orient was produced and collected in an archive of knowledge that creates and re-creates the conditions of its existence.

I propose to introduce the conditions by which the North can be understood, first as an "other" to Europe, and secondly as an "other" to Canada. In short, I will argue that the North continues to be produced by a discourse of power, and is contained within an archive of knowledge that is continually created and re-created through research.

In this final sample, the primary writer borrows a set of theoretical ideas, even as he indicates a readiness to use others. This mixing and matching reinforces the flexibility of theory:

Theory in an Introduction

Robert E. Terrill
Spectacular Repression: Sanitizing the Batman

This work [on Batman] remains predominantly within a Jungian framework, both because doing so facilitates framing this critique as an extension of the earlier Jungian analysis (Terrill, 1993) and because Jung offers a particularly rich vocabulary for discussing the presentation of archetypal images in contemporary public discourse. However, as the argument develops it borrows from other theoretical vocabularies, particularly toward augmenting Jung's rather sketchy discussion of homosexuality as it relates to the presentation of archetypes.[4]

Defining Key Terms

We have already noted that some papers begin with a definition of key terms, providing a more down-to-business version of context. Alternatively, definitions of key terms could come later in an introduction. This is the case in I.S. MacLaren's paper below. In the fourth paragraph of the introduction to a paper on modes of landscape perception in Franklin's first expedition, MacLaren defines the particular terms he uses.

I. S. MacLaren
Retaining Captaincy of the Soul: Response to
Nature in the First Franklin Expedition

The sublime arose as eighteenth-century Britain's aesthetic of vastness. From great landscapes of literary conception, such as Milton's scenes of hell, to immense natural landforms such as the Swiss and cisalpine mountains, the deserts of the Levant, and the fjords of Scandinavia, the sublime represented an ineffable realm whose properties, if they were governed by an order at all, were governed by one which could not be discerned by rational powers of the human mind.

Posing a Research Question

Frequently, introductions to research papers will pose one or more questions. These questions typically indicate the investigative concerns of the paper. If it is possible to identify a primary research question, the answer to that question is very often the thesis of the paper.

T. D. MacLulich

Canadian Exploration as Literature

... to argue that exploration writing is literature simply on the grounds that it can be approached as literature is surely to avoid the real issues. The pertinent questions are: Have the explorers' literary qualities arisen by accident or design? And are these literary qualities pervasive and consistent enough to constitute a set of literary conventions?

As MacLulich's paper develops, the second question emerges as the most important, and MacLulich's detailed answer to this question constitutes his thesis.

Stating a Thesis

A thesis expresses the overarching knowledge claim that a writer is attempting to substantiate. Thus, if the research site and prestige abstraction form topic, thesis is the *argument* that emerges from topic. Emerging from topic (and, perhaps, from a theoretical framework), the thesis comprises an individual writer's knowledge-making message to the academic community. Whereas structural forecasts, for example, explain how a paper is organized, a thesis statement explains the position that a paper takes. Myers explains that "all researchers are faced with decisions about the level of claim they might wish to make. The higher the level of claim, the more likely that it will involve contradicting large bodies of the relevant literature ..." (as cited in Swales, 1990, p. 117).

In the humanities and social sciences, a thesis frequently appears at or near the end of the introductory section of a paper. In some cases, readers may be able to highlight a single sentence that best conveys the writer's overarching knowledge claim. Sentences such as this mark important moments in the knowledge-making process and so they are often flagged by their own brand of *metadiscourse* – by metadiscursive verbs such as "argue," "demonstrate," "indicate," "show," "illustrate," and so on. Alternatively, readers may find it difficult to isolate a single sentence as the best version of thesis. In cases like this, several things could be going on. For example, the thesis may not be in the introduction! In other instances, the thesis may be spread throughout several sentences or even an entire paragraph.

An Introductory Paragraph in which Readers May Find It Difficult to Foreground a Single Sentence as Thesis

Richard C. Davies
Thrice-Told Tales: The Exploration Writing of Sir John Franklin

Subtly but consistently, as one moves from journal through fair copy to narrative, one encounters an image of native people that grows gradually more disparaging and condemning. The narrative casts Indian and Inuit in the role of predatory antagonist to civilization and portrays them as the chaotic, irrational enemy of order, a disapprobation that is considerably intensified from what appears in the journal. I must emphasize that the differences are not extreme: Franklin's desire to avoid subjective evaluations prevents any dramatic alterations. Nevertheless, it seems to fair to say that many of the indigenous North Americans who appear in the narrative are portrayed as savages opposed to such European virtues as industry, trust, and reason.

In Davies' paper, perhaps several of the sentences vie for our attention as the one that best states thesis.

In the following paper, thesis is again spread throughout the paragraph, but this time, metadiscourse emphasizes the first sentence as an attempt to crystallize the argument. We've underlined the key passage. In the second example, metadiscourse crystallizes thesis at the end of a paragraph. Again, we've underlined the key passage.

An Introductory Paragraph in Which a Single Sentence is Foregrounded as Thesis through Metadiscourse

Dana L. Cloud

Hegemony or Concordance?: The Rhetoric of Tokenism in "Oprah" Winfrey's Rags-to-Riches Biography

This article argues that the content, pervasiveness, and popularity of the "Oprah" narratives warrant the recognition of a "terministic screen" or genre of discourse called tokenist biography, defined as biological narratives that authorize a person from a marginalized or oppressed group to speak as a culture hero on the condition that the person's life story be framed in liberal-capitalist terms. Like Clarence Thomas during his Supreme Court confirmation hearings (see Morrison, 1992), "Oprah" is constructed in the biographical narratives that frame her rise to stardom in the late 1980s as a black person who, refusing identification with the politics of black liberation, "proves" that the American Dream is possible for all Black Americans.

A Thesis Sentence Embedded in an Introductory Paragraph that Contains Other Rhetorical Features

Annette Hill

Fearful and Safe: Audience Response to British Reality Programming

This article will focus on two BBC reality series, *999* and *Children's Hospital*, and will examine why these series are popular with British audiences, in particular, focusing on the "entertainment potential" (Kilborn, 1994, p. 425) of programs that depict victims of accidents and life-threatening illnesses. Audience response to these series is linked to public trust in the BBC and program makers, and an "aesthetics of attraction" (Corner, 1995, p. 29), in which viewers experience fear and relief as the victims of a life-threatening accident or illness are saved by brave and hardworking emergency services and medical staff. The construction of a caring society in reality programs screened on a public service channel may not be an accurate reflection of healthcare in Britain, but the findings in this study indicate that audiences are attracted to life-affirming factual programs.

In the interest of clarity, we advise student writers in the humanities and social sciences to provide compact thesis statements at the end of an introduction (comparable to the last sample above), unless they have a compelling reason to avoid this strategy. Because a thesis is such an important rhetorical feature, it may be worth repeating, but such repetition is sometimes most effective when it occurs at strategic points in the core of a paper. Another alternative would be to delay the presentation of thesis until the conclusion. However, this pattern is more common in the natural sciences, where papers begin with a **hypothesis** (see Chapter 9).

Statement of Relevance

As previously noted, statements of relevance situate knowledge claims in a larger social and/or historical context, and in doing so they speak to the broader significance or meaning of academic research. In this sense, a statement of relevance often has moral implications — it frequently deals with what *should* or *ought to be* done to improve a situation (Giltrow, 2002, pp. 15, 314). Statements of Relevance may appear in introductions, but they are perhaps more common in conclusions (see Statement of Relevance, Chapter 8).

IDEAS FOR FURTHER STUDY

1. Block and label introductory rhetorical features in the sample introductions presented below:

Sample Introduction 1

Cheryl Kirschner

Desperate Measures: Commercial Interests and the Murders at St. John's Fort

From the place which we quitted this morning the west side of the river displayed a beautiful succession of the most beautiful scenery I had ever beheld. . . . This magnificent theatre of nature has all the decorations which trees and animals of the country can afford it; and their intervals are enlivened with vast herds of elks and buffaloes.

— Alexander Mackenzie

Alexander Mackenzie's description of the banks of the Peace River, in May of 1793, hardly sounds like the setting for famine, collusion, and carnage. Nonetheless, on November second and third, in 1823, at St. John's Fort, on the upper Peace River, four local natives murdered five Hudson's Bay Company employees: one clerk and four voyageurs.[1]

Over the past decade, scholars have discussed the causes and effects of the murders at St. John's Fort. According to Robin Ridington, in "Changes of Mind: Dunne-za Resistance to Empire," the native people claim that the murders were "justified retaliation" for the mysterious death of a native hunter who had requested to leave the post in order to return to his band.[2] Conversely, in *Delayed Frontier: The Peace River Country to 1909*, David Leonard writes: " the perpetrators were reported to have been Beaver Indians who were angry at the pending closure of the post . . ."[3] In "Early Fur-Trade History in the Peace River District of British Columbia, 1794–1824," Finola Finlay focuses on the effect of the murders: "The murders at St. John's have been cited by all authorities as the cause of the closure of the Peace River forts."[4] Despite such scholarly activity, little has been written to acquaint us with the business tactics and concerns of the Hudson's Bay Company administrators who oversaw the Peace River Forts. Accordingly, this essay examines the St. John's Fort murders in relation to the commercial interests of the Hudson's Bay Company.

First, I will present profiles of the two key HBC administrators, William McIntosh and George Simpson, who decided to close St. John's Fort. I will then describe the murders and the company's reaction to them. Finally, my analysis will situate the murders in relation to the corporate strategy of the HBC. I will argue that William McIntosh and George Simpson deliberately provoked the St. John's murders in order to justify the withdrawal of fur trading operations in a region that no longer offered viable profits.

Sample Introduction 2

Shelley Ergang, Sarah Filmer, Robert French, Pat Jansen, Jasveen Jhand, Aviva Jones, Julie Hindbo, Raffaella Loro, Karen MacIsaac, Jonathan Meyer, Alison Newth, Steve Roe, and Karen Wiltse

"If the Story Could Be Heard": Colonial Discourse and the Surrender of Indian Reserve 172

Heaven, according to Charlie Yahey [a Beaver Dreamer], is like Where Happiness Dwells. It is a place where people come

together and greet their relatives they have not seen for an
entire year.

— Robin Ridington, *Trail to Heaven*

1   Archeological studies indicate that aboriginal peoples inhabited
Northeastern British Columbia more than 10,000 years BP.[2] The history
of the Beaver people[3] reaches back into these bygone millennia.
Traditional Beaver culture revolved around the seasons: hunting and
berry picking during the summer and trapping in the winter. According
to Hugh Brody, such activities combined to create an annual system that
comprised a whole: each part made a unique contribution to the entire
unit.[4] In the eighteenth and nineteenth centuries, an expanding fur trade
economy began to deplete food resources. The situation reached a crisis
point by the end of the nineteenth century, when the Klondike gold rush
brought unprecedented pressure to bear on the aboriginal people of the
region. Responding to encroachments on their territory, the Beaver people
established a blockade that interrupted the flow of prospectors.[5] Treaty
8, signed partly in response to such tensions, recognized all entitlement
to reserve lands for native groups in Northern Alberta, Northeastern
British Columbia, and the Northwest Territories.

2   On April 11, 1916, pursuant to Treaty 8, members of the Fort St. John
Beaver Band chose 18,168 acres of rolling prairie, seven miles north of
Fort St. John, as their reserve. Traditionally referred to as "Suu Na Chii
K' Chi Ge" (The Place Where Happiness Dwells), the territory newly
designated as Indian Reserve 172 (I.R. 172) had long served as an important
summer gathering place for the Beaver people.[6] By the end of World
War I, however, white settlers began to lobby for the sale of I.R. 172.
Political pressure for a sale mounted in the early 1940s, when it became
apparent that returning World War II veterans would need land to settle.
Finally, on September 22, 1945, the Fort St. John Beaver Band purportedly
executed a surrender of I.R. 172 to the Government of Canada, "to sell or
lease."[7]

3   The subsequent history of I.R. 172 is fraught with political and legal
turmoil. In 1948, the reserve was sold to the Department of Veterans'
Affairs, for considerably less than its appraised value. Shortly thereafter,
in 1949, oil and gas deposits were discovered on I.R. 172, and profits

from these discoveries eventually accrued to the newly established settlers. In the early 1950s, the Fort St. John Beaver Band consented to the purchase of two smaller reserves, farther north of town. Some families moved to the Doig River (I.R. 206), while other families relocated along the Blueberry River (I.R. 205). Thirty years later, in September 1978, Chiefs from both the Doig and Blueberry communities began joint legal action against the Government of Canada, claiming damages for the improvident surrender and improper transfer of I.R. 172.[8] The plaintiffs' case was dismissed at the Federal Court Trial Division in 1987, and the dismissal was later upheld by a split decision at the Federal Court of Appeal in 1992.[9] The Band appealed again, and in 1995 the Supreme Court of Canada found that the Crown breached its fiduciary obligation by selling the Band's mineral rights and making no effort to correct its error.[10] By 1997, the plaintiffs negotiated an out-of-court settlement for $147 million as restitution for oil and gas royalties.[11]

4   Scholarly studies of the surrender of I.R. 172 are limited. In "Improvident Surrenders and the Crown's Fiduciary Obligations," David Knoll explores the pre-surrender fiduciary duties of the Crown and how the Supreme Court's ruling has the potential to influence judicial decisions in similar cases.[12] In "Crown Fiduciary Duty, Indian Title, and the Lost Treasure of I.R. 172," J. Paul Salembier also discusses the Crown's fiduciary obligations.[13] Finally, in "Cultures in Conflict: The Problem of Discourse," Robin Ridington looks at how "the issue of communication between cultures [is] central to [questions about] whether the surrender was taken as a responsible exercise of the government's trust responsibility." Ridington suggests that "[a]ttempted discourse between different cultures may create conflict, ambiguity, even oppression."[14]

5   Building on Ridington's discursive approach, this essay examines colonial discourse in relation to the surrender of I.R. 172, focussing on governmental correspondence and newspaper journalism from 1933–1946. Our primary intention is not to provide definitive answers to historical questions about aboriginal consent or governmental responsibility, but to describe colonial habits of mind in the area and period at issue. First, we will analyze governmental correspondence in the decade that preceded the surrender of I.R. 172, from 1933 to 1944. Second, we will discuss governmental records amid the period of the surrender itself, during the summer and fall of 1945. Third, we will comment on newspaper journalism immediately before and after the surrender, from 1944–1946. Given the era that we are dealing with, it should come as no surprise that governmental and journalistic discourse portrayed native culture disparagingly, nor that various attitudes and decisions were framed in terms of the "superior" values of European Canadians. Less obvious, however, are the conceptual nuances that inform these assumptions. We will demonstrate that the surrender of I.R. 172 exemplifies a complex network of discursive habits that attempted to legitimize the interests of a dominant, settler culture. We hope that our approach will shed light on colonialist constructions of racism and thereby contribute to ongoing struggles against such practices.

6   Our study draws on a substantial scholarship relating to the language of colonialism, both in British Columbia and throughout Canada. Hugh Brody, for example, contextualizes settler and governmental attitudes toward the Beaver people of Northeastern British Columbia by explaining that colonial discourse itself is based on racist assumptions about aboriginal inferiority.[16] According to Brody, aboriginal difference was misinterpreted as evidence of inferiority.[17] Indeed, many years after initial contact, little was understood about the aboriginal people who inhabited the land. The concept of a hunting and gathering culture was especially elusive. Hunters were "seemingly haphazard, wasteful, greedy, impoverished, and yet indifferent to material goods."[18] They were savage—and if savages "were not really human, or if their ways of life were neither civilized nor Christian, then they had no right—least of all any right of ownership to the lands they occupied."[19] Hunters of the north, in particular, were judged to have no real viable economy of their own.[20] They were the "non-economic" people, unresponsive to benevolent attempts to change them. This unresponsiveness, in turn, fueled the negative stereotype. Not only were the hunters perceived as poor, but they were thought to be "too ignorant even to appreciate the fact."[21]

Sample 3

Christy Gerlinsky
Streamers in the Sky: The Picturesque and
the Sublime in the Diary of Monica Storrs

Later the rays turned into search light beams of milky light, and then these began to curve into strange shapes, like a very slowly moving snake curling around the Northern horizon,

and fading into faint rose and green, like a rainbow seen in the
dark.[1]

— Monica Storrs

W.L. Morton's edited version of Monica Storrs' diary, *God's Galloping
Girl: The Peace River Diaries of Monica Storrs*, provides an account of the
years 1929–1931, in which Storrs emigrated to Canada as a missionary,
travelled across the country, and finally settled in the Peace River region
of northeastern British Columbia. Storrs was reared as a gentlewoman
in Britain, and Christian beliefs were deeply instilled in her character.
She came to the Peace River region at a time of new settlement, to serve
in the Sunday schools, and to help both the Girl Guide and Boy Scout
groups. Storrs herself did not have an easy childhood. Morton explains
that at the age of two, Storrs was stricken with tuberculosis of the spine,
which left her bedridden until the age of twelve, when she had to learn
to walk again. The suffering experienced by Storrs as a child may explain
her strong desire to work with children of the Peace River.[2] Except for
Morton's own research, Storrs' experience in the Peace has received little
scholarly attention. In an effort to fill this gap, I examine how Monica
Storrs constructs place in her diary, particularly in relation to the sublime
and picturesque.

In "The Aesthetic Map of the North, 1845–1859," I.S. MacLaren says
that "the discovery of the North entailed a . . . process of identification
that combined human expectation and fact, illusion and empirical reality,"
meaning that the explorers used "metaphors" accepted in their own
culture to measure the Canadian north, as well as the other places they
travelled to.[3] According to MacLaren, such metaphors were used by
explorers to relate an uncharted and unknown land to a familiar setting.
This process of identification is a characteristic of human intelligence,
facilitating the emotional need for home and familiarity. Even beyond
one's natural home, there is an instinct to construct the new setting in
relation to a setting that is already well known.[4] Similarly, in "Retaining
Captaincy of the Soul: Response to Nature in the First Franklin
Expedition," MacLaren suggests that the way an individual perceives
nature is dependent upon the way their culture sees nature.[5] MacLaren's
ideas can be traced back to J. Wreford Watson's "The Role of Illusion in
North American Geography: A Note on the Geography of North
American Settlement," which tells us that "mental impressions" often
"condition" responses to place; thus, "lack of facts, misconceptions, and
preconceptions" all lead to guesses and assumptions, which precede true
findings.[6]

In relation to Storrs' construction of place, it is worth noting that the terms "sublime" and "picturesque" were used throughout the time of British exploration to describe the Canadian landscape. MacLaren notes that the sublime refers to wide open spaces which can not be defined and stretch beyond the horizon; these spaces appear to be threatening, places that would not sustain human habitation but yield impression and grandeur ultimately associated with God. Some examples of the sublime are mountain peaks or the far-stretching ocean. Natural wonders such as tornadoes, thunderstorms, and blizzards are also defined as being sublime.[7] The picturesque, on the other hand, involves a more inviting, pastoral setting, often with peaceful rivers, hazy mountains, and clusters of leafy trees backed by a sunset. Virtually all of the English countryside was conceived as picturesque.[8]

In the Introduction to Storrs' diary, Morton comments: "The wonder is how Monica went on serenely between the faith by which she lived and the reality in which she moved."[9] Perhaps the answer to this puzzle can be found in Storrs' culturally conditioned construction of place. Indeed, I will demonstrate that Monica Storrs used the sublime and picturesque to familiarize her surroundings and create serenity for herself. In short, Monica Storrs employed British habits of landscape appreciation to make the Peace River region seem more like her own home.

2. Reading well-written abstracts can help you learn how to write a good abstract. The ProQuest database provides abstracts to dissertations and master's theses that have been published in North America in the past two years. This database can be accessed at:

http://wwwlib.umi.com/dissertations

Answer the two questions on that page to proceed to the next page, where you can do a basic search of the ProQuest database.

As a sample search, try the following:

First Search Term:	feminist	in	Keyword (KEY)
Second Search Term:	Canadian	in	Subject (SU)
Third Search Term:	literature	in	Subject (SU)

Click on Search . This search brings up information on dissertations or master's theses. Scroll down to the first item and click on Citation + Abstract . As you read through the abstract, note its rhetorical features.

Check out some of the other abstracts in this search.

Next, try a search of your own, using search terms that interest you. Use keywords from several disciplines. Read some of the abstracts. Are there noticeable differences between abstracts in the sciences and abstracts in the social sciences? Between English and the sciences?

3. Building upon your proposal, begin to think about the shape of the introduction to your paper.

REFERENCES

Abel, K. (1989). Of two minds: Dene response to the Mackenzie missions, 1858-1902. In K.S. Coates and W.R. Morrison (Eds.), *Interpreting Canada's north: Selected readings* (pp. 77–93). Toronto: Copp Clark.

Arruda, T.F. (1998). "You would have had your pick": Youth, gender, and jobs in Williams Lake, British Columbia, 1945-75. In R. Sandwell (Ed.), *Beyond city limits: Rural history in British Columbia* (pp. 225-234). Vancouver: UBC Press.

Blaisure, K.R., & Koivunen, J.M. (2002). Family science faculty members' experiences with teaching from a feminist perspective. *Family Relations, 52,* 22-32.

Cloud, D.L. (1996). Hegemony or concordance?: The rhetoric of tokenism in "Oprah" Winfrey's rags-to-riches biography. *Critical Studies in Mass Communication, 13,* 115-137.

Cruikshank, J. (1992, Winter). Images of society in Klondike gold rush narratives. *Ethnohistory, 39*(1), 29-49.

den Ouden, P. (1998, Winter). "My Uttermost Valleys": Patriarchal fear of the feminine in Robert Service's poetry and prose." *The Northern Review: A Multidisciplinary Journal of the Arts and Sciences of the North, 19,* 113-121.

Egan, S., & Helms, G. (1999, Winter). The many tongues of mothertalk: Life stories of Mary Kiyoshi Kiyooka." *Canadian Literature, 163,* 47-77.

Fetveit, A. (1999). Reality T.V. in the digital era: A paradox in visual culture? *Media, Culture, and Society, 21,* 787-804.

Friesen, D.W., & Orr, J. (1998). New paths, old ways: Exploring the places of influence on the role identity. *The Canadian Journal of Native Education, 22*(2), 188-200.

Gerlinsky, C. (2002). Streamers in the sky: The sublime and the picturesque in the diary of Monica Storrs. Unpublished paper.

Gillespie, G. (2002). "I was well pleased with our sport among the buffalo": Big-game hunters, travel writing, and cultural imperialism in the British North American west, 1847–72. *The Canadian Historical Review, 83*(4), 555–84.

Giltrow, J. (1994). *Academic writing: Writing and reading across the disciplines.* 2nd ed. Peterborough: Broadview Press.

Giltrow, J. (2002). *Academic writing: Writing and reading in the disciplines.* 3rd ed. Peterborough: Broadview Press.

Grant, S. (1989). Myths of the north in the Canadian ethos. *The Northern Review: A Multidisciplinary Journal of the Arts and Sciences of the North, 3–4,* 15–41.

Hamer, D. (1999). Wildfire's influence on yellow hedysarum digging habitat and its use by grizzly bears in Banff National Park, Alberta. *Canadian Journal of Zoology, 77,* 1513–1520.

Harrison, S. (2001). Making the grade: Creating a successful learning environment for post-secondary students with learning disabilities. For a revised, published version of this paper, see Harrison, S. (2003, Spring). Creating a successful learning environment for postsecondary students with learning disabilities: Policy and practice. *Journal of College Reading and Learning, 33* (2), 131–145.

Hill, A. (2000, May). Fearful and safe: Audience response to British reality programming. *Television and New Media, 1*(2), 193–213.

Hinds, E.J.W. (1992, Winter). The devil sings the blues: Heavy metal, gothic fiction, and "postmodern" discourse. *The Journal of Popular Culture, 26,* 151–164.

Hookimaw-Witt, J. (1998). Any changes since residential school? *The Canadian Journal of Native Education, 22*(2), 159–170.

Hopkins, J.S. (1991). West Edmonton Mall: Landscape of myths and elsewhereness. *Canadian Geographer, 34,* 2–17.

Hyde, P. (2000, August). Managing bodies — managing relationships: The popular media and the social construction of women's bodies and social roles from the 1930s to the 1950s. *Journal of Sociology, 36*(12), 157–169.

Iacovetta, F. (1999, Dec.). Gossip, contest, and power in the making of suburban bad girls: Toronto, 1945–60. *Canadian Historical Review, 80*(4), 585–623.

Killian, K.D. (2002). Dominant and marginalized discourses in interracial couples' narratives: Implications for family therapists. *Family Process, 41*(4), 603–618.

Kirschner, C. (1998). Desperate measures: Commercial interests and the murders at St. John's Fort. Unpublished paper.

Knowles, R.P. (1995). Post-, "grapes," nuts and flakes: "Coach's corner" as post-colonial performance." *Modern Drama, 38,* 123–130.

Lewis, G.H. (1997, Winter). Lap dancer or hillbilly deluxe?: The cultural constructions of modern country music. *Journal of Popular Culture, 31*(3), 163–173.

MacAulay, S. (2002). The smokestack leaned toward capitalism: An examination of the Middle Way Program of the Antigonish Movement. *Journal of Canadian Studies 37*(1), 43–67.

MacDonald, S.P. (1994). *Professional and academic writing in the humanities and social sciences.* Carbondale: Southern Illinois University Press.

MacLaren, I.S. (1984). Retaining captaincy of the soul: Response to nature in the first Franklin expedition. *Essays on Canadian Writing, 28,* 57–92.

MacLulich, T.D. (1979). Canadian exploration as literature. *Canadian Literature, 81,* 72–85.

Northey, M., & Knight, D.B. (1992). *Making sense in geography and environmental studies: A student's guide to research, writing, and style.* Toronto: Oxford University Press.

Parpart, L. (2002). Adapting emotions: Notes on the transformation of affect and ideology from "We So Seldom Look on Love" to *Kissed. Essays on Canadian Writing, 76,* 51–82.

Perry, A. (1998). Bachelors in the backwoods: White men and homosocial culture in up-country British Columbia, 1858-71. In R. Sandwell (Ed.) *Beyond city limits: Rural history in British Columbia* (pp. 180–194). Vancouver: UBC Press.

Ridington, R. (1990). "When poison gas come down like a fog": A native community's response to cultural disaster. In R. Ridington, *Little bit know something: Stories in a language of anthropology* (pp. 206–224). Iowa City: University of Iowa Press.

Ryan, J. (1995). Experiencing urban schooling: The adjustment of native students to the demands of a post-secondary education program. *The Canadian Journal of Native Studies, 15*(2), 211–229.

Share, D.L., & Silva, P.A. (2003). Gender bias in IQ-discrepancy and post-discrepancy definitions of reading disability. *Journal of Learning Disabilities, 36*(1), 4–14.

Smyth, H. (1998). "Lords of the world": Writing gender and imperialism on northern space in C. C. Vyvyan's *Arctic Adventure. Studies in Canadian Literature, 23*(1), 211–229.

Tam, C.M., et al. (1999, Dec.). Feng shui and its impacts on land and property developments. *Journal of Urban Planning and Development, 125*(4), 152–163.

Terrill, R.E. (2000, Dec.). Spectacular repression: Sanitizing the Batman. *Critical Studies in Media Communication, 17*(4), 493–509.

Valery, J.H., et al. (1997, Summer). The nature and amount of support college-age adolescents request and receive from parents. *Adolescence, 32*(126), 323–337.

York, L. (1999). "What it took and took/ to be a man": Teaching Timothy Findley and the construction of masculinities. *Journal of Canadian Studies, 33*(4), 15–30.

West, D.A. (1991, Summer). Re-searching the north in Canada: An introduction to the Canadian northern discourse." *Journal of Canadian Studies, 26*(2), 108–119.

INTRODUCTION TO THE READINGS

In the published readings that follow, academic introductions progressively become more densely layered with rhetorical features. Amid other stylistic features, Nancy Theberge, a sociologist, takes a position (provides a thesis) and offers a description of her methodology. Pamela den Ouden, writing as a literary critic, devotes even more space to getting her argument under way, and in doing so presents a series of carefully calculated "moves." Thus, both papers lend themselves to a rhetorical analysis that is grounded in the concepts discussed in this chapter.

NANCY THEBERGE

A Feminist Analysis of Responses to Sports Violence: Media Coverage of the 1987 World Junior Hockey Championship

Abstract: This paper analyzes media accounts of a dramatic and highly publicized incident of sport violence. In a game between the Canadian and Soviet teams at the 1987 World Junior Hockey Championship, a fight broke out that escalated into a brawl involving all members of both teams. After some 20 minutes of fighting, the game was declared over and both teams were suspended from the tournament. The analysis shows that newspaper accounts framed the incident primarily as a technical failing that could have been prevented if some individuals had acted responsibly. Interpretations that located the incident in the culture and organization of the sport assumed the status of secondary accounts. The dominance of the primary definition meant that a critique of the social basis of violence in sport never received a full airing. More significantly, the opportunity to initiate fundamental change in one of the social bases of hegemonic masculinity was lost.

1   On January 4, 1987, during the second period of a game between the Canadian and Soviet teams at the World Junior Hockey Championship tournament in Piestany, Czechoslovakia, a fight broke out that escalated into a brawl involving all members of both teams. Leading the game by a score of 4–2, the Canadian team was assured of a bronze medal in the tournament; it had a good possibility of winning a silver medal and a chance to win a gold medal. The Soviet team was out of medal contention. After some 20 minutes of fighting, the officials left the ice and turned off the lights in the hockey arena. The game was declared over and both teams were suspended from the tournament. The suspension meant that the Canadian team lost its medal.

2   The brawl and suspensions generated considerable reaction both in Canada and in international hockey circles. As well, they received extensive coverage in the Canadian media, where they were front page news for several days and the subject of regular coverage for nearly two weeks. This paper provides a discussion and analysis of newspaper coverage of the event and its aftermath. Although the amount of coverage was extensive, the contents were focused largely around a few themes. The analysis concentrates on two of the most prominent themes, which are closely related: What went wrong? And who was responsible for this "wrong"? (The other major theme emphasized in the coverage is a political interpretation of the events, which involved presentation of the incident in the context of a rivalry between the Canadian and Soviet hockey systems. Some accounts presented this as a contrast between political systems and ideologies.)[1]

3   As the following account shows, the events of the World Junior Hockey Championship were framed primarily — although not exclusively — as a technical failure that could have been prevented if some person or persons had acted responsibly. Alternative interpretations, specifically that the event was but an instance of a systemic malaise in a sport that celebrates and reproduces a violent, and in Bruce Kidd's (1983, p. 48) term "barbaric," masculinity, were reduced to the status of secondary accounts of the affair.

Methods and Procedures

4   The data for this analysis were taken from a content analysis of five English-Canadian daily newspapers for a two-week period following initial coverage of the event on January 5. The papers examined are the *Halifax Chronicle-Herald*, the *Montreal Gazette*, the *Toronto Star*, the *Vancouver Sun*, and the *Globe and Mail*, which is published nationally. These papers were chosen to provide a representative sample of English-Canadian newspapers from across the country. The analysis considered all material published in the papers that was related to the incident. There was considerable similarity in the five papers' news reports of the incident and its aftermath. This is to be expected, as all the papers relied heavily for their news material on wire service reports, particularly reports from the Canadian Press. In addition the *Globe and Mail*, which maintains a Moscow bureau, published reports on the event by its Moscow correspondent. There was greater variation among the papers in the contents of editorial commentary and stories produced by staff writers. Most stories by staff writers were concerned with local reactions to the incident and subsequent developments.

5   The discussion below provides an analysis of material in the five papers, taken together. Because of the papers' reliance upon common sources and the similarity in material published, the analysis does not focus on a comparison of newspapers.

Accounts of the Fight and Subsequent Developments

6   Coverage of the event and its aftermath offered the views of a variety of observers. This included a cross-section of members of the Canadian hockey community, others in the Soviet and international hockey communities, and interested observers outside hockey, including members of the media.

7   Among members of the Canadian hockey community, the question of how the event occurred was almost always framed as an issue of responsibility or, more accurately, a failure to act responsibly. Central to virtually all explanations was the argument that some person or group had failed to do their job. There was disagreement in views presented of who was to blame, however. One individual who was the target of much criticism is Bert Templeton, coach of the Canadian team. The first day's coverage highlighted his statement that he would "take the blame" but that the Canadian Amateur Hockey Association (CAHA) "better not hang me out to dry." On this and subsequent days, he was criticized by National Hockey League (NHL) players who were interviewed for their reactions,[2] by Dennis McDonald, Canadian representative to the International Hockey Federation (IHF),[3] and by Dave King, coach of the Canadian Olympic team. King's criticism of Templeton was indirect; he noted that restraint in international hockey is necessary and that he had personally held back players to prevent them from starting or joining a fight.[4] Criticism of Templeton was also fueled by stories in several papers profiling the coach and highlighting a history of involvement in fights and violence throughout his career.[5]

8   Templeton received support from other quarters. Not surprisingly, he was universally supported by his players.[6] He was also absolved of responsibility by Alan Eagleson, who by virtue of his several positions as an agent and negotiator is probably the most influential Canadian in international hockey. Eagleson indicated that the players and coaches "did what any red-blooded Canadians would have done." The players were also exonerated by Otto Jelinek, then Minister of State for Fitness and Amateur Sport, who said, "you really can't blame the kids."[7]

9   Eagleson and Jelinek assigned major responsibility for the incident to the International Hockey Federation and to its Canadian representative, Dennis McDonald. The IHF was especially faulted for failing to assign competent officials; Jelinek called the officiating "disgraceful."[8] Eagleson also criticized Dennis McDonald who, as the director of operations for the Canadian team, was "the man in charge."[9]

10   The comments by Eagleson and Jelinek are especially significant because of their power and stature in international and Canadian sport. The Minister's sentiments were given added force when he appeared with the President of the CAHA at a press conference on January 14 to announce the results of the Association's investigation of the event. The report absolved the players and coaches and blamed both the "poor refereeing" and the Soviet players who "precipitated" the incident with their roughhouse tactics.[10]

11   Criticism of the officiating figured prominently in the coverage. By all accounts, the referee had "lost control of the game."[11] This official was Norwegian. The presence of an allegedly incompetent referee from a country not known for its hockey prowess provided a particularly convenient target for blame.

12   It should be noted that comments from some observers within the Canadian hockey community did recognize the wider context of issues. The president of the CAHA, Murray Costello, described the incident as "a blow to the entire program." Costello indicated that the CAHA "will be looking into everything as best we can to see how it came about and whether it was an isolated incident."[12] Such observations, however, were overshadowed by accounts that the "problem" was one of failed responsibility by some individual or group.

13 Coverage of the incident also included several reports of comments by Soviet officials and citizens. These reports were taken from statements issued by officials in Canada at the time of the event and from stories filed by the *Globe and Mail's* Moscow correspondent. The tone of remarks is similar to those offered by Canadians in that individuals were singled out for their part in the incident. Like the Canadians, Soviet commentators assigned blame to a number of parties. These include the Canadian players, who "caused" the event by their aggressiveness, the officials who failed to control the game, and the International Hockey Federation for expelling the teams.[13]

14 Explanations from Canadian and Soviet representatives are marked by an expected difference and some important similarities. There is predictable disagreement in statements from the two countries regarding which team was the main instigator and aggressor. Officials from both countries agreed, however, that the game officials and the IHF must share responsibility for the event. Most significantly, explanations from Soviet officials, like those from their Canadian counterparts, characterized the incident as an instance of failed responsibility by some individual or group.

15 Coverage also included extensive commentary from persons outside hockey, such as from members of the media in the form of newspaper editorials and columns by sportswriters. As with news accounts, the comments of sports columnists presented a variety of reactions and interpretations of the incident. These included defense and praise for the Canadian players and coaches as well as criticism of the players, coaches, game officials, and IHF officials. A column in the *Globe and Mail* of January 5 blamed the Soviet players, the International Hockey Federation, and Canadians who criticized the players' actions.[14] The players are exonerated, for they "did little more than any sane, healthy person would do in similar circumstances." In a similar vein, a column in the *Vancouver Sun* of January 6 was titled "Yea: Junior Hockey Players Did Canadians Proud."[15]

16 Another view presented in some columns and many editorials is that the incident was the outcome of a systemic problem in hockey that goes well beyond the actions of individuals. The *Vancouver Sun* of January 6 cautioned against blaming the players. Rather, it said "hockey's tragedy" is that "it has taught young people that violence is normal human behavior." The *Sun* commented further that the event may "help shock the world of hockey into cleaning up its act."[16] On the same day, the *Halifax Chronicle-Herald* commented that "what will be required in international hockey is not so much a change of rules as a change of attitude," and that the IHF and CAHA "have an obligation to ensure the game does not degenerate into the kind of gladiator sport that was on display" in Piestany.[17]

17 Although interpretations locating the problem in the culture and social organization of the sport were in the minority among the views of sportswriters, the comments of one writer stood out as an exception. *Vancouver Sun* sports columnist James Lawton wrote a series of impassioned pieces condemning the incident and all who took part. On January 5 Lawton wrote that the event was a crude and brutal betrayal of reason and "any sense that Canadian hockey might finally strip itself of the illusion that masculinity and thuggery are in some way inextricably mixed."[18] On January 7 he stated that the crime of the incident "is not the rather pathetic failure of [the players] to keep control of their feelings. It is the systematic corruption of the idea of sport that goes into the training of so many of those players."[19] On the 16th he wrote of "the normality of the jungle" that characterizes hockey, and said that the "episode made nonsense of the concept of sport." Lawton's column on this day was titled "Jelinek Totally Wrong," a reference to the minister's decision to appeal the suspension of the Canadian team by the IHF. He argued that the decision was "morally bankrupt" and "the point that should be hammered now is that there were alternatives to such full-blooded involvement in the brawl." He concluded this column by urging an international review of the game.[20] Throughout his pieces, Lawton criticized those who defended the actions of the Canadian players on any grounds. More significantly, his analysis placed the event in a larger context by directing attention to the need for fundamental change in the sport.

18 Letters to the editor published during this period also gave support to the view that the incident reflected a systemic problem in the sport. A total of 24 letters were printed in the papers between January 10 and 17.[21] A preliminary examination of letters to the editor revealed several themes. Accordingly, a classification scheme was devised and the letters were coded for the appearance of themes. The most prominent theme was criticism of the hockey "system" that encourages fighting. This sentiment was expressed in nine letters; many of them excused the behavior of the players, who were seen as victims of the system. Eight letters specifically criticized the coaches and players on the Canadian team. Four letters were statements of support for the Canadian team, and one letter supported and defended the coach, Bert Templeton. Five letters directed criticism toward the Soviet team or Soviet hockey system.

A Critique of the Ideology of Masculinity

19 For feminists, the events surrounding the 1987 World Junior Hockey Championship represented the worst of the ideology of masculinity in sport. The fight between the Canadian and Soviet teams was a vivid illustration of the reality of sport as a masculine practice, and the responses to the incident failed to focus discussion on key issues of concern to feminists. Notwithstanding distaste for the events and the majority of accounts and responses to them, it may be instructive to try to unravel the significance of the representation of the incident that was presented in the media.

20 Feminist critiques have of course paid considerable attention to the masculine ideology of sport. Sport is a cultural practice that embodies qualities of toughness, aggression, and physical dominance. Not only is it a setting wherein individual males learn these traits; in sport the cultural meaning and social reality of masculinity are continually reinforced and reproduced. Moreover, the apparent "naturalness" of gendered experiences of sport, based upon their assumed basis in physical differences between the sexes, makes sport a particularly powerful setting for the reproduction of hegemonic masculinity (Hargreaves, Jennifer, 1986, p. 113).

21 The events at Piestany certainly reinforced this image and reality. For feminists, a key issue in an analysis and critique of media accounts of the events in the Junior Hockey Championship lies in the treatment of violence as a problematic of the events. The discussion above indicated that the fight between the two teams (and the resulting suspensions) certainly was an issue of debate and disagreement. That is, definitions and interpretations of the incident were vigorously contested. As emphasized in the earlier review, however, the debate was largely limited to an interpretation of the event as an issue of failed responsibility. The counter-interpretation of the fight as an instance of a systemic malaise in the sport, a position argued forcefully and eloquently by some, was largely overtaken by the primary interpretation of the event as a technical and individual failing.

22 None of the columnists and writers who presented an alternative view of the events at Piestany was identified as a feminist. Indeed, there is no evidence that any of the newspaper commentators saw the events in Piestany as a feminist concern. The centrality of violence to the imagery and practice of sport, however, has been the subject of some of the most significant feminist critiques of sport. These critiques have mainly taken two forms. First is the argument that violent sport forms are antithetical to feminist values and goals. On this basis, some feminists reject "typically" violent sports such as football and ice hockey. A second critique is directed toward the violence against women that is practiced in some masculine sport settings. Jennifer Hargreaves (1986, p. 111) has argued that the character of violence against women in sport has become more varied and complex than in previous times. An example is provided in Eric Dunning's discussion of violence against women that is central to the subculture of rugby. This violence is depicted in the traditions of the subculture that are enacted after a match, including a male striptease and obscene songs that "embody a hostile, brutal but, at the same time, fearful attitude towards women and the sexual act" (Dunning, 1986, p. 84).

23 A review of media accounts and interpretations of the Junior Hockey Championship extends the feminist critique to a further consideration. The public response and interpretation of the events offered a powerful affirmation of both the "naturalness" and legitimacy of violence as a masculine practice. Contemporary analyses and critiques of gender relations have shown the centrality of violence to the construction of masculine hegemony. This takes a myriad of forms, including wife beating, sexual harassment and assault, pornography, and some media imagery of women. It is critical to understand these experiences not as isolated encounters between individual women and men or as inevitable oppression due to men's dominant position. Rather, violence against women is woven into the fabric of social life and is supported by a complex of institutions — economic, political, and social. One of the most significant projects of feminism is to uncover the social bases of violence against women and to bring discussion of its elimination to prominence on the public agenda. Such a project, however, is not simple.

24 In a critique of theories of gender relations, Bob Connell (1987, pp. 54–58) discusses a theoretical approach that he calls categorical. Features of this approach include a close identification of opposed interests in sexual politics with specific categories of people, and a focus of the argument on the social category as a unit. Among prominent writers Connell associates with this perspective are Mary Daly, Susan Brownmiller, and Andrea Dworkin. The works of these and other writers offer much to interpretations of gender relations, particularly in their emphasis on the connections between gender, power, and opposing interests. As Connell notes, however, these theories are also characterized by some serious problems. Of particular interest here are the presentation of the categories of men and women as absolutes and the focus within these approaches on "representative individuals." These problems result in a kind of essentialism that masks or even denies the social basis of gender construction. Connell (1987, p. 57) offers as a case in point "the treatment of male sexuality in much of the literature on violence against women." As he suggests, to theorize abuses of power as the direct outcome of masculinity misses "the social arrangements that give a particular kind of masculinity a hegemonic position in sexual politics and that marginalize others. And in many arguments it misses the social processes that construct this kind of masculinity in the first place" (Connell, 1987, p. 58).

25 One of the social processes that contributes to the construction of this masculinity is the definition of violence in sport as legitimate and natural. The centrality of sport to masculine socialization and as a "signifier" (Kidd, 1987b, p. 253) of masculinity ensures this contribution. The acceptance of the place of violence in hockey was woven throughout media discussions of the events at the Junior Hockey Championship. In some cases the message was explicit, as in the comment that the players and coach "only did what any red-blooded Canadians would have done." Such statements reflect the most vulgar of categorical interpretations of behavior. (And we may be sure that here "red-blooded" means male Canadian.) A more subtle — and therefore likely more powerful — statement was contained in the primary definition of the event as a failure of responsibility. The dominance of this view over the counterinterpretation of a systemic problem in the sport meant that the critique and analysis of this problem never received a full airing. As a result, the opportunity to initiate meaningful change in one of the cultural bases of hegemonic masculinity was lost.

26 In conclusion, it is important to acknowledge that public discussion has included the presentation of alternative views and definitions. As the account presented here has shown, this view was evident in some newspaper accounts of the World Junior Hockey Championship but was overtaken by the dominant presentations of primary definers. Other alternative accounts were given. (See Bruce Kidd, 1987a, "Of Ice and Men.") Moreover, North Americans are also treated — occasionally — to the sport of ice hockey in alternate forms. In the same year in which the debacle of the World Junior Hockey Championship took place, Canadian and Soviet teams again met on the ice. This time the competition was between the very best senior players from both countries. In the finals of the Canada Cup tournament in September 1987, spectators were treated to a version of hockey that was at times breathtaking for the display of skill, artistry, and control. The contrast between this version of the sport and the thuggery that is regularly displayed in the National Hockey League and in junior hockey was at times astounding. Sadly, such interpretations and experience of the sport are rare exceptions to the dominant practice, which celebrates an antifeminist masculinity. For this reason, the tragedy of the 1987 World Junior Hockey Championship was not the lost medal or honor but the lost opportunity to challenge this dominant definition and practice.

NOTES

1. "'We've been cheated,' Canadians say." *Montreal Gazette*, January 5, 1987, p. D3. "Canada, U.S.S.R. clear the benches." *Toronto Star*, January 5, 1987, p. C1.
2. Mike Beamish, "Junior brawl disturbs Canucks." *Vancouver Sun*, January 5, 1987, p. C2.
3. "Eagleson dislikes decision to deny Canadians medal." *Vancouver Sun*, January 6, 1987, p. F1. Paul Hunter, "Canadian coach 'not ashamed.'" *Toronto Star*, January 6, 1987, p. F3.
4. Jim Proudfoot, "Canadian hockey teams must learn to bite the bullet." *Toronto Star*, January 6, 1987, p. F1.
5. "Canada, U.S.S.R. clear the benches." *Toronto Star*, January 5, 1987, p. C1. Mike Beamish, "Hockey fights a large part of Templeton past." *Vancouver Sun*, January 6, 1987, p. D6. David Shoalts, "'Soviet club to blame for hockey brawling', Canadians contend." *Globe and Mail*, January 6, 1987, p. A1.
6. "Hockey brawl spurs ouster of Canada, Soviet Union." *Globe and Mail*, January 5, 1987, p. A1. "Canada, U.S.S.R. clear the benches." *Toronto Star*, January 5, 1987, p. C1. "Juniors defend role in fight on ice." *Vancouver Sun*, January 5, 1987, p. A1. Paul Hunter, "'We're not ashamed of what we did,' Canadians in hockey brawl insist," *Toronto Star*, January 6, 1987, p. A1. Mike Beamish, "Juniors would repeat in same circumstances." *Vancouver Sun*, January 6, 1987, p. D7.
7. Mary Ormsby, "Jelinek 'can't blame the kids.'" *Toronto Star*, January 5, 1987, p. A1. James Davidson, "Eagleson raps CAHA official." *Globe and Mail*, January 6, 1987, pp. D1, D3.
8. Mary Ormsby, "Jelinek 'can't blame the kids.'" *Toronto Star*, January 5, 1987, p. A1. Scott White, "Brawl called 'black stain.'" *Halifax Chronicle-Herald*, January 6, 1987, p. 19.
9. "Eagleson, Jelinek blame officials for junior brawl." *Montreal Gazette*, January 6, 1987, p. C2. James Davidson, "Eagleson raps CAHA official." *Globe and Mail*, January 6, 1987, p. D1, D3. Frank Orr, "Eagle blows the whistle on European officials." *Toronto Star*, January 6, 1987, p. F1.
10. Graham Cox, "Canada appealing IHF ruling." *Halifax Chronicle-Herald*, January 15, 1987, p. 31.
11. "Hockey brawl spurs ouster . . ."; Shoalts, "Soviet club to blame . . ."; Ormsby, "Jelinik 'can't blame the kids'"; "Eagleson, Jelinek blame officials . . ."; Lawrence Martin, "Vasiliev ordered player off bench." *Globe and Mail*, January 8, 1987, p. D3. "'Ronning in over head,' says longtime NHL ref." *Globe and Mail*, January 8, 1987, p. D2.
12. Ken McKee, "It's a black eye for Canada." *Toronto Star*, January 5, 1987, p. C1.
13. Lawrence Martin, "Soviet hockey official lays blame on Canada." *Globe and Mail*, January 7, 1987, p. D1. Patricia Legras, "Junior players take a beating in Soviet papers." *Toronto Star*, January 7, 1987, p. C1. "Soviets blaming Canada for brawl." *Vancouver Sun*, January 7, 1987, p. F2. "Soviet official says Canada

started brawl." *Montreal Gazette*, January 7, 1987, p. B6. "Soviets criticize media." *Halifax Chronicle-Herald*, January. 8, 1987, p. 8.

14. Al Strachan, "Soviets to blame for fight disgrace." *Globe and Mail*, January 5, 1987, p. C1.

15. Earl McRae, "Yea: Junior hockey players did Canadians proud." *Vancouver Sun*, January 6, 1987, p. D6. This column was paired with another column presenting an opposing view, titled "Nay: Winning possible gold more vital than fighting." The author of the column is James Lawton, whose position on the incident is discussed elsewhere in this article.

16. "Take it out of the brawl game." *Vancouver Sun*, January 6, 1987, p. B4.

17. "Gladiators on skates." *Halifax Chronicle-Herald*, January 6, p. 6.

18. James Lawton, "Past success betrayed." *Vancouver Sun*, January 5, 1987, p. C1.

19. James Lawton, "Honor not at stake." *Vancouver Sun*, January 7, 1987, p. Fl.

20. James Lawton, "Jelinek totally wrong." *Vancouver Sun*, January 16, 1987, p. D1.

21. These letters were distributed unevenly: The *Toronto Star* published 16, the *Globe and Mail* published 10, and the *Montreal Gazette* published 1. No letters on the incident were published in the *Vancouver Sun* and the *Halifax Chronicle-Herald*. Not all letters were concerned solely with the events of the tournament. A few were concerned with issue of hockey violence generally, but clearly were written in response to the tournament incident.

REFERENCES

Connell, R.W. (1987). *Gender and power*. Stanford, CA: Stanford University Press.

Dunning, E. (1986). Sport as a male preserve: Notes on the social sources of masculine identity and its transformations. *Theory, Culture and Society*, 3(1), 79–90.

Hall, S., Critcher, C., Jefferson, T., Clarke, J., & Roberts, B. (1978). *Mugging, the state and law and order*. London: MacMillan.

Hargreaves, J[ennifer]. (1986). Where's the virtue? Where's the grace? A discussion of the social production of gender relations in and through sport. *Theory, Culture and Society*, 3(1), 109–121.

Hargreaves, J[ohn]. (1986). *Sport, power and culture*. Cambridge: Polity Press.

Kidd, B. (1983). Skating away from the fight: Canadian sport, culture and personal responsibility. In W. J. Baker & J. A. Rog (Eds.), *Sport and the humanities: A symposium* (pp. 3-54). Orono: University of Maine at Orono Press.

_____. (1987a, June). Of ice and men. *Integral: The Magazine for Changing Men*, 1, 16.

_____. (1987b). Sports and masculinity. In M. Kaufman (Ed.), *Beyond patriarchy: Essays by men on pleasure, power and change* (pp. 250–265). New York: Oxford.

PAMELA DEN OUDEN

"My Uttermost Valleys": Patriarchal Fear
of the Feminine in Robert Service's Poetry and Prose

"We get from a writer what we bring to him, and sometimes we get
more than he intended. Our intelligence fuses with his, and his
words go deeper than he ever purposed."

— Robert Service[1]

1   The bronze plaque on the wall of the former post office in
Kilwinning, Scotland, Robert Service's boyhood home, calls Service
"the celebrated bard of the Yukon." Although he spent only eight of
his eighty-four years in the Yukon, Service staked his claim as a "real
bonafide Sour-dough" in a 1948 speech to the Yukoners Association,
in which he described his relationship with the North as an intimate
one: "I know the land, I know the spirit of the North, I've communed
with it and it got under my skin; it forced me to write: I take no credit
for anything I've done, it's the spirit of the North and that's what you
all have in you—it all go into you and it did something to you; it
made you better and finer people than you'd ever have been if you
hadn't gone to the North because the North has *personality*, and it
does things to you" (Service, "Gold Rush," italics mine).

2   In *Strange Things: The Malevolent North in Canadian Literature*,
Margaret Atwood contextualizes Service's attitude toward the
Canadian North in terms of gender. According to Atwood, Service
"habitually personifies the North as a savage but fascinating female"
(18). In their well-known 1979 study of the patriarchal literary tradition,
entitled *Madwoman in the Attic: The Woman Writer and the Nineteenth
Century Literary Imagination,* Sandra Gilbert and Susan Gubar, two
American feminist critics, provide a theoretical framework for
Atwood's observation. Gilbert and Gubar argue that many male
writers, including such luminaries as Dante, Milton, Swift, and Dickens,
have presented their female characters as angels (21–27) or as monsters
(27–35). The angel is characterized by "contemplative purity" (21),
while the monster, like a man, seeks "a life of significant action" (21).

3   According to Gilbert and Gubar, whose work draws on the writings of earlier feminists, including Karen Horney, Simone de Beauvoir and Dorothy Dinnerstein, these objectifications of women represent male ways of coping with psycho-sexual anxieties produced by a female Other. Male authors allay their fears of monstrous women by calling them names — "witch, bitch, fiend, monster" (Gilbert and Gubar 28). Of the woman who exemplifies contemplative purity, a male author may tell himself there is no need for him to dread a being who has a "clear line of literary descent from divine Virgin to domestic angel" (20). Building upon Gilbert and Gubar's theoretical perspective, this essay examines patriarchal fear of the feminine in the poetry and prose of Robert Service. For Service, the Canadian North becomes a white, blank page upon which he inscribes his own fantasies about the female Other. Indeed, Service draws these two faces of women — angel and monster — on the face of the northern landscape, thereby revealing what Karen Horney refers to as "men's secret dread of women" (136).

4   In *Ploughman of the Moon*, the first volume of his autobiography, Service also says that "childish memories seem trivial but they reveal traits that were to distinguish [his] whole life" (9). This seems to indicate the possibility that Service's attitude toward women was "stamped" on him during his formative years — from the time he was a toddler till he was nine years old he lived, not with his mother and father and nine siblings, but in the care of his grandparents and four maiden aunts. Being sent away from his family may have seemed like a rejection to him, and such a rejection may have been the origin of the inferiority complex from which Service says he "never" recovered (39). Several of his early memories recall his guardian aunts. For instance, this from the time he was five years old: "my aunts wore black silk skirts, and as they sat in front of the fire they drew them up over their knees. I was supposed to be too young to notice but the fatness of their legs disgusted me" (4). He also tells about "dar[ing] to peep" while his Aunt Jeannie was changing her chemise: "What I saw made me duck my head under the blankets. If women undressed are as ugly as that, I never want to get married" (14–15). He goes on to say that although his aunts were "gentle," they were "never demonstrative": "Sweethearts kissed and mothers kissed, but outside of that osculation was taboo. I never saw any kissing in my family. If

I had I think I would have been shamed" (10). He notes that "any show of emotion embarrassed [him]" (11). Consequently, he merely shook hands when he parted from his aunts; he was embarrassed when his Aunt Jeannie cried at the station. In addition to illustrating a Victorian repression that was typical of the times, these examples from Service's childhood also show his strong sense of anxiety about himself and his relationship to the women in his life.

5   Furthermore, Service goes on, in several places in his autobiography, to speak about his inferiority complex. "Banking for me would have been a blind alley; but, as I see it now, with my unstable temperament, all of my life would have been a blind alley. I was as destined to failure as the sparks fly upward" (*Ploughman* 129). Telling of his early time in British Columbia, in a settlement "glorified by the Old School Tie," he says, "Can it be wondered that my inferiority complex flourished in their midst and that I felt a grubby vulgarian" (152). Later, in California, when he could not get a hotel room, he accepted an offer to use a chicken house as accommodation: "Mr. Koenig charged me a quarter for sleeping in his chicken house. I was so weak I had no guts to protest. I mention this to show to what a new low my inferiority complex had fallen. If I had had a tail I would have tucked it between my legs. Every one was handing me a dirty deal, and I was taking it like a yellow dog ... I was a proper sap" (217). Service says he might have had more respect for himself if he "had learned to do at least one thing well" (20). In *Harper of Heaven*, the second volume of his autobiography, Service again takes up the theme of his feelings of inferiority. He describes himself in Paris around 1911: "So I bought [a monocle] in a pawnbroker's. . . . Behind it I concealed *my inferiority complex*. Screwing it in my eye I looked superciliously at the world" (97, italics mine).

6   This inferiority complex governed the way Service related to women. As a shy young man, Service cultivated a "manly disdain for women"; he says: "For years I scarcely spoke to a girl ... *I was afraid of them*, and if by chance I met one I was self-conscious and tongue-tied" (*Ploughman* 117, italics mine). He was a "lone dog": he says, "Never was I more happy, and this because I felt so blissfully alone" (52). He names Thoreau, "who fostered the recluse in [him]," as one of the greatest influences in his life. Service saw himself as one "of the

race of men who don't fit in" (65), as a "dreamer and fumbler" and "escapist" (26). He tells of feeling sorry for a friend who, at age 23, was already married with two children—"in a trap, done for" (27). Service compared this with his own blissful state: "Oh, how glad I was to be free. . . . Free with the promise of a future" (27).

7   At the age of 20, after working for seven years in a bank, Service decided to leave "the ledger for the land" (127). Wanting "escape, freedom, and adventure," he decided to go to Canada where he "would be a man in a world of men" (131). Service says he "made himself an authority on the Dominion" (131). Perhaps he felt, that by "throwing over the traces" and living the life of a cowboy (131), he would free himself from his past and his anxieties. In telling of this decision, he engenders the land as female: "Canada held out *her* arms to me. *She* won" (131, italics mine).

8   Turning now to another part of Service's writing, I'd like to consider some of the poems in which he further engenders the land as both an angelic and monstrous female. In "The Law of the Yukon," Service presents the land as "monster," one who carries out "significant action" against the "misfits and the failures" (Service, *Collected* 10). In rejecting the "foolish and feeble," the monster-Yukon proclaims her ruthlessness: "Wild and wide are my borders, stern as death is my sway;/ From my ruthless throne I have ruled alone for a million years and a day" (10). Service embodies the North's desire for a life of "significant action " in strong verbs:

> One by one I dismayed them, frighting them sore with my glooms;
> One by one I betrayed them unto my manifold dooms.
> Drowned them like rats in my rivers, starved them like curs on
>   my plains,
> Rotted the flesh that was left them, poisoned the blood in their
>   veins;
> Burst with my winter upon them, searing forever their sight,
> Lashed them with fungus-white faces, whimpering wild in the
>   night. (11)

9   So the land, the North, pits herself against those who trespass on her territory. In addition, this monstrous female Yukon takes on the traditionally held male role of dispenser and interpreter of the law:

"she makes it plain." Like the Old Testament prophet, Habakkuk, whom God told to "write the vision and *make it plain* (Habakkuk 2:2, italics mine), the female-North prophesies the destruction of those who cannot live up to the law which operates in her territory. This law is simply that the Strong thrive, the Fit survive, but the Weak perish (Service, *Collected* 13).

10 In "The Law of the Yukon," by using words reminiscent of those written by Emma Lazarus for the inscription of the Statue of Liberty, Service invites a comparison between these two women: the monstrous female Yukon and the "angel-woman" characterized by purity, service, and selflessness. The Yukon declares that those who are strong, "men of her mettle" are those who will establish her fame: "winning me honor, not shame; / Searching my uttermost valleys, fighting each step as they go" (12). These are men with "hearts of Vikings. . . . Desperate, strong and resistless, unthrottled by fear or defeat" (12). Service emphasizes the self-effacement of Lazarus' angel by not mentioning her specifically, but by only alluding to Lazarus' "mighty woman with a torch" (Bell 845). Liberty's cry, "Send these, the homeless, tempest-tossed, to me" (Bell 845) are inverted in the words of the Yukon: "Send not your foolish and feeble" (Service, *Collected* 10). Like the Yukon, Liberty also has the power of nature at her fingertips: the torch's "flame / Is the imprisoned lightning" (Bell 845). However, this angel-woman does not use the power of nature to destroy, as does the monster-Yukon, but to send out a message of "world-wide welcome." The invitation of Liberty is universal and open, while the invitation of the Yukon is discriminatory and selective. Although both the female Yukon and the Statue of Liberty are portrayed as mothers, they are opposites — angel and monster: selfless Liberty is the "Mother of Exiles" (Bell 845), a comfort to those cast out from other lands, while the Yukon, "monstrous, moody, pathetic" (Service, *Collected* 12), draws to her bosom and mothers only those who are worthy, only those able to survive the harshness of her landscape.

11 Similarly, in "The Lure of Little Voices," first published in the 1907 collection *Songs of a Sourdough*, the North becomes a rival, a femme fatale, eager to steal a man from another woman who realizes she is helpless to withstand the wiles of such a seductress. First, the man says he hears "the Little voices all a-begging [him] to go"; however, this siren song quickly acquires a sharper focus: "a-begging me to *leave* you" (Service, *Collected* 47, italics mine). In her boldness, the North gives the man a message to pass on to his woman: "He was ours before you got him, and we want him once again" (47). In the fourth stanza, the narrator equates the North with "the womb of desolation": the place where desolation is nurtured and brought forth. In this poem, as in "The Law of the Yukon," the North is seeking men. In her quest, she strips them of their masculinity and virility. The narrator says: "The spell of them is on me and I'm helpless as a child" (48). First the North is a rival, then a stern mother. The man is singular; the woman is plural, with a multiplicity of power. In addition, as the man turns his ear to the "lure of the Little Voices," he begins to be overshadowed and overcome by the cruel nature of the North. This causes him to treat his woman cruelly: "softly in the sleep-time from your love I'll steal away" (49). In light of the fact that feminist critic Dorothy Dinnerstein suggests that male anxieties about female autonomy probably go as deep as everyone's mother-dominated infancy (Gilbert and Gubar 28), perhaps in this poem we are seeing Service holding a mirror to his own face, expressing the fear that in entering into a deep relationship with a strong woman, he would be reduced to the status of a child.

12   On the other hand, in "The Spell of the Yukon," Service emphasizes the angelic side of the Yukon. Gilbert and Gubar explain that male authors fit masks over woman's face to lessen the "dread" of her inconstancy and to allow them to possess her. The North is described as mystic, mighty, and majestic. The narrator seems infatuated and enraptured by the land, even though he recognizes the potential dangers. Especially in the fourth stanza, and then on through the rest of the poem, the language used to describe the landscape is descriptive and expansive, echoing the grandeur of the land itself:

> I've stood in some mighty-mouthed hollow
>   That's plumb-full of hush to the brim:
> I've watched the big, husky sun wallow
>   In crimson and gold, and grow dim,
> Till the moon set the pearly peaks gleaming,
>   And the stars tumbled out, neck and crop;

And I've thought that I surely was dreaming,
With the peace o' the world piled on top. (3-4)

13 This mystic and benevolent view of the North, a mask that Service creates to cover the other face, the terrible killing face of the North, allows men to feel superior to the North, thereby lessening their dread of "her." This dread, at its heart, is a dread of the land, which as Simone de Beauvoir suggests, represents the female body: "She is the earth, man is the seed. . . . The sod, broken by the plowman's labor, passively receives the seed within its furrows" (163).

14 In "Men of the High North," first published in the 1909 collection *Ballads of a Cheechako,* Service shows this bifurcated nature of the female North in a single work. He engenders the land as female and describes the North in soft, glowing terms. For instance, in the line "Islands of opal float on silver seas" (Service, *Collected* 78), the open, long vowel sound of "i" and "o," coupled with the sibilant "s," give a "rounded" and "feminine" feel to the words. Furthermore, in the fourth stanza, the man of the High North is pictured as a monarch ruling over a kingdom "unravished and gleaming," having been lured to *"her* vastness *taintlessly sweet"* (78, italics mine). This is the angelic side of the Female North, one who can crown a man king. If "he" is the king, then "she" must be his subject. However, the other, more threatening side of the North is also evident—not only can she crown him, she can also slay him: "Suffer her fury, cherish and love her—/ He who would rule must learn to obey" (79).

15 Shortly after Service decided that he was "ready for the greatest of all life's adventures—Marriage" (Service, *Harper* 51), he proposed to Germaine Bourgoin, whom he had known for three weeks. In describing his "peculiarly Scotch" approach to marriage, Service says: "I wanted a wife who would be willing to black my shoes of a morning. I remembered how my dear mother shone the boots of myself and four brothers before we went to school, spitting on them to make the blacking go further. . . . I dreaded a wasteful woman" (52).

16 Through his description of his relationship with his wife, he shows his desire to maintain traditional male superiority. Service says he feels "a certain restraint" in telling about his domestic life, that "there are matters too sacred to be revealed even to the most sympathetic reader" (Service, *Harper* 54). This "restraint" prevents him from so much as mentioning the name of the woman he marries. Throughout the rest of the book, if he refers to her at all, he objectifies her, calling her "the wife" (55) or "the Missus" (58). Here, Service provides a clear example of a male author killing his female character into his art. In this case, the character that he stills and silences, the one to whom he denies not only voice but also separate existence, is not a fictional character, but Germaine Bourgoin, the woman he married.

17 This small sampling of the poetry and prose of the "Bard of the Yukon" (Berton 133) suggests that Service's life and art are one. Service's poetry portrays the North as a frigid and unforgiving land where only the Fit and the Strong survive. Service gives archetypal expression to a deep-rooted male anxiety: in a relationship with a woman, a man must face his fear that he may not be one of the Fit and the Strong, but may instead fall into the other category, the despised, weak, "crippled and palsied" (Service, *Collected* 10) in the sight of that woman. Furthermore, "a man in a world of men" (Service, *Ploughman* 131) must contemplate the fact that although he may be stronger, and may be able to overpower a woman physically, such strength is no proof that he has searched her "uttermost valleys" (Service, *Collected* 12), finding out and discovering those deepest recesses within her. The sexual act itself exemplifies this anxiety: although the man penetrates the woman, she swallows him, surrounding him with herself until he is no longer seen. In *This Sex Which is Not One*, a landmark collection of essays, French feminist critic Luce Irigaray states: "Women's desire is often interpreted, and feared, as a sort of insatiable hunger, a voracity that will swallow [men] whole" (29). This deep searching and consequent swallowing up is what men both ardently seek and desperately fear.

18 Although plagued by self-doubt throughout his life, Service was instrumental in writing the mythology of the Canadian North as a place where men pit themselves against the environment and where only the Strong survive. Toward the end of his life, he questioned whether he could call himself a "real honest to God sourdough": "I never packed a piano over the White Path—I never fought prize fighters in the ring beneath the midnight sun; I never saw the shooting of Dan McGrew; I never cremated Sam McGee. . . . No, I did none of those things (Service, "Gold Rush"). What he did was capture the popular imagination. According to biographer James Mackay, it has often been stated that Robert Service is the most widely read poet of this century (397); Service called himself a "versifier, not a poet" (381) who wrote not for the "highbrows" but for the "common people" (380). He believed himself to be "the only living writer who [had] made $1,000,000 out of writing verse" (387). Service acknowledged his debt: "All I have and am I consider I owe to the North" (Service, "Gold Rush"). With his fame came the renown of the Yukon, a Janus-faced landscape, at once terrible and beautiful, savage and fascinating.

NOTES

1.   Epigraph from *Ploughman of the Moon*, page 158.

WORKS CITED

Atwood, Margaret. *Strange Things: The Malevolent North in Canadian Literature.* London: Clarendon, 1995.
Bell, James B. "Statue of Liberty." *World Book Encyclopedia.* 1991 ed.
Berton, Pierre. *My Times.* Toronto: Doubleday Canada, 1995.
De Beauvoir, Simone. *The Second Sex.* New York: Vintage, 1974.
Gilbert, Sandra, and Susan Gubar. *The Madwoman in the Attic: The Woman Writer and the Nineteenth Century Literary Imagination.* New Haven: Yale UP, 1979.
Irigaray, Luce. *This Sex Which is Not One.* Ithaca: Cornell UP, 1985.
Service, Robert. "Gold Rush in the Yukon." Address to Yukoners Association. Vancouver, 1948. Transcribed from a telediphone recording, D.L.O. 38945. Reading, England: BBC Archives.
_____. *Collected Poems of Robert Service.* Toronto: McGraw-Hill Ryerson, 1960.
_____. *Harper of Heaven.* New York: Dodd Mead, 1948.
_____. *Ploughman of the Moon.* New York: Dodd Mead, 1945.

Core Paragraphs
in a Research Paper

I thank you for your voices, thank you,
Your most sweet voices.

—Shakespeare

In general, the middle section or core of a research paper in the humanities or social sciences develops a thesis. It is here, in the core paragraphs, where writers often begin to draw extensively on their sources, in an effort to present "low-level" details as evidence (Giltrow, 2002, p. 86). Such writing requires careful forethought, involving another set of rhetorical considerations that address not only broad organizational patterns, but the finer nuances of managing and presenting reported speech. Accordingly, this chapter deals with the skills that you will need to develop your thesis claim. An appropriate metaphor for the whole process of thesis development might be diving. We are now in a position to go deep.

METHODS OF DEVELOPMENT

Texts and syllabi for traditional composition classes often stress "methods of development," not to be confused with the Methods sections that appear in some articles. Throughout a term, students may be asked to write a descriptive essay, a narrative essay, a process analysis essay, a definition essay, a comparative essay, an argumentative essay, and so on. The catalogues of these methods of development or "rhetorical modes" vary little from handbook to handbook, or from anthology to anthology. For example, in *Patterns for a Purpose* (1995), a handbook and anthology combined, argumentation is not regarded as a separate rhetorical mode; the editor claims that it is part of all the others. In any event, the modes themselves are foregrounded as central principles that guide writing. In *Canadian Content* (2000), a widely used anthology, the catalogue looks like this:

- Narration
- Description
- Exemplification
- Process (or Chronological) Analysis
- Classification and Division
- Comparison and Contrast
- Cause and Effect
- Definition

There is nothing wrong with the methods-of-development approach to writing, which certainly has influential supporters, but it tends to give a simplistic view of the writing process, particularly in the case of discipline-based research papers. Indeed, methods of development may provide a way of thinking about the overall structure of a paragraph or of an entire paper, but these methods do not address the rhetorical nuances of academic writing, partly because the methods themselves are not very sensitive to the demands of particular writing situations. Historically, in fact, instructors of rhetoric in ancient Greece and Renaissance Europe used these same methods to provide their students with strategies for spontaneously elaborating on a range of subjects. Methods of development are generic, all-purpose tools.

We are familiar with methods of development, both as students ourselves and as instructors. The following e-mail, sent several years ago, reflects the concerns that led to our adoption of a more discipline-based approach to writing.

Hi Steve,

I've been looking at a lot of the composition texts that are here in the English T[eaching] A[ssistant]'s office. They are all the same, with essays grouped under [concepts] such as reflecting, reporting, explaining, arguing, persuading, comparing and contrasting, etc. Most talk somewhere about audience, but usually not about an academic audience in a specific sense.

When I look through academic journals — and I have been looking at ones outside of English as well as examples of ones [familiar in English Studies] — I don't see articles that can be categorized according to these groups. Certainly, an author will argue a point, or compare something to something else within the context of the whole article but these articles have a certain sophistication (?) or tone (?) that cannot be reduced to a "compare and contrast" or "argumentative" or "persuasive" essay.

. . . Maria Montessori (1870–1952) [was] an Italian doctor and educator who [worked] with supposedly ineducable children. . . In a Montessori classroom, three- and four-year-olds learn to handle crystal and fine china (instead of plastic) dishes; they learn to care for their immediate environment, learn to cook without burning down the school or getting third-degree burns on their hands! They learn specific names for things as opposed to group names (Aberdeen Angus, Jersey, Guernsey, Holstein, Charolais — instead of just "cow.")

It seems to me that the attitude or philosophy of most writers of composition texts is that first-year college or university [students] can't handle or can't be trusted with the "fine china and crystal" of the academic essay. . . . Probably nowhere, except in "composition" class, are students asked to "write an essay comparing skiing and snowboarding" (this is a current assignment from [an] English class).

Pamela

In short, the methods-of-development approach to composition is "pre-disciplinary." It does not adequately address the real world of academic writing.

Nevertheless, this does not mean that rhetorical modes should be relegated to the scrap heap. Provided they are situated amid a more detailed array of rhetorical moves, they can still be useful as organizational starting points. Thus, once you have written a proposal or drafted an introduction and have a sense of what your thesis might be, you could begin to think about a method (or methods) of development that will enable you to validate your thesis. At this stage, it would probably be best to think about methods of development in relation to the core as a whole, but sooner or later you may find that particular paragraphs entail their own developmental structure.

Thinking about the core, you could ask yourself questions like this: Does the thesis require the presentation of major examples? Does it obligate me to compare two or more things? Should I be describing or narrating a series of events? Finding simple answers to these questions may be difficult because it is likely that any given paper will do many of these things. Accordingly, there is an aspect of make-believe in isolating one or two rhetorical modes: chances are, numerous other modes will be at work in the overall structure of your paper, and some readers may regard these other modes as more dominant than the one(s) you highlighted. Even so, the organizational modes that you consciously acknowledge and try to refine should help you to communicate with others. And that, after all, is the purpose: in terms of overall structure, methods of development reflect general patterns. The handbooks and anthologies that devote considerable space to the explication and demonstration of methods of development will have more to say about how these methods can be used.

Here, we will simply take one essay as a case study, Tony Arruda's "'You Would Have Had Your Pick': Youth, Gender, and Jobs in Williams Lake, British Columbia, 1945–1972" (1998). We suggest that Arruda uses comparison and contrast as a dominant organizational principle that structures his entire essay, although chronology also plays a role in how he arranges his material. Arruda's thesis, contrary to the allusive phrase, is that during the study period young people did not have their "pick" of part-time jobs in Williams Lake. In short, he argues that gender determined job opportunities: boys could work in relatively high-paying industrial jobs, but girls were limited to poor-paying jobs as office and domestic helpers. Notice how the thesis itself seems to call for an argument that is based on comparisons. This is how the comparison plays itself out, section-by-section, paragraph-by-paragraph:

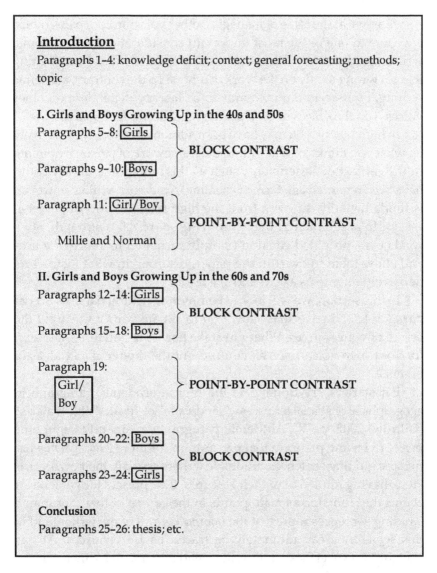

Introduction
Paragraphs 1–4: knowledge deficit; context; general forecasting; methods; topic

I. Girls and Boys Growing Up in the 40s and 50s
Paragraphs 5–8: Girls
> BLOCK CONTRAST
Paragraphs 9–10: Boys

Paragraph 11: Girl/Boy
> POINT-BY-POINT CONTRAST
Millie and Norman

II. Girls and Boys Growing Up in the 60s and 70s
Paragraphs 12–14: Girls
> BLOCK CONTRAST
Paragraphs 15–18: Boys

Paragraph 19:
Girl/
Boy
> POINT-BY-POINT CONTRAST

Paragraphs 20–22: Boys
> BLOCK CONTRAST
Paragraphs 23–24: Girls

Conclusion
Paragraphs 25–26: thesis; etc.

This kind of organization does not happen by accident. Clearly, Arruda had a plan or blueprint that was based on a fairly distinctive method of development. Your own thesis may not call for comparison and contrast, but you should have an understanding of your own overall organizational principles.

MANAGING OTHER VOICES IN CORE PARAGRAPHS

As we arrive at the issue of managing other voices in core paragraphs, we come to one of the most important considerations for academic writers. Students, in particular, need to know that in academic writing it is not wrong to rely on the work of others. To the contrary, academic writing, by its very nature, tends to be heavily dependent on other voices—on the voices of both primary and secondary sources.

In high school, you may have been admonished to rely exclusively on what you think, to write within the framework of personal opinion. In the context of assignments such as this, going to a library could have been regarded as a form of cheating. Academic writing, however, is fundamentally different from the high school world of personal essays. In academic writing, employing sources is a strength, not a weakness—provided you don't simply surrender to the other voices and allow them to overrun the paper, resulting in what instructors derisively refer to as a "cut-and-paste job."

In this section, we will look at common structural patterns in core paragraphs, patterns that allow you to situate your voice amid the voices of your sources. What's at stake here is negotiating "a space" for your own voice, even as you present the thoughts and ideas of others.

For starters, try to imagine the typical academic paragraph in geographical or spatial terms, as a "landscape" of "peaks" and "valleys" (Giltrow, 2002, p. 77). Academic paragraphs frequently begin on a peak or viewing platform that presents one or more *guiding sentences*. In these guiding sentences, academic writers speak in their own voice. Here, having mulled over their research, they present judgements or claims that function as main points in the course of their argument. Guiding sentences represent the *informed* views of the writer, and in this sense they can ultimately be traced back to sources. At this "height," however, academic writers tend to stand above their sources and offer generalizations. Like advance scouts, guiding sentences chart a route forward.

Thereafter, core paragraphs tend to descend very quickly into a valley of *low-level details*. These valleys tend to be filled with dense thickets of *reported speech*. Here, along the valley floor, writers embrace their sources, presenting evidence for guiding sentences by quoting, paraphrasing, or summarizing other voices. Some paragraphs end on the valley floor, with low-level detail, so that readers must await the next paragraph before once again ascending to higher ground. Alternatively, paragraphs may climb back up on their own and offer *retrospective* or *transitional sentences*. Retrospective sentences essentially recap and emphasize opening generalizations, while transitional sentences anticipate terrain in the next paragraph.

The paragraph topographies look like this:

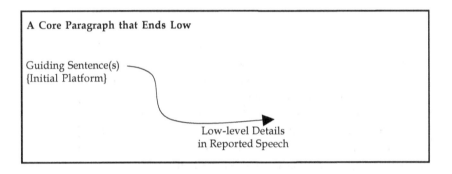

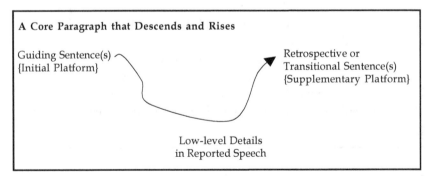

The basic rhetorical features under discussion have been blocked in Sample 1. Identify these patterns in the other samples that follow.

Sample 1

Nancy Theberge
A Feminist Analysis of Responses to Sports Violence

Although interpretations locating the problem in the culture and social organization of the sport were in the minority among the views of sportswriters, the comments of one writer stood } *Initial Platform*

out as an exception. *Vancouver Sun* sports columnist James Lawton wrote a series of impassioned pieces condemning the incident and all who took part. On January 5 Lawton wrote that the event was a crude and brutal betrayal of reason and "any sense that Canadian hockey might finally strip itself of the illusion that masculinity and thuggery are in some way inextricably mixed."[18] On January 7 he stated that the crime of the incident "is not the rather pathetic failure of [the players] to keep control of their feelings. It is the systematic corruption of the idea of sport that goes into the training of so many of those players."[19] On the 16th he wrote of "the normality of the jungle" that characterizes hockey, and said that the "episode made nonsense of the concept of sport." Lawton's column on this day was titled "Jelinek Totally Wrong," a reference to the minister's decision to appeal the suspension of the Canadian team by the IHF. He argued that the decision was "morally bankrupt" and "the point that should be hammered now is that there were alternatives to such full-blooded involvement in the brawl." He concluded this column by urging an international review of the game.[20] Throughout his pieces, Lawton criticized those who defended the actions of the Canadian players on any grounds. More significantly, his analysis placed the event in a larger context by directing attention to the need for fundamental change in the sport. *Low-Level Details* / *Supplementary Platform*

Sample 2

Tony Arruda
"You Would Have Had Your Pick"

In response to the general question, "What sorts of part-time jobs were there for girls after school?" women who entered their teens in the 1940's or early 1950's invariably cited a very limited range of options: "the drug store," "the grocery store," or "Mackenzie's department store." Relatively few girls actually worked outside their homes or family-run enterprises. Camille Summerland recalled she was the only girl in a class with over a dozen girls who worked part-time after school for wages. As another woman put it, "[i]t was mostly boys that worked after school." In her early to mid-teens, Katie-Jean Kurtz was restricted from working outside the home after school by her parents, particularly her father. Katie-Jean was quite vigorous as she described the general context: "When I was young, boys had a great number more opportunities than girls—there's no doubt about it. My brother left home at sixteen and earned a man's salary . . . When I was a child, my parents wanted—felt—that I should be a secretary—that would be an excellent job for a woman. That would mean I wouldn't have to scrub floors." Her experience illuminates the simple but important point that "family life" is actually experienced differently by each individual member of the family. It also illustrates that parental fear of what might befall an unaccompanied female is one critical underpinning of the sexual division of labour within a patriarchal system.

Sample 3

Mark Kirby
Feminist, Populist, Humanitarian?:
Progressive Thinking and Images of Princess Diana

The claim that Diana was an inspiration to women, whose life contained some commentary on gender politics seems to be the strongest argument and was aired quite widely in the media. Beatrix Campbell, for example, argued that Princess Diana had survived victimhood to realise her true self identity (Channel 4's "After Dark" special, 14/9/97). Similarly, Suzanne Moore noted: "Had she been born 20 years earlier she would have been expected to put up with her husband's infidelity, to grin and bear it. In refusing to do so, she laid open the cynical workings of monarchy, patriarchy and hereditary privilege that had used her as little more than a brood mare. When the fairy tale fractured we saw another story altogether, one that many, particularly women, could relate to" (*Independent*, 1/9/97). Writing from this same perspective, Joan Smith claimed: "Diana's unhappy marriage charted a familiar course for millions of women and made them feel that, however disastrous their lives, they were not alone" (*Guardian*, 2/9/97). Yet Smith was also willing to point to the tendency to overlook the faults of Princess Diana in all of this (*Independent on Sunday*, 14/9/97). The *Cosmopolitan* editor, Mandi Norwood, writing in the *Express on Sunday* (14/9/97), even went so far as to argue that: "Diana personified feminism, new feminism — a force of nature rather than a mere brand of politics," and went on to argue that she, along with Mother Teresa, showed that "feminine" values of kindness, compassion, radiance and good humour were "worth a lot." This was rejected by Nicci Gerard (*Observer* 21/9/97) who also noted that she felt like "the personal had washed the political away." Gerard presents a more hard-headed view of feminism than allowed for by the adulation of Diana, and highlights the criticisms of Joan Smith made by Beatrix Campbell who, she says, argued that there was a problem with "Smith's insufficiently reverential attitude to Diana."

Sample 4

Donna Cox
Diana: Her True Story: Post-modern Transgressions in Identity

In the classic scenario of romance fiction, there is an evacuation of identity in the jouissant encounter of one and other so that two subjectivities merge in a fantasized situation of perfect blissful union. Lacan refers to "jouissance" as an intense and excessive pleasure/pain associated with sexual coming and religious mysticism (Lacan, 1982). In *A Touch of Love*, the heroine experiences "an ecstasy and a rapture that was indescribable sweep through her body. It was so vivid, so intense that it was partly a sharp pain" (p. 158). [Barbara] Cartland [one of Diana's favourite novelists] goes on to associate this with the "very essence of love" which results in an ultimate out-of-body experience for the united couple (p. 158). The undoing/dissolution of "I" is here so intense that it evacuates identity and translates into the bodily location by which we orientate ourselves in time and space. In his study of the structure of romance, Northrop Frye identifies its "structural core [as] the individual loss or confusion or break in the continuity of identity"' (Frye, 1976, p.

104). Here is a romantic diaspora of dispossessed identity which Diana had textual recourse to, writing herself into the heroine's place so that textuality might be said to have had its effects in her lived bodily experience.

Sample 5

Annette Hill
Fearful and Safe: Audience Response to British Reality Programming

The connection with American commercial television and popular factual entertainment led to accusations that European reality programming was populist and an example of the lowest common denominator television. Bondebjerg (1996, p. 28) noted how programs such as *SOS liveller dod* (Sweden), *Sagan ukopklaret* (Denmark), and *999* (United Kingdom) exported and adapted the format of American reality programs to fit "European . . . [and] formerly very traditional public service cultures." Similarly, Dauncey (1996) commented on how French reality programs such as *La Nuit des heros* (France 2, 1991), *Urgences* (La Cinq, 1991), or *Temoin No. 1* (TF1, 1993) also developed out of the American tradition of reality TV (Dauncey, 1996, p. 95). In France, concern about reality programming led to debate about the negative impact of reality TV, specifically its tendency to encourage tabloidization and voyeurism (Dauncey, 1996, pp. 97, 99, 101). Dauncey (1996) criticizes the American and British approaches to popular factual entertainment that, according to him, sacrifice quality in favour of commercial interests: "France should realise that by producing its own, inexpensive, popular and populist television in the form of reality shows, it is undermining its higher order ambitions to be the foremost purveyor of quality culture" (p. 101).

Remember that the samples above merely present *common* patterns. Clearly, there will be exceptions: sometimes, for example, core paragraphs may consist only of brief, high-level comments that forecast the direction of a particular section in the core; or perhaps low-level details will comprise first-hand observations of the writer and not involve a lot of reported speech; alternatively, the topography of a paragraph may present a series of rises and dips (generalizations and evidence) somewhere in the middle; on other occasions, readers may encounter paragraphs that actually seem to begin low, with reported speech. In any event, the typical patterns that we have foregrounded can serve as useful models for researchers who are not familiar with the conventions of academic prose. More often than not, core paragraphs in student papers should probably look like the ones we have selected.

> **Core paragraphs** in the humanities and social sciences are generally typified by different levels: in the high places (at the outset and perhaps at the end), we hear the voice of the primary writer; in the lower middle-ground, we hear the voices of others.

The basic patterns that we are emphasizing raise some questions about proportion. First, it is evident that variations in elevation produce core paragraphs that are quite bulky. The low-level detail, in particular, takes up a lot of room, so that paragraphs as a whole may extend to half a page or more. Further, given the amount of space devoted to the presentation of low-level detail, it would seem that a large percentage of the core of a research paper may consist of reported speech.

These assumptions are supported by the samples. Sample 1 consists of eleven sentences. Four present the observations of Theberge, the primary writer; seven entail reported speech that presents the observations of someone else. Thus, about 63 percent of the paragraph involves another voice — that of sports columnist James Lawton. The figures for Sample 2 are similar. Depending on how one accounts for ellipses, this paragraph also consists of eleven sentences. Once again, four present the observations of Arruda, the primary writer; seven present the observations of Williams Lake residents. If this pattern were to hold true in other papers in other disciplines, more than half of the core in research papers would involve reported speech.

In actuality, a wider sampling of core paragraphs, even within Theberge's and Arruda's respective papers, would probably reveal a lower ratio of reported speech, but the overall percentage would remain quite high — probably within 35 to 55 percent. Thus, real examples of academic writing, involving discipline-based articles published by professional scholars, indicate that other voices play a *major role* in the language of research.

Given the precedents established by published research, the temptation to simply give in to other voices may be strong. This impulse can become even stronger when writers are pressed for time or when they feel intimidated by other voices in the knowledge domain. Surrounded by experts, student writers may begin to doubt the value of their own ideas and become reluctant to claim even the high-level room for themselves. Remember, however, that the high-level observations are rarely pulled out of thin air; they are born, instead, from the assimilation and synthesis that accompany careful research and reading. In this sense, even the high-level points are founded on other voices — on accumulated evidence that will be presented in due course. Thus, academic writers neither surrender to other voices nor ignore them: the whole concept of academic argumentation hinges on the interplay between generalization and evidence, a process whereby academic writers strategically situate their own voice in relation to others.

PLATFORM OUTLINE

Given the discussion of methods of development and paragraph structure, we are now in a position to think about outlining the core of a paper. Techniques for outlining vary, and may range from rough notes or diagrams to enumerated subsets of sentences. Most students are familiar with the latter technique, which results in what is sometimes called a formal outline. The example below reviews formal outlines by focusing on a core paragraph from a paper by Diane Thompson, entitled "Canadian Women Over Four Centuries." Thompson's thesis is that "Many seemingly ordinary women in Canadian history were, in fact, quite extraordinary and deserving of acclaim." A paragraph from the core of Thompson's paper looks like this:

Madame de la Peltrie founded an Ursuline convent in Quebec, but yearned for even greater hardship. Thus, she later appealed to go to the Huron Mission field. Perhaps she sought the martyrdom of Jesuit Priests. In any event, the Jesuits refused her offer of service. In Quebec, Peltrie met Jeanne Mance. Since her youth, Mance had wanted to be a missionary in Canada. Accordingly, Mance joined an expedition to found a mission at Montreal. Yet the Quebec governor opposed the project because the mission site was deep in Huron territory. Mance, Peltrie, and the other women were undeterred. They arrived safely in Montreal and immediately raised an altar to celebrate mass.

A formal outline of the paragraph might look like this:

I. Madame de la Peltrie founded an Ursuline convent in Quebec, but yearned for even greater hardship.
   A. She appealed to go to the Huron Mission field.
      1. Perhaps she sought the martyrdom of Jesuit Priests.
      2. Yet the Jesuits refused her offer of service.
   B. In Quebec, Peltrie met Jeanne Mance.
      1. Since her youth, Mance had wanted to be a missionary in Canada.
      2. Mance joined an expedition to found a missionary at Montreal.
         (a) The Quebec governor opposed the project because the mission site was deep in Huron territory.
         (b) However, Mance, Peltrie, and other women were undeterred.
            (i) The women arrived safely in Montreal.
            (ii) They immediately raised an altar and celebrated mass.

Notice how the formal outline reinforces the concept of levels. Indeed, if the outline were turned clockwise, on its side, the topography of Thompson's paragraph would graphically depict the levels.

Whichever outlining technique you choose, outlines can help the development of a paper, but outlining may not be for everyone. Some writers like the embellished sense of direction that comes with an outline and prefer to draft with a kind of blueprint in front of them. Other writers find it very difficult to compose an outline before they begin drafting and prefer to discover their sense of direction by working in the environment of rough paragraphs. Thus, as we consider outlining, we are again faced with the uncertainties of the writing process. Different writers work differently, and it would be foolish to recommend universal procedures.

At most, this text simply asks you *to consider* a certain kind of outline, one that strikes a compromise between the very rough and the very detailed. This kind of outline merely focuses on *high-level platforms* in core paragraphs, providing a bird's-eye view of an essay's peaks or hilltops, the places that are so crucial to management and direction. Essentially, such outlines consist of a list of *guiding sentences* at the beginning of individual paragraphs (*retrospective* or *transitional* sentences could be developed later, in the draft). Moreover, writers are free to compose such an outline at a self-selected stage in the writing process. If you are among those who are uncomfortable outlining before drafting, you could experiment with a platform outline after a draft is complete. In any event, the merit of such an outline is that it enables you to examine the overall *coherence, proportion,* and *relevance* of the core of your paper.

Coherence: platform statements should logically follow one another (in effect, they should tell an intelligible story).

Proportion: platforms should reflect an appropriate distribution of emphasis on main points (one main point should not threaten to eclipse others).

Relevance: platforms should stay in touch with topic and contribute to thesis development.

The platform outline presented below charts peaks in the core of Jon Swainger's "American Crime Comics as Villains: An Incident from Northern Canada." The outline begins by establishing topic and thesis. Subheadings in the core are designated by roman numerals, and core paragraphs are marked by arabic numerals. Ellipses indicate the presence of low-level details that come between initial and supplementary platforms.

In preparing this outline, we had to study every paragraph individually. Indeed, while we assumed that the first sentence or two in each paragraph would offer high-level guiding sentences, we consistently checked this. We are particularly struck by how the high points in this author's paragraphs keep topic in view and by how these high points tell a coherent narrative or story as they engage in thesis development.

Platform Outline for Jon Swainger's "American Crime Comics as Villains: An Incident from Northern Canada"

RS: The comic book murder [underlined]
AB: crime-free Peace[bold]

Topic: **The Crime-Free Peace** and the Comic Book Murder

Thesis: The local response to the comic book murder underscored a deliberate communal attempt to preserve the illusion of a **crime-free Peace**.

I. THE "CRIME FREE PEACE" [Development of the key abstraction as background information in the core]

1. In contrast to the prairies of southern Canada, non-native settlement arrived in the Peace region relatively late. . . . [Intervening low-level details]. . . . Chaotic and inconsistent, the slow migration of settlers continued until the 1920s and 1930s when, ironically, farm families on the southern prairies experienced droughts, and **the Peace emerged as the last best land for those hoping for another fresh beginning.**

2. Despite the opportunity the Peace offered, the flow of new immigrants was little more than a trickle. . . . [Intervening low-level details]. . . . Given that [the few] residents were on isolated homesteads or in small communities where most individuals were recognizable by almost everyone, it is hardly surprising that **the level of reported crime was not that great**.

3. [However,] [t]hrough the pages of the *Peace River Block News*, residents of the Peace were well-informed of all manner of local criminal activity.

4. [Thus,] [r]esidents were aware that, notwithstanding its rural nature, the region was certainly not crime free. Yet, despite the evidence, **the belief persisted that the region was not particularly affected by criminal activity.**

5. This discrepancy between the observable presence of crime and lawlessness and the publicly maintained assertion that the region was relatively **crime free**, sets the context for the comic book murder of November 1948.

6. The greatest tests for **this willing suspension of [belief]** came in the form of the United States Army Corps of Engineers who poured into the Peace to initiate construction of the Alaska Highway in 1942.

7. While there may not have been an orgy of crime, there was significant increase in police investigations along with significant increase in drunkenness, theft, and personal violence during the war years. . . . [Yet] [t]he region emerged from the war years with its **crime-free image** intact and it would be **that image** which provided the backdrop for the "comic book murder."

II. THE COMIC BOOK MURDER [A more detailed examination of topic; the success of the argument depends on the persuasiveness of this section, which begins by saying more about the research site]

1. On the evening of November 12, 1948, two boys, aged 11 and 13 years, stole a 30-30 rifle and ammunition from an unlocked car parked on Second Avenue in Dawson Creek, British Columbia.

2. Having attended a movie in Dawson Creek, sixty-two-year-old James Watson and his family were returning home to Kilkerran by car, when they were confronted by the waiting aspiring bandits just before 10 p.m. . . . [Intervening low-level detail]. . . . Four days later on November 16th, Watson died in St. Joseph's hospital at Dawson Creek.

3. At the inquest held on November 22nd the events surrounding the shooting were outlined before M.S. Morrell, police magistrate and acting coroner, with an empaneled six man jury. . . . [Intervening low-level

detail]. . . . As a consequence, the 13-year-old was committed to the Industrial Home for Boys in Coquitlam, BC, while the 11-year-old was committed to the care of the Superintendent of Child Welfare, in Vancouver.

4. Reaction to the fatal shooting, the youthfulness of the two accused, and the pronounced role of American crime comics was immediate. . . . [Intervening low-level detail]. . . . Apparently, crime comics represented all that was evil in an increasingly complex world.

5. By stressing an alleged relationship between crime comics and the death of James Watson, local editorialists and law enforcement officials remained true to the fiction of the crime-free Peace. [Nice repetition of thesis at the end of this section]

III. THE COMIC BOOK PERIL [This section places the xenophobic reaction to the comic book murder and to American crime comics in a larger, national context; in doing so, however, the section risks compromising the claim that there is a particular ideology at work in the Peace]

1. The tragedy of James Watson's death provided an opportune moment for Canadian activists alarmed by crime comics. . . . [Intervening low-level detail]. . . . After six days of persistent, if not terribly aggressive advocacy, combined with the submission of an example of the comic book literature to Liberal Minister of Justice, J.L. Isley, [Davie] Fulton obtained the minister's commitment to draft a suitable amendment to the *Criminal Code.*

2. When Fulton pressed the matter a week later, however, Isley had softened his commitment to act. . . . [Intervening low-level detail]. . . . Fifteen months would elapse before the government would finally take action.

3. A number of events took place in the interim.

4. When Parliament reconvened after the Liberals' return to power and with the appointment of Stuart Garson as Minister of Justice, public

mood and political will had shifted decidedly in favour of action against the crime comics. Indeed, from the moment that Fulton introduced Bill 10, to amend the *Criminal Code* on the portrayal of crime, it was evident that the legislation would succeed.

5. Fellow parliamentarians voiced support in favour of Fulton's bill.

6. Although it was evident that with government backing, the Fulton bill would pass, aspects of the legislation nonetheless drew critical attention.

IV. THE PERIL VANQUISHED [Conclusion]

1. By the time the Fulton bill became law, much of the uproar over crime comics in the Peace had subsided even as the *Peace River Block News* and the *Alaska Highway News* engaged in a flurry of editorial hand-wringing.

2. For residents of the Peace region of northeastern British Columbia, the murder of James Watson was a horrific incident in the midst of what most believed was a law-abiding and orderly community. This sort of crime was not supposed to happen in the Peace country; adults assumed that the younger generation subscribed to the homesteaders' ideals of the 1920s and 1930s. Demonizing American comic books bolstered the notion that a single identifiable set of values had existed and remained intact despite the cultural changes brought on by the construction of the Alaska Highway. . . . [intervening low-level detail]. . . . [R]ather than wrestle with the implications of the murder, it was far easier to characterize the shooting as a freakish tragedy caused by a morally degenerate and insidious outside force: American crime comics.

3. The belief that juvenile delinquency was inspired by crime comics offered a convenient explanation for the murder. . . . [intervening low-level detail]. . . . Thus, when these two boys decided to re-enact a comic book robbery, the hard-working parents of the Peace sought an explanation in the plague of crime comics as a symbol of the broader invasion of their once isolated and idealized Peace River country.

4. The Peace was not merely a geographic location, it was a way that people felt about law, order, and respect for authority which, in turn,

> was grounded in the very reason that settlers came to the region in the
> first instance.... [intervening low-level detail]. ... Scapegoating American
> crime comics not only reassured the community of its **distinctive
> character**, it also helped redefine **that identity** in response to the
> encroaching North American culture.

The above outline enables us to evaluate Swainger's paper in terms
of *coherence, proportion,* and *relevance,* and for this reason the outline is
a valuable tool. Whether outlines are prepared before or after a first
draft, they can be used to assess your own work.

STYLES OF DOCUMENTATION

Different disciplines have different ways of acknowledging
information borrowed from sources. Thus, once you are ready to begin
drafting, it is probably a good idea to know what style of
documentation your paper calls for. In academic writing, there are
four major styles of documentation: the Chicago (or Turabian) style,
the American Psychological Association style (APA), the Council of
Biology Editors style (CBE), and the Modern Language Association
style (MLA). The Chicago style, which involves bibliographic footnotes
or endnotes, is commonly used in history. APA is used in the social
sciences, in disciplines like psychology and sociology. CBE is standard
in the sciences, and for disciplines such as engineering. MLA is used
in English studies and philosophy. While all of this may seem daunting
to someone approaching styles of documentation for the first time,
documentation is actually a fairly straightforward process, one that is
governed by genre expectations that reflect social needs.

The various styles of documentation may look different, but they
share an underlying structure in that all four involve a *two-step process.*
Regardless of style, documentation at the first step involves some
sort of *in-text citation:* APA, CBE, and MLA all use parenthetical
citations that provide bits of information in round brackets, or
parentheses; Chicago, on the other hand, uses raised or superscript
numerals. At the second step, these in-text citations usually correspond
to *a list of sources* at the end of the paper. Step 1, involving the citation,

indicates that the primary writer is drawing on a source. Step 2, the list, provides complete information about the source.

Since citations and lists complement each other, they can be envisioned as partners in a dance.

The samples below show the two-step process of documentation in randomly chosen passages:

MLA **Step 1: From** **Pamela den Ouden's** **"My Uttermost** **Valleys"**	In their well-known 1979 study of the patriarchal literary tradition, entitled *Madwoman in the Attic: The Woman Writer and the Nineteenth Century Literary Imagination*, Sandra Gilbert and Susan Gubar, two American feminist critics, argue that many male writers, including such luminaries as Dante, Milton, Swift, and Dickens, have presented their female characters as angels (21–27) or as monsters (27–35).

Works Cited

Gilbert, Sandra, and Susan Gubar. *The Madwoman in the Attic: The Woman Writer and the Nineteenth-Century Literary Imagination*. New Haven: Yale UP, 1979.

Step 2: From the Works Cited at the end of the paper

APA
Step 1: From Shari Harrison's "Empowering Life Long Learners: Using Authentic Assessment to Enhance Learning in Post-Secondary Writing Courses"

According to Fischer and King (1995), "authentic assessment is a positive and dynamic form of evaluation. It is a system that documents what students can do; promotes the collaboration of teacher [and] student . . . in the learning process; and places ownership of learning on the student" (p. 33).

References

Fischer, C., & King, R. (1995). *Authentic assessment: A guide to implementation*. Thousand Oaks, CA: Corwin Press.

Step 2: From the list of references at the end of the paper

ANOTHER EXAMPLE OF APA
Step 1: From Alice Carlick's "The Girl and the Grizzly"

Anthropologists suggest that narratives provide windows on the way people think about and live in the world (Ridington, 1988, p. 70; Cruikshank, 1983, p. 5).

References
Cruikshank, J. (1983). *The stolen woman: Female journeys in Tagish and Tutchone narrative.* National Museum of Man Mercury Series, paper No. 87. Ottawa: National Museums of Canada.

Ridington, R. (1988). *Trail to heaven: Knowledge and narrative in a northern Native community.* Vancouver: Douglas and McIntyre.

Step 2: From the list of references at the end of the paper

**CBE
Step 1: From Chapter 3 in the CBE Manual**

A detailed source on phonetic symbols is *Phonetic Symbol Guide* (Pullum and Ladusaw 1986).

References
Pullum GK, Ladusaw WA. 1986. *Phonetic symbol guide.* Chicago: Univ. Chicago Pr.

Step 2: From the list of references at the end of the paper

**ANOTHER EXAMPLE OF CBE
Step 1: From David Hamer's paper on grizzly bears in Banff**

In years of high fruit production, roots are dug infrequently by grizzly bears during autumn, but if the buffaloberry crop fails, roots can dominate the diet from August until hibernation in later October or November (Pearson 1975, Russell et al. 1979, Hamer and Herrero 1987a).

References

Hamer D, Herrero S. 1987a. Grizzly bear food
and habitat in the Front Ranges of Banff National
Park, Alberta. Int. Conf. Bear Res. Manage. 7:199–
213.

Pearson AM. 1975. The northern interior grizzly
bear Ursus arctos L. Canadian Wildlife Service
Report Series No. 34. 84 p.

Russell RH, Nolan JW, Woody NG, Anderson,
GW. 1979. A study of the grizzly bear in Jasper
National Park, 1975–1978. Final report. Canadian
Wildlife Service, Edmonton, Alberta. 136 p.

Step 2: From the list of references at the end of the paper

**CHICAGO
Step 1: From I.S.
MacLaren's
"Retaining
Captaincy of the
Soul"**

Conventional modes of perceiving nature
comprised no less a part of the Arctic explorer's
baggage than they did the Grand Tourist's
because, as Stephen Fender has stated recently in
his study of the response to landscape in the early
American West, "People confronted by
unfamiliar landscapes have often needed the
reassurance of frames or focussing devices,
whether physical or conceptual, brought along
from their own cultural base."[1]

Notes

[1] Stephen Fender, *Plotting the Golden West:
American Literature and the Rhetoric of the
California Trail* (Cambridge: Cambridge
University Press, 1981), p. 16.

Step 2: From the list of notes at the end of the paper

The precise mechanics for each style of documentation vary according to the nature of the source. For example, Step 2 entries for books look a little different from Step 2 entries for journals. It is also worth remembering that some publishers use their own versions (in-house versions) of a given style, so that APA and CBE formatting, in particular, may differ from journal to journal. In the case of papers prepared for college and university classes, students should follow the advice of individual instructors. Some instructors may accept variations on established styles and merely insist on consistency. In this situation, you could simply follow the precedents established by a published paper in your discipline. Other instructors, however, may require papers to be formatted in strict accordance with the official style manuals listed below:

CBE: *Scientific Style and Format: the CBE Manual for Authors, Editors, and Publishers,* 6th ed.

APA: *Publication Manual of the American Psychological Association,* 5th ed.

MLA: *MLA Handbook for Writers of Research Papers,* 6th ed.

Chicago: *The Chicago Manual of Style,* 14th ed. University of Chicago Press.

Turabian: *A Manual for Writers of Term Papers, Theses, and Dissertations,* 6th ed.

Normally, these style manuals can be found in the reference section of your library, and they are often supplemented by a host of abridged style manuals. Many composition handbooks also provide abridged information on the different styles, as do innumerable Web sites devoted to documentation. The problem with Web sites, however, is that they can be "here today, gone tomorrow." The following sites may be accessible:

Documentation Guide: APA and other Styles
library.concordia.ca/services/citations.html

The Official APA Site
www.apa.org

Documentation and Style Guide for Chicago Style
www.msoe.edu/gen_st/style/

Ready Reference: Style Manuals
www.gwu.edu/gelman/ref/readyref/style.html

The Official MLA Site
www.mla.org

If your instructor requires a particular style, it would be a good idea to ask him or her to approve abridged style manuals, whether they are in print or on-line.

Documentation can be a tedious and time-consuming process. Nevertheless, it deserves your careful attention, for meticulous documentation enables readers to check and verify information for themselves. In relation to genre theory, then, thoroughness serves a scholarly need for precision, accuracy, and reliability. It will impress your instructors, just as it impresses journal editors.

Our intention is to present documentation in this text as a demonstration of the patterns we discuss. Thus, rather than providing more instructional material on Step 2 here, we invite readers to examine our own chapter references, which are formatted in APA style; reference lists for sample papers use various documentation styles. For the remainder of this chapter, we will elaborate on Step 1 of the process.

SENTENCE-LEVEL CONSIDERATIONS AND REPORTED SPEECH

Once you know what style of documentation you will be using, there are some further sentence-level considerations that warrant attention as you acknowledge sources in core paragraphs. Each time you employ a source, you need to decide whether you will

- quote, or
- paraphrase

and whether you will acknowledge the source

- directly, by identifying it in an attributive expression (see below), or
- indirectly, by identifying the source in the citation only.

It is possible to mix and match these choices in a variety of ways. You may provide the following:

- direct reference with quotation
- direct reference with paraphrase
- indirect reference with quotation
- indirect reference with paraphrase

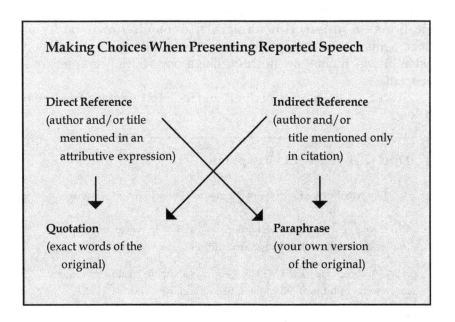

Making Choices When Presenting Reported Speech

Direct Reference
(author and/or title
    mentioned in an
    attributive expression)

Indirect Reference
(author and/or
    title mentioned only
    in citation)

Quotation
(exact words of the
    original)

Paraphrase
(your own version
    of the original)

Quotation or Paraphrase

As mentioned in the discussion of summary writing, the general rule is to quote only when the precise words of the source are important. Otherwise, paraphrase is preferable. Note, however, that it is possible to strike a compromise between quotation and paraphrase: quoted phrases can appear embedded inside a paraphrase.

Direct and Indirect Reference

Remember that direct reference occurs when a researcher identifies a source in an *attributive expression* that comes before a citation (cf. Swales, 1994, pp. 148–9). More specifically, when direct reference occurs, attribution is incorporated into the grammatical relationships of a sentence so that sources (author's names, titles, and/or personal pronouns) appear as one of the following:

- the subject of a verb
- a possessive adjective
- the object of a preposition
- the object of a prepositional phrase

Indirect reference, on the other hand, marginalizes attribution, pushing it exclusively into citations, the form of which (parenthetical citations or superscript numerals) depends on the style of documentation. In indirect reference, then, attribution is an isolated aside in which citations function like a non-restrictive appositive element.

Some Step 1 examples of direct and indirect reference are shown below:

Direct Reference with Paraphrase

(An Attributive Expression [Phrase or Clause] Plus a Citation)

Chicago: According to Christy, Bedaux's ability to create a favourable impression of himself led to the multimillionaire's success.[1]

APA: According to Christy (1980), Bedaux's ability to create a favourable impression of himself led to the multimillionaire's success (p. 23).

MLA: Christy argues that Bedaux's ability to create a favourable impression of himself led to his success (23).

Indirect Reference with Paraphrase

(A Citation Only)

Chicago: Bedaux's ability to create a favourable impression of himself led to his success.[1]

APA: Bedaux's ability to create a favourable impression of himself led to his success (Christy, 1980, p. 23).

MLA: Bedaux's ability to create a favourable impression of himself led to his success (Christy 23).

When you employ direct reference, you are shining a spotlight on your source, as though it were at centre stage. When you employ indirect reference, sources are more shadowy figures that inhabit peripheral regions. The use of direct and indirect reference is a discretionary art, not an exact science. Just be aware of your stylistic choices, and try to make informed, sensitive decisions. Here are some guidelines:

Use Direct Reference
   ✓ When referring to an important source for the first time
   ✓ When referring to an important source at the beginning of a paragraph
   ✓ When returning to an important source after employing other sources
   ✓ On an intermittent basis, just because it sounds good

Use Indirect Reference
   ✓ When providing a brief description of a tradition of inquiry
   ✓ Whenever you do not feel a need to draw attention to a source
   ✓ When ongoing statements of attribution amid low-level paragraph detail may begin to clutter up your writing.

More on Grammatical Constructions in Direct Reference

Certain grammatical patterns occur in the construction of direct reference. We've presented some of these patterns below.

Source passage: The decision whether or not to marry belongs properly to individuals, not to the government. (Thomas Stoddard, "Marriage is a Fundamental Right," p. 45). The samples below employ MLA documentation.

- Attributive expressions may be written as prepositional phrases before, between, or sometimes after a quotation or paraphrase.

   > According to Thomas Stoddard, "[t]he decision whether or not to marry belongs properly to individuals, not to the government" (45).

   > "The decision whether or not to marry," according to Thomas Stoddard, "belongs properly to individuals, not to the government" (45).

   > "The decision whether or not to marry belongs properly to individuals, not to the government," according to Thomas Stoddard (45).

- Attributive expressions may be written as subordinate clauses preceding a quotation or paraphrase. In these cases, the quotation or paraphrase must comprise a main clause.

   > As Thomas Stoddard notes, "[t]he decision whether or not to marry belongs properly to individuals, not to the government" (45).

   > As Thomas Stoddard notes, choices about marriage are matters of individual discretion, rather than governmental decree (45).

- Attributive expressions may be written as part of a main clause, consisting of a subject and a transitive verb. The quotation or paraphrase (often the object of the transitive verb) may complete the main clause.

> In "Marriage is a Fundamental Right," Thomas Stoddard argues that "[t]he decision whether or not to marry belongs properly to individuals, not to the government" (45).

> In "Marriage is a Fundamental Right," Thomas Stoddard notes that choices about marriage are matters of individual discretion, rather than governmental decree (45).

- Attributive expressions may also be written as complete main clauses that precede a quotation.

> Thomas Stoddard argues that personal freedom is a paramount concern: "The decision whether or not to marry belongs properly to individuals, not to the government" (45).

Choosing Attributive Verbs for Direct Reference

When direct reference involves subject/predicate constructions, you have a host of attributive verbs to choose from. Writers can indicate their attitude toward a source by exploiting the connotative meaning of such verbs. "Claims," for example, may imply the subjective construction of information and could be used to suggest that you are standing at a critical distance from what the source says (cf. Giltrow, 2002, p. 251). "Illustrates," on the other hand, has a more objective, authoritative ring, possibly because it implies the existence of empirical evidence, and can be used to accredit information. Sample attributive verbs are listed below:

argues	emphasizes	relates
asserts	explains	reports
believes	illustrates	reveals
claims	implies	says
comments	insists	sees

concludes	maintains	shows
condemns	notes	speculates
considers	observes	suggests
declares	points out	writes

On occasion, the colouring force of attributive verbs can be emphasized through the use of adverbs. Consider the effect of the adverb/verb constructions in an essay by Kerry Abel, entitled "Of Two Minds: Dene Response to the Mackenzie Missions, 1858–1902":

> Even those who would agree with revisionist historians that the fur trade did not cause as great a disruption as once believed, still would argue that the case of the missionary was quite different. As one author confidently asserts,
>
> > Things started to change permanently and fundamentally when the missionaries started to take over the souls of native people . . . There is no question that the practical result has been the destruction of one of the cornerstones of native culture.[5]

In this case, Abel proceeds to disagree with this "confident" assertion. Perhaps, then, the confidence that Abel attributes to the source signals what *she* regards as an overly confident approach to knowledge-making. Such interrelationships suggest that the production of knowledge is a complicated and potentially adversarial business in which writers occasionally pit themselves against their sources. However, ethics of politeness are part of academic culture, so debate should be carried on in a respectful manner.

Maintaining Contact with Sources

It is important to maintain ongoing contact with your sources. You should not, for example, introduce a source once, through direct or indirect reference, then continue to draw on it without further attribution, leaving your reader to guess where information is coming from. This means that direct and indirect reference, two basic patterns involved in reported speech, should make ongoing appearances throughout the core of your essay. In the paragraph that follows, all of the information after the guiding platform (the first sentence) has been drawn from John Berger. Passages One and Two provide weak examples of reported speech; Passages Three and Four provide better examples.

Passage 1

[inadequate reporting: the beginning of the frame is vague]

When we look at art, whether portraits, photographs, or advertisements, we should note where people in the picture are looking. In advertisements in women's magazines, for example, there is a tendency for men to act and women to appear; men look at women and women watch themselves being looked at. In such cases, women are depicted as conscious recipients of a male gaze. Similarly, in Renaissance paintings of female nudes, the woman's expression reflected her subordination to the male owner of the painting. Accordingly, the ideal viewer is typically male and the female model appeals to his ego (Berger, 1972, pp. 52–64).

Passage 2

[inadequate reporting: the frame dissolves too soon]

When we look at art, whether portraits, photographs, or advertisements, we should note where people in the picture are looking. According to Berger (1972), in advertisements in women's magazines, for example, there is a tendency for men to act and women to appear; men look at women and women watch themselves being looked at (p. 52). In such cases, women are depicted as conscious recipients of a male gaze. Similarly, in Renaissance paintings of female nudes, the woman's expression reflected her subordination to the male owner of the painting. Accordingly, the ideal viewer is typically male and the female model appeals to his ego.

Passage 3

[adequate but cumbersome documentation: consecutive citations]

When we look at art, whether portraits, photographs, or advertisements, we should note where people in the picture are looking. In advertisements in women's magazines, for example, there is a tendency for men to act and women to appear; men look at women and women watch themselves being looked at (Berger, 1972, p. 52). In such cases, women are depicted as conscious recipients of a male gaze (Berger, 1972, p. 54). Similarly, in Renaissance paintings of female nudes, the woman's expression reflected her subordination to the male owner of the painting (Berger, 1972, p. 55). Accordingly, the ideal viewer is typically male and the female model appeals to his ego (Berger, 1972, pp. 52–64).

Passage 4
[adequate and unobtrusive documentation: the envelope technique]
When we look at art, whether portraits, photographs, or advertisements, we should note where people in the picture are looking. According to Berger (1972), in advertisements in women's magazines, for example, there is a tendency for men to act and women to appear; men look at women and women watch themselves being looked at. In such cases, women are depicted as conscious recipients of a male gaze. Similarly, in Renaissance paintings of female nudes, the woman's expression reflected her subordination to the male owner of the painting. Accordingly, the ideal viewer is typically male and the female model appeals to his ego (pp. 52–64).

In Passage Four, the citation that accompanies direct reference is delayed so that the attributive frame encompasses more information. This "envelope technique" can be clear and economical, but if the frame becomes too large, readers may lose track of its borders.

CASE STUDY: STAYING IN TOUCH WITH SOURCES

This chapter concludes with a case study of how attribution can be improved in successive drafts. Here, we witness a student paper progressing from a first draft to a second draft, with improved attribution along the way. For emphasis, the attributive expressions are in bold, and citations are highlighted by arrows.

First Draft of an Introduction: Weak Attribution
Champagne and Caviar: Geographical Exploration and the Bedaux Expedition

> [Bedaux was] a rich nut . . . a five-foot-six egotist trying desperately and not very effectively to be noticed.[1]

In the summer of 1934, the Bedaux expedition rolled into the Peace country on its way to find a gateway to the Pacific. Charles E. Bedaux, the leader of the expedition, was born in the small French village of Charenton-le-Pont. Bedaux's father, a railroad engineer, and his mother, a dressmaker, both hoped that their son would aspire through school and become a lawyer; however, a year and a half before he was to have graduated, Bedaux was expelled. For the next couple of years, Bedaux worked at several part-time jobs but was consistently drawn towards the "red-light" districts of urban France. After working as a hawker for night clubs, he met a pimp who offered to teach him the tricks of his trade. One aspect of this education was a keystone to Bedaux's success: "the necessity of keeping up a front no matter how down on his luck he might be."[2] This, along with his ability to convince men of their need for his services and his alluring personality, led to his success in selling his efficiency system which eventually made him a multimillionaire. It also led to his two marriages and numerous extracurricular affairs. After setting a record for crossing the Sahara Desert for the first time in rubber-tired vehicles, touring the South American rain forest region, and sailing throughout the South Seas, Bedaux turned towards what he considered the last unconquered corner of the world, the northern section of British Columbia.

Notes
1. Jim Christy, *Rough Road to the North* (Toronto: Doubleday, 1980), p. 23.
2. Jim Christy, *The Price of Power* (New York: Knopf, 1981), p. 21.

Second Draft of an Introduction: Adequate Attribution
Champagne and Caviar: Geographical Exploration and the Bedaux Expedition

> [Bedaux was] a rich nut . . . a five-foot-six egotist trying desperately and not very effectively to be noticed.
>   — Jim Christy, *Rough Road to the North*.[1]

In the summer of 1934, the Bedaux expedition rolled into the Peace country on its way to find a gateway to the Pacific. In *The Price of Power*, Jim Christy chronicles Bedaux's early life: the leader of the expedition was born in the small French village of Charenton-le-Pont; Bedaux's father, a railroad engineer, and his mother, a dressmaker, both hoped that their son would aspire through school and become a lawyer; however, a year and a half before he was to have graduated, Bedaux was expelled; for the next couple of years, Bedaux worked at several part-time jobs but was consistently drawn towards the "red-light" districts of urban France; after working as a hawker for night clubs, he met a pimp who offered to teach him the tricks of his trade.[2] According to Christy, one aspect of this education was a keystone to Bedaux's success: "the necessity of keeping up a front no matter how down on his luck he might be."[3] This, Christy asserts, along with Bedaux's alluring personality and his ability to convince men of their need for his services, led to his success in selling his efficiency system which eventually made him a multimillionaire. Christy adds that Bedaux's ability to create a favourable impression of himself also led to the multimillionaire's two marriages and numerous extracurricular affairs.[4] After setting a record for crossing the Sahara Desert for the first time in rubber-tired vehicles,[5] during the South American rain forest region, and sailing throughout the South Seas, Bedaux turned towards what he considered the last unconquered corner of the world, the northern section of British Columbia.

Notes
1. Jim Christy, *Rough Road to the North* (Toronto: Doubleday, 1980), 23.
2. Jim Christy, *The Price of Power* (New York: Knopf, 1981), 21.
3. Ibid.
4. Ibid., p. 22.
5. Ibid., p. 23.

PLAGIARISM

Plagiarism is representing someone else's work as your own. More specifically, it involves a failure to fully acknowledge one's use of sources, whether such use involves quotation or paraphrase. Plagiarism is a serious academic offence. For students, the penalties for plagiarism range from failing grades to suspension or expulsion. The most blatant forms of plagiarism involve deliberate, wholesale copying or purchasing a paper from someone else and turning it in as your own. However, most student plagiarism probably results either from inexperience with the conventions of formal attribution or from simple carelessness. In these instances, writers inadvertently present someone else's words or ideas as their own. The best way to avoid plagiarism is to pay strict attention to the nuances of attribution. Remember the following:

- Use quotation marks and citations when you are quoting;
- Remember that even paraphrased material requires attribution; and finally,
- Remember to stay in touch with your sources — consistently provide your reader with attributive frames.

Common Knowledge

Most handbooks inform students that common knowledge does not require attribution or documentation. Thus, common knowledge is presented as an exception to the rule that all borrowed information must be documented. However, this exception is neither as simple nor as reliable as it may sound. In this book, we would like to make a distinction between common non-disciplinary knowledge that does not require attribution and common disciplinary knowledge that does require attribution.

Common non-disciplinary knowledge is not generated under the carefully monitored conditions of academic research. For example, easily accessible biographical or historical information can be regarded as common non-disciplinary knowledge:

- Ernest Hemingway was born in 1899 in Oak Park, Illinois.
- Canadian Confederation occurred in 1867.

This kind of common knowledge does not require documentation. Even though it may not technically constitute *common* knowledge in the sense that people walk around with such information in their heads, such facts are part of a general cultural inheritance and may be found in popular sources such as encyclopedias and other reference books. Generally speaking, this kind of knowledge is not produced through any original thinking or empirical investigation.

On the other hand, common disciplinary knowledge embodies generally accepted understandings that have been developed through academic research and original thinking in particular fields. For example:

- Although he adopted an anti-intellectual persona in his public life, Hemingway, the writer, employed many of the literary techniques associated with the high modernism of writers such as T.S. Eliot.
- The influences that led to Canadian confederation were fundamentally different from the processes that led to American nationhood.

This kind of common knowledge should be documented. In fact, such assertions have likely emerged from a tradition of inquiry, and we already know that scholars are under an obligation to acknowledge the work of their disciplinary predecessors, even when the previous studies present a scholarly consensus.

In the student paper below, the attributive frame begins a little too soon—Black's birth date is common non-disciplinary knowledge and doesn't require attribution, although the curriculum at the "ladies' school" probably does:

From Gold Rush Pioneer to the Second Female Member of Parliament: Martha Black's Trek to Success

According to William Morrison, Martha Black was born in Chicago in February 1866. She was a child of privilege with a taste for pranks, and she attended proper ladies' schools, where she learned the skills meant to assure wealthy girls of her day a successful marriage: deportment, needlework, elocution, tennis, riding, and botany.[1]

At the end of the day, writers may still experience some uncertainty about the type of common knowledge they are dealing with, and whether, in fact, it does require attribution. When in doubt, cite. Use and acknowledge sources extensively, but make sure that your own voice retains a managing role at the higher levels.

IDEAS FOR FURTHER STUDY

1. Identify a primary method of development for your paper.

2. Prepare a platform outline for an essay that you have found during your research. Does the outline demonstrate the kind of narrative coherence that was evident in the outline of Jon Swainger's paper?

3. Using concepts discussed under "Sentence-Level Considerations and Reported Speech," analyze the management of other voices in the paper that you outlined.

CHAPTER REFERENCES

Arruda, T.F. (1998). "You would have had your pick": Youth, gender, and jobs in Williams Lake, British Columbia, 1945–75. In R. Sandwell (Ed.), *Beyond city limits: Rural history in British Columbia* (pp. 225–234). Vancouver: UBC Press.

Clouse, B.F. (1995). *Patterns for a purpose.* New York: McGraw-Hill.

Cox, D. (1999). *Diana: Her true story:* Post-modern transgressions in identity. *Journal of Gender Studies, 8*(3), 323–37.

Hill, A. (2000, May). Fearful and safe: Audience response to British reality programming. *Television and New Media, 1*(2), 193–213.

Kirby, M. (1998). Feminist, Populist, Humanitarian?: Progressive thinking and images of Princess Diana. *Class and Capital, 64,* 2941.

Theberge, N. (1989). A feminist analysis of responses to sports violence: Media coverage of the 1987 World Junior Hockey Championship. *Sociology of Sport Journal, 6*(3), 247–256.

Swainger, J. (1998). American crime comics as villains: An incident from Northern Canada. *Legal Studies Forum, 22,* 215–231.

Thompson, D. (1996). Canadian women over four centuries. In N. Waldman and S. Norton (Eds.), *Canadian content.* 3rd ed. (pp. 96–105). Toronto: Harcourt Brace.

Waldman, N., & Norton, S. (Eds.). (2000). *Canadian content.* 4th ed. Toronto: Harcourt Brace.

INTRODUCTION TO THE READINGS

Bernard Gallagher's essay on Stephen King illustrates some of the stylistic features that we have discussed in this chapter. It is worth paying particular attention to Gallagher's management of other voices; do you see guiding platforms and low-level details here? The paper by Jennifer Mitchell, produced in a first-year academic writing course,

shows that student papers can exhibit many of the characteristics of
published research. Like Gallagher's, Mitchell's paper meticulously
manages reported speech. The guiding platforms for core paragraphs
are especially impressive insofar as they present thesis-driven narrative
coherence.

BERNARD J. GALLAGHER

Reading Between the Lines: Stephen King and Allegory

1   Without a doubt, Stephen King is the one popular novelist whose
earnings and reputation have undergone a horrifyingly meteoric rise.
In 1982 King pocketed two million dollars for all his works (Gray 87);
in 1986 he pocketed three million dollars alone as an advance on his
novel, *It* (Booth and Kanfer 74). In 1982 *Time* magazine's Paul Gray
claimed that King represented a threat to serious book lovers
everywhere. In 1986 *Time* magazine's Stefan Kanfer and Cathy Booth
aim no poison darts at King and his works. At worst their breezy and
irreverent style implies a critical attitude toward King and his works.
At best, they attempt both to explain the tradition of horror fiction
and to locate King within the context of that tradition.

2   *Time* magazine's shift in attitude, to some degree, reflects a
corresponding shift in the halls of libraries, high schools, and colleges.
I don't mean to suggest that King is about to replace Shakespeare. I
do, however, want to suggest that a cultural phenomenon of such
proportions deserves scrutiny. Moreover, I want also to suggest that
a good number of the readers, fans, and critics of Stephen King, as do
Time's reporters, ignore what eventually may be regarded as the most
important book in the King corpus, Stephen King's *Danse Macabre*. This
book of quasi-criticism not only brings an interesting and sometimes
incisive critical vision to the work of horror, it also reveals an implicit
critical method which opens up a realm of interpretive possibilities
for popular fiction, film, and television. What I propose to do, then, is
to clarify King's discussion of critical method in his *Danse Macabre* and
then demonstrate how this method might apply in close readings of
[popular fiction].

3   The insight which King offers into the work of horror is based upon a bimodal or dualistic vision which insists upon the necessity of reading between the lines. The first mode or level which King describes is the "gross out" level—i.e., that level at which a cultural norm is violated for shock effect (4). Examples of the gross-out include Reagan's vomiting on the priest's face in *The Exorcist* or the monster in Frankenheimer's *The Prophecy* crunching off a helicopter pilot's head (4). The second and subtextual level – the level between the lines, so to speak—he describes is the artistic level (4), that is, a second level at which horror novels seek to probe "phobic pressure points" (4) which address archetypal, "political, economic, and psychological rather than supernatural fears" (5). Examples of this second and artistic level include the fear of death implicit in *Ghost Story* (262), the xenophobia implicit in Christopher Nybey's *The Thing* (152), and "economic unease" in *The Amityville Horror* (142). This second level, according to King, gives the work of horror its "pleasing allegorical feel" (5).

4   At this point, things become much less straightforward. King offers us little help in defining and understanding what he means by "pleasing allegorical feel." On one occasion, King treats allegory as a "symbolic way" of saying "things that we would be afraid to say right out straight" (31), a way for readers to "exercise emotions which society demands we keep closely in hand" (31). On another occasion he refers to the preceding notion of allegory as subtext or the "liaison formed between" our fantasies and our real fears (129). On still another occasion he talks about "symbols" and "symbolic mirrors" in general (144). And on other various occasions, he mentions "archetypes" (57) and "mass dreams" (144). Clearly, the pleasing allegorical feel about which King speaks has little to do with the allegory of the Middle Ages. The phrase, as he applies it, does not offer a system of symbology that extends and operates in the fashion of *The Pearl* or *The Romance of the Rose*. It is not a multi-modal system of symbols which offers the possibility of simultaneous interpretations on the literal, moral, anagogical, and allegorical levels.

5   Instead, the "pleasing allegorical feel" about which King speaks is a peculiar kind of psychological allegory, for the readings between the lines to which King invites us invariably discuss political, social, and economic anxieties of the contemporary individual. For example,

Carrie, according to King, is actually a feminist novel which confronts a young woman's psychic conflict when she attempts to live as a strong and autonomous individual in a culture that would prefer to see her as a passive and powerless piece of femininity (172). Moreover, *The Amityville Horror*, according to King, is really a story of economic unease which traces the demise of a young couple who buy a home they can't afford (142).

6   Once we recognize that King's bimodal vision of allegory places extraordinary emphasis upon hidden psychological anxieties or upon reading between the lines, we begin to see that a surprising number of parallels exist between the structure of King's allegory and the structure that Freud attributes to the dream. . . . Freud divides the dream into two basic levels of meaning just as King divides the work of horror into the levels of gross-out and subtext. The first and most obvious level of meaning in a dream, according to Freud, is the manifest or dream content-level (218). Physical experiences as recalled by the memory comprise this level. In other words, remembered movements, colors, sensations, and experiences compose the dream's first level of meaning. The second level of meaning in a dream, according to Freud, is the psychic or latent content level. Desires springing from the unconscious comprise this second level (218, 238). These desires, of course, invariably involve the wish-fulfillment of an infantile sexual impulse (495).

7   Both the systems of Freud and King, then, are bimodal. Moreover, both men argue that their bimodal systems result from the need of the individual to generate a superficial level of meaning which will disguise or hide a deeper and more disturbing level of meaning. King writes that horror fiction allows us to say "things that we would be afraid to say right out straight" (31), and Freud argues that the psyche creates the manifest content of the dream to "evade censorship" and to allow the dreamer to continue to sleep while expressing his suppressed and potentially disruptive desires (485). The schemes of both King and Freud, then, operate on the assumption that the surface level in either the work of horror or the dream generates its symbolic structure in order to protect the individual from the internal conflicts which he finds disruptive. . . . [T]he similarities between King's method for interpreting the work of horror and Freud's universal method for

interpreting dreams imply that King's critical method has applications extending far beyond the work of horror.

8   For instance, we do not need to scrutinize Ludlum's *The Bourne Identity* too closely in order to discover that it possesses the "pleasing allegorical feel" about which King speaks. On the gross-out or manifest level, the novel traces the odyssey of David Webb, alias Jason Bourne, who has experienced a total loss of memory while in the middle of a counter-insurgency spy mission designed to draw out and destroy the super assassin, Carlos. On the artistic or subtextual level, though, the novel explores the problem of human identity. In short, it asks the same question Christopher Lasch asks in his book, *The Minimal Self: Psychic Survival in Troubled Times*: has the invasion of "culture and personal life by the modern industrial system produced . . . A loss of autonomy . . . [And] a tendency to confuse self-identification with the exercise of consumer choices?" (41–42). Lasch's answer is a resounding yes. According to him we live in a narcissistic culture, that is, a culture in which the individual, like the Narcissus of Greek Myth, can no longer clearly distinguish between himself and his environment. Ludlum's answer to the question is also a resounding yes; and he, too, suggests that the individual who is self-reliant has at least a slight chance at independence and personal identity.

9   We can easily begin to support the notion that *The Bourne Identity* symbolically explores the problems of personal identity in an indifferent, or perhaps even hostile, technological world by first identifying, as did King and Freud, the incidents and characters in which everything the novel does well is "summed up" (King 143). And without a doubt, the novel's protagonist, David Webb, provides us with a perfect example of King's summing up . . . When Webb, alias Jason Bourne, nearly drowns at the outset of the novel, we encounter what I consider to be the key to understanding the story's subtextual discussion of the perils of personal identity.

> He felt the cold water envelop him, swallowing him, sucking him under . . . And there was heat, a strange moist heat at his temple that seared through the freezing water that kept swallowing him . . . He felt these things, acknowledging his own panic as he felt them. He could see his own body turning and twisting, arms and feet working

frantically against the pressures of the whirlpool . . . yet strangely
there was peace. It was the calm of the observer, the uninvolved
observer, separated from the events. . . . Then another form of panic
spread through him. . . . He could not submit to peace. Not yet. (14)

What you've just read, on the manifest level or the level of the gross-
out, is the description of the near-drowning of David Webb after he
has been wounded and washed overboard into a stormy sea. This
near-drowning, however, takes on new significance when we read
the comments made by Doctors Washburn and Panov. Washburn
clearly establishes Webb as a sort of white Anglo-Saxon everyman
when he describes Webb as "the prototype of the white Anglo-Saxon
people seen everyday on the bitter cricket fields, or the tennis court"
(22). At the conclusion of the novel, Doctor Panov expands Washburn's
guess at Webb's everyman role when he says, "In a way, he's [meaning
Webb] a functioning microcosm of us all. I mean, we're all trying to
find out who the hell we are, aren't we?" (522). In short, Ludlum has
condensed contemporary man into the character of David Webb.

10   Moreover, since the novel deals with the problems of an amnesiac
everyman trying to discover his true identity, we also realize that the
whirlpool and storm which threaten Webb represent much more than
the far-reaching horrors of immediate drowning. At the subtextual
level, in fact, these two elements of natural destruction actually serve
as metaphoric expressions of the individual's desire to relinquish his
personal identity. What tempts Webb is not the agony of drowning at
sea but the peace that follows the abandonment of the struggle to
survive. And what nearly kills Webb is not the sea itself but the calm
detachment which renders him apathetic to his condition. Once we
realize that the storm and the whirlpool have only drawn out attitudes
that were already present, we also realize that the emphasis in this
particular scene resides not in the physical presence of the sea but in
Webb's psyche. And since Webb functions as an everyman, we also
realize that we supposedly share in the same psychic weaknesses.
Consequently, we can then see evidence of the transference to which
King indirectly refers in his interpretation of *The Amityville Horror*, a
way of intensely expressing our fears of losing our identities. Reading
between the lines as King would, we also see, then, that a displacement
has occurred and that Webb's temptations and near-drowning

metaphorically express the contemporary American's temptations to abandon the struggle for personal identity in favour of the calm and peace of the unobtrusive and minimal self (Lasch 33–36).

11 Once we establish the subtextual concern of *The Bourne Identity* with the temptations and problems faced by the individual interested in developing an authentic personal identity, nearly every incident in the novel refashions and repeats the opening crisis of the near-drowning in Chapter 1. Indeed, Ludlum seems to run Webb through a checklist of institutions in order to demonstrate the inability of any institution to form an authentic personal identity. For instance, the novel opens with a "Preface" which offers two seemingly authentic news releases about the shadowy figure, Carlos. As we read through both releases, we see that in both instances these newspapers offer very little real information. In fact, the only thing about which we can be sure is that the newspapers are not sources of hard information or personal identity. Later on in the novel, Marie St. Jacques – the romantic interest – confirms our suspicions about newspapers when she says:

> "Both [stories] are constructed out of lies, the first connected to the second by tenuous speculation – public speculation – on a banking crisis that would never be made public. . . . And that second story – the patently false statement that millions were stolen from Gemeinschaft – was tacked onto the equally false story that I'm wanted for killing three men in Zurich." (278)

Newspapers in Ludlum's *The Bourne Identity* are sources of misinformation and are, therefore, incapable of aiding the individual in understanding either himself or his world.

12 *The Bourne Identity*, however, is democratic in its criticism. It not only damns the press, it also damns the military industrial complex and the United States government. In spite of an incredible amount of planning and an equally incredible amount of secrecy, the United States Government's plan to trap Carlos falls apart because government officers, due to circumstances beyond even their control, can no longer make sense of what has happened to Webb (292). Not only did their scenario fail to consider the possibility of Webb's injury, it also failed to consider Webb as a human being. Consequently, they are invariably puzzled by Webb's actions, largely because he has forgotten the identity they manufactured for him and has begun to act according to a set of internal values that emphasize love and loyalty. Furthermore, once Webb begins to operate consistently on a set of values, he also begins to abandon his chameleon-like identity for an identity which is both personal and authentic.

13 Ludlum's criticism of institutions as potential sources of personal identity extends beyond newspapers and government to include even the sacred cows of banking and medicine. For instance, Webb begins his search for identity at a bank in Zurich, believing somehow that the factual nature of his relationship with the bank will help him overcome his amnesia. Ironically, just the opposite happens. Once in the bank, Webb mistakes his alias, Jason, for his real name. He also wrongly surmises that the codename, Treadstone, is the name of a business firm for which he works. He also mistakenly believes that Mr. Koenig, an employee of the bank, is trustworthy. At the root of these three mistakes, however, we find one truly serious mistake, that is the assumption that a bank and money can somehow help him discover who he is. Although the newspapers, government, and Swiss Bank are all venerable institutions promoting the established order, they cannot provide our everyman with an authentic identity.

14 Doctors and medicine are also inadequate sources of the individual's identity — they are far too materialistic and quantitative. However, both Doctor Washburn and Doctor Panov seem to understand that their profession is limited and that the individual alone must be the source of his personal identity. Washburn warns Webb early on that the task he is about to undertake is not easy and that he alone must be the source of his identity. He says:

> "I think I know what's going through your mind. A sense of helplessness; of drifting without a rudder to put you on course. I've been your rudder, and I won't be with you; there's nothing I can do about that. But believe me when I tell you, you are not helpless. You will find your way." (35)

15 Washburn's metaphor of the ship and rudder, of course, harkens back to the opening metaphors of the sea and the whirlpool in Chapter

1, and his statement is essentially a reaffirmation of Webb's earlier decision to brave the storm and whirlpool rather than to abandon himself to the whims of circumstance. Panov, at the end of the novel, makes a similar kind of assertion. He says:

> "I've too much respect for the human mind to deal you chicken soup psychology; there's too damn much of it floating around in the wrong hands. . . . It's true we can go in with a knife and reach the storm centres, reduce the anxieties, bring a kind of peace to him. Even bring him back to what he was, perhaps. But it's not the kind of peace he wants. . . ." (522)

16 In other words, Washburn and Panov both recognize that authentic personal identity resides not in institutions but in the individual and his attempts to confront the turmoil of life. Indeed, Ludlum's novel, *The Bourne Identity*, and Christopher Lasch's book, *The Minimal Self*, both seem to advise us that authentic personal identity resides not in the lobotomized peace of a minimal and chameleon self but in the tension and struggle of the individual to balance his individuality against the claims that nature and society make upon him.

17 It takes little imagination to realize that the list of popular [books,] films, and programs to which we can apply Stephen King's method of interpretation could go on and on. Indeed, the possibilities for reading between the lines seem endless. Of more consequence, perhaps, is the realization that works of popular culture, if they are to be understood and appreciated for what they are, should be subject to continuously critical reading and viewing — the very kind of reading and viewing that King advocates in his *Danse Macabre*. Consequently, it seems to me that King is far too modest in his discussion of the existence of the subtextual or the allegorical in horror fiction. He may well have been able to argue that the pleasing allegorical feel found in horror fiction is also found in many popular American movies, novels, and television programs and that works of popular culture often provide a quiet forum in which the viewers and readers of America symbolically address serious concerns of the day.

WORKS CITED

Booth, Cathy, and Stefan Kanfer. "King of Horror." *Time* 6 Oct. 1986: 74–83.

Freud, Sigmund. *The Interpretation of Dreams*. New York: Vintage, 1900.

Gray, Paul. "Master of Postliterate Prose," *Time* 30 Aug. 1982: 87.

King, Stephen. *Stephen King's Danse Macabre*. New York: Everest House, 1981.

Lasch, Christopher. *The Minimal Self: Psychic Survival in Troubled Times*. New York: Norton, 1984.

Ludlum, Robert. *The Bourne Identity*. New York: Marek, 1980.

JENNIFER MITCHELL

Indian Princess #134: Cultural Assimilation at St. Joseph's Mission

1   Throughout the 1800s, many religious organizations proselytized throughout Canada to convert all persons of other faiths, particularly Aboriginal peoples. In 1866, the Catholic Church opened a mission in the heart of the interior of British Columbia, approximately twelve miles southwest of Williams Lake. St. Joseph's Mission was built and run by the Oblates of Mary Immaculate. Its main objective was "to bring the Indian to lead a Christian life" (Whitehead, 1981, p. 19). Over the next century, until St. Joseph's Mission closed in the 1980s, it became an industrial boarding school for Native children. Leaving their Native heritage behind, the children at St. Joseph's learned prayer, reading, writing, and, most of all, the Euro-Canadian lifestyle. According to the missionaries, the objective was "to raise [the Indians] to the level of the whites" (Haig-Brown, 1988, p. 29). The Roman Catholic Church and the Canadian government cooperated in this endeavour, as both presumed to understand what was in the best interest of the "savage" Indians.

2   There is a growing body of scholarship on residential schools in B.C. and throughout Canada. In *Resistance and Renewal: Surviving the Indian Residential School* (1988), Celia Haig-Brown studies the effects residential school life has had on Natives who attended residential institutions in B.C. between 1907 and 1967, focusing mainly on the Kamloops Residential School. In *Victims of Benevolence: The Dark Legacy of the Williams Lake Residential School* (1992), Elizabeth Furniss discusses two tragic events in the history of the Williams Lake Residential School, the institution at issue here. Other studies include J.R. Miller's *Shingwauk's Vision* (1996) and John S. Milloy's *A National Crime* (1999).

Drawing on Haig-Brown and Furniss in particular, this essay examines cultural assimilation at St. Joseph's Mission, with an emphasis on the experiences of my mother, Beverley Mitchell. First, I will discuss the history of the residential school system. Second, I will concentrate on life at St. Joseph's Mission school. Third, I will comment on the long-term effects residential schools have had on the children who attended them. My paper will demonstrate that attendance at St. Joseph's Mission negatively affected the cultural identity of the Native children who were schooled there, including my mother.

Methods
3   Interviews with my mother, Beverley Mitchell, are an integral part of my research. At her birth in Williams Lake, B.C., in 1954, she was given the name Mary Bob. Beverley attended St. Joseph's Residential Mission (also known as the Williams Lake Residential School), from the time she was four years old until she was eight years old. There she was given the first name of "Beverley," as there were too many children with the Christian name of "Mary." Later on in life, she changed her name to Beverley Marie, "to have my own identity." She arrived at the mission in 1958 and did not leave until 1961. Beverley is from the Sugar Cane Band of Williams Lake and is of Shuswap (Secwepemc) ancestry. Interviews with Beverley, about her experience at St. Joseph's, were conducted at her home in Fort St. John, over a two-day period between October 19–20, 2001.

An Historical Overview of the Residential School System
4   The Canadian government and the Roman Catholic Church worked together to assimilate the Native population into a supposedly more civilized and superior European style of living. Furniss (1992) notes that the state saw the Natives' way of life as something to be destroyed and absorbed into mainstream culture, a process that would resolve the "Indian problem" (p. 13). Furniss adds that the Federal government sought to transform all Native peoples into a physical and cultural image that was more pleasing to Euro-Canadian sensibilities (p. 16). The common ideal of the Catholic Church and Canadian officials was to assimilate the Native culture as quickly as possible.

5   The policy of assimilation was formally adopted in the *Indian Act* of 1880. This *Act* was initially created by the Canadian government as

a 25-year plan for the liquidation of the "Indian problem," the elimination of the Indian culture, and the eradication of Indians from Canadian society. The goal was clearly expressed in a statement made by a government official in the 1920s:

> Our objective is to continue until there is not a single Indian in Canada that has not been absorbed into the body politic and there is no Indian question, and no Indian department, that is the whole objective of this Bill. (Haig-Brown, 1988, p. 32)

The *Act* also made it illegal for Natives to practice their cultural traditions. As part of the assimilation process, Native children were required to attend day schools or industrial boarding schools (Haig-Brown, 1988, p. 31).

6   The government of Canada provided the Catholic Church with funds for the operation of residential schools. The benefits of collaborating on Indian education were two-fold: for the government, it was a cost-effective way to eliminate Native culture without being directly involved; for the missionaries, cooperation was a way to manage schools as they saw fit (Furniss, 1992, pp. 26, 27). Thus, the government clearly supported the missionaries in their role as front-line workers in the assimilation of the Indian, a process that involved aggressively Christianizing and civilizing the "Other."

7   The priests, nuns, and teachers who ran the missionary schools were devout in the Christian belief that the second coming of Christ would occur only when the gospel had been spread throughout the world (Furniss, 1992, p. 16). Moreover, Native culture had to be destroyed if there were to be any chance of saving the Natives' souls, an objective that the missionaries saw as being in the Native peoples' best interest. The salvation of the Native people depended on their acceptance of Christianity and on their renunciation of pagan beliefs. Furniss (1992) notes that the missionaries felt it was crucial to remove the Native children from their homes and families, influences that were viewed as deleterious to cultural adjustment. According to Haig-Brown (1988), the resulting segregation of children and families reveals the invasive nature of the missionaries' work (p. 35). Native children were taught the European way of life on a live-in, full-time basis.

Life at St. Joseph's

8 Mission schools were intentionally situated away from Native communities and families, and St. Joseph's Mission was no exception. A bus would routinely pick up children attending the school. According to Haig-Brown (1988), this bus was originally called the "school truck" and, later, the "cattle truck." The arrival of this bus often involved Native peoples' introduction into a way of life that was dramatically different from the one they had always known. Native children began to recognize and fear the mission school bus and its arrival in their community (pp. 47, 48). Indeed, Beverley remembers the bus in a negative light: "[A] bus came and got us and took us to the mission. I never left for four years. No one came to get me; no one came to visit me" (personal communication, Oct. 19, 20, 2001). Beverley finds this memory, of the bus taking her away from her home, especially vivid. Others who attended residential schools have similar memories of a first bus ride (Haig-Brown, 1998, p. 48). Perhaps the memory is so vivid because the experience marked the loss of home and family.

9 Given their distance from Native communities, residential schools limited the contact between children and families. Furniss (1992) explains that the Oblates saw "the physical removal of children from their families and communities [as] a central ingredient of the residential school system" (p. 51). Beverley remembers that there were older students at St. Joseph's who told her that they had been her age when they first arrived there. The school went up to grade eight and the children would not be allowed to leave until they had completed grade eight. Beverley cannot recall a time at St. Joseph's that her mother was allowed to visit her. She recalls receiving a gift from her mother only once during her stay at the mission: one Christmas she received a plastic candy cane filled with chocolates. She had no other contact with her family in her four-year stay (personal communication, Oct. 19, 20, 2001). This form of segregation was normal within residential schools in British Columbia. Distancing Native children from their families, including siblings at the same school, was seen as beneficial to the missionary goal of bringing Natives into Euro-Canadian society.

10 Upon their arrival at the mission, Native children were immediately submerged in a lifestyle alarmingly different from their own. Haig-Brown (1988) reveals that Shuswap children were taught by watching and learning, with no real time constraints or schedules (p. 37). Conversely, virtually every moment of the students' time at the missionary schools was under constant supervision and direction (Haig-Brown, 1988, p. 47). When asked what she spent most of her time doing at the mission, Beverley described a typical weekday:

> We got up at five in the morning, we got dressed and made our bed. It was like in barracks, if you didn't do it right they'd rip it all up. We washed, got dressed, brushed our teeth, went to pray. Then we went to breakfast and to school. School was like a regular school day. Then we were done and we'd have some free time to play in the playroom. Then you had supper. Then you went to church, and to bed. Probably around nine at night we'd go to bed. (personal communication, Oct. 19, 20, 2001)

This regimented style of living and learning marked a drastic change from the relaxed, participation-and-example approach to living that Shuswap children had been used to.

11   As Native children lost the way of life they had known, they also lost all sense of personal identity. Haig-Brown (1988) notes that upon the children's arrival at the mission school, "personal identification became a number written in ink on [the children's] wrists and [on their] cupboards, where they stored their few belongings" (p. 48). Beverley's memories of lining up to get a laundry roll once a week support Haig-Brown's observation. Beverley recalls that the roll consisted of fresh sheets, a pillowcase, a clean uniform, and underwear: "[Y]ou stood in line to pick up your roll, with your number on it. I was number 134; if you forgot your number you were in big trouble" (personal communication, Oct. 19, 20, 2001). In effect, then, in reducing the children to mere numbers, the missionaries redefined their identities.

12   In addition to isolating Native children, missionaries also sought to transform them through discipline. According to Furniss (1992), this was very clear in the Oblates of St. Joseph's educational philosophy: "Strict discipline, regimented behavior, submission to authority, and corporal punishment were to be the central characteristics of education" (p. 49). Thus, the missionaries shared the popular belief that physical punishment was a perfectly acceptable tool for teaching, and they made this strategy a central component in the assimilation of Native people.

13 Since teaching Catholicism to the Natives was an important part of the missionary objectives, prayer was a large part of the students' day-to-day lives. Beverley recalls praying for two to three hours every morning, then again at breakfast and dinner. She recalls praying at least four times a day and remembers that Sundays were reserved solely for prayer. Beverley recollects:

> I was howling one time. I was howling so bad, one of the nuns gave me a cookie. They never gave out cookies. It was unheard of. I was four years old and had been on my knees praying for two hours. I was in pain. (personal communication, Oct. 19, 20, 2001)

To worsen the confusion, prayers were often given in Latin. Thus, children who could not understand English were subjected to yet another language in church. Haig-Brown (1988) explains that Native children would suffer through prayers in silence and confusion or reap the punishment dealt them (p. 59). Moreover, this schedule was followed regardless of a child's understanding or previous belief system.

14 An integral part of the mission schools' focus on cultural suppression and assimilation involved the ultimate extinction of the Native languages. Haig-Brown (1988) states that the missionaries felt that the Native children should be made to speak English, not through formal instruction, but by hearing English and being forced to speak it themselves. Haig-Brown further asserts that upon their arrival at the mission, Native children were not permitted, and were even forbidden, to speak their Native language, even though many of the children knew no other form of speech. Deviation from the rule was dealt with strictly and harshly (pp. 56–57). A particularly harsh punishment involved pushing sewing needles through the tongues of children caught speaking their language (Haig-Brown, 1988, p.16). This was a routine form of punishment for language offenders in several residential schools, and Beverley remembers observing this practice during her stay at St. Joseph's. Beverley recalls another common form of corporal punishment: "If you spoke your own language, the nuns

would punch you in the face and would often pull your ears." Other children who attended residential schools concur that there was no transition time to learn and to understand the new language (Haig-Brown, 1988, p. 82). By striking at Native languages, missionaries undermined the very base of Aboriginal cultures.

15 Furthermore, missionaries gained the obedience of Native students through punishment that incorporated public humiliation. Beverley recalls that, at St. Joseph's, the nuns commonly spanked children who had wet their sheets. The nuns would further induce shame by making the children wear the soiled sheets on their heads, in front of everyone. In other cases, the soiled sheets were put back on the beds until change day (personal communication, Oct. 19, 20, 2001). Another form of public humiliation involved public head-shavings (Haig-Brown, 1988, p. 84). Given traditional associations, this form of punishment was among the most embarrassing. Beverley recollects an incident when she had been berry-picking with a small group led by a few nuns. She did not hear the whistle that was blown as a signal for everyone to return and line up. According to Beverley,

> They cut my hair because they said I tried to run away. I didn't hear it [the whistle], so they made me stand on a stool in front of everyone and they cut all my hair off, then they shaved my head. (personal communication, Oct. 19, 20, 2001)

The humiliation and shame caused by these public displays have lingered in the minds of St. Joseph's students, even much later in their lives.

16 Poor food, food shortages, and constant hunger were as common at St. Joseph's as punishment and humiliation. Haig-Brown (1988) recounts the stories of children who remember drinking blue milk and eating rotten fish-stew on Fridays. Such meals were staples at the residential schools. "If you're hungry enough," one child explained, "a person will eat anything" (pp. 60, 69). For her part, Beverley recalls drinking milk that had gone so bad it was lumpy and had a bluish tinge to it, and everyone called it "blue milk." Nevertheless, they had no choice but to drink. Beverley has particularly vivid memories of one dinner at St. Joseph's:

> It was Friday and they made fish-head stew and it stunk to high heaven. I'm sure it was all rotten. "Fish Friday" they called it. They made this stew, it just smelled so awful. I thought, "I can't eat this," and she came and whacked me on the head and said, "Eat." So I went to eat and I got some of it down, and I puked. I puked back into my bowl, she saw me do it too and when everyone got up from the rows to leave, she came over and put her hand on my shoulder and said, "You'll stay until you eat it." I sat there all night and all the next day. I finally ate it, I finished it. To this day if I smell fish I want to be sick. (personal communication, Oct. 19, 20, 2001)

Furniss (1992) observes that although school officials initially cited a lack of government funding as the reason for such a poor diet, neither the nuns nor the priests showed any remorse at the paltry portions and often rancid food that was served to the children. The missionaries themselves, meanwhile, had their own cooks who served them their meals in a separate dining room (pp. 18, 61). Thus, food shortages among the student populace did not appear to have any effect on the missionaries of St. Joseph's.

17 Another painful aspect of the residential school system was the eventual return home. What should have been a happy time was often rife with stress, confusion, and emotional pain as students who had been forced to learn one way of life were suddenly thrown back into another, which, by then, they barely understood or remembered. The problem was particularly prevalent in children who began their residency at a young age and did not go home in the summertime. Beverley remembers when her mother came to get her:

> There was this strange woman standing there. I remember thinking that she was a very beautiful woman. She was what I thought an Indian Princess would look exactly like. I was hiding behind the nun because she had come with a white man, and I think you naturally come to fear the white man there. I went with her kicking and screaming. They said, "You're going with your mom," which meant nothing to me. I hadn't known anyone else since I was four and she was a stranger to me, with a white man. The word "mom" meant nothing to me, and I was supposed to go with them. (personal communication, Oct. 19, 20, 2001)

Beverley's memory suggests the extent to which practices at missionary schools dissociated children from their families.

The Long-Term Effects of Residential Schools

18   For former students, the long-term effects of residential schools are potentially devastating. Beverley has found that many of the things she does today are in some way related to the treatment she was subjected to at St. Joseph's. For example, Beverley finds changes in her routine very disconcerting. She attributes this to the strictly ordered existence that she followed while living at St. Joseph's Mission (personal communication, Oct. 19, 20, 2001). Other students, such as Randy Fred of the Port Alberni Residential School, turned to alcohol or to other forms of abuse in an effort to cope with the past (Haig-Brown, 1988, pp. 15–24). Children who have attended residential schools also try to cope with their experience by blocking much of it out. Beverley herself has used this psychological device: "It's like you lose so much time in your life because you block it out. You suppress it so bad, so it's like it didn't exist until you face up to it." In a related way, Beverley also recalls that for most of her adult life she did not directly relate herself to the child who attended St. Joseph's. She set herself apart from that period in her life by imagining the little girl to whom bad things had happened as someone else (personal communication, Oct. 19, 20, 2001). Thus, in their adult lives, many former residential school children struggle to find ways of coping with what they have endured in their pasts.

19   The contrast between Catholic beliefs and traditional spirituality in Aboriginal communities is also a cause of much present-day confusion among those who attended residential schools. Haig-Brown (1988) notes that some students have been able to combine the two forms of worship into a belief system that they are comfortable with, but others have abandoned religion and spirituality altogether (p. 122). When asked why she still believes in Christianity, Beverley replied, "[B]ecause it's ingrained in you every day from a young age so much that, how can you not? I need to believe in something, and maybe now not their Christianity, but in God and The Creator. We were taught religion for hours every day, how could you not believe" (personal communication, Oct. 19, 20, 2001).

20 Summarizing her life at St. Joseph's, Beverley does not recall ever feeling loved or cared for by the nuns:

> No, not ever. That's not what they were about, not part of what we were there for, I guess. I never thought about it or missed it much. I was too busy trying to do what they wanted and stay out of trouble. I was too busy being hungry and trying to take care of myself to think too much about love, or miss it much, I guess. (personal communication, Oct. 19, 20, 2001)

Beverley adds that having to spend a period of her life with her feelings shut off is probably a reason why she cares so much and shows love so freely now (personal communication, Oct. 19, 20, 2001). Nevertheless, in reflecting on St. Joseph's and its effects on her, there are a few things today that awaken old fears in Beverley. Because the nuns wore heavy rosary beads that rattled when they walked, whenever Beverley hears beads rattle today, the hair stands up on the back of her neck. Similarly, whenever Beverley walks by a shoe store, she is reminded of getting only one pair of shoes a year at St. Joseph's, regardless of how much she grew. Beverley also recalls her feelings of helplessness when the nuns were hurting other kids; she recalls wanting so much to help them but knowing what would happen to her if she did.

Conclusion

21 In British Columbia, the last residential school closed in the 1980s. Ten years after this last closure, the leaders of St. Joseph's Mission formally apologized for the damage that residential schools have inflicted upon Native communities (Furniss, 1992, pp. 31, 32). Nevertheless, many church officials continue to defend the residential school system. Moreover, there has yet to be any public apology or acceptance of responsibility on the part of the Canadian government for its role in funding these institutions and making assimilation a part of Canadian law.

22 Through corporal punishment, humiliation, destruction of language, segregation, prayer, and other tactics, the missionaries of residential schools, including St. Joseph's, tried to destroy Native culture. In doing so, they created confusion about identity, faith, and personal self-worth among the Native students. As they turned into

42

DESIGNS FOR DISCIPLINES

adults, many of these former students felt they did not belong in the society they had been pushed into. Today, this confusion still manifests itself in self-loathing, self-destruction, alcoholism, and other abuses.

23 Beverley, however, has been lucky in many ways. Even though it has taken her many years to begin to heal, she has, indeed, begun this long journey. Realizing her long-ago wish to help other children, she now works as a teacher's aide for Native students. Moreover, in coming forward with her own story, Beverley might help other Native people understand their experiences at residential schools. Indeed, courageous individuals like Beverley are bringing to light events that have been buried in the past for much too long.

REFERENCES

Furniss, E. (1992). *Victims of benevolence: The dark legacy of the Williams Lake Residential School.* Vancouver: Arsenal Pulp Press.

Haig-Brown, C. (1988). *Resistance and renewal: Surviving the Indian residential school.* Vancouver: Secwepemc Cultural Education Society.

Miller, J.R. (1996). *Shingwauk's vision: A history of Native residential schools.* Toronto: University of Toronto Press.

Milloy, J.S. (1999). *"A national crime": The Canadian government and the residential school system, 1879 to 1986.* Winnipeg: University of Manitoba Press.

Whitehead, M. (1981). *The Cariboo Mission: A history of the Oblates.* Vancouver: Sono Nis Press.

Scholarly Conclusions

The end crowns the work.
— Anonymous

Perhaps the major function of conclusions in the humanities and social sciences is to confirm what has already been said. For this reason, many conclusions in fields such as English or sociology do not labour under the kind of intense knowledge-making burdens that introductions are prone to. That is, putting the finishing touches on an argument may not be quite as difficult as getting the argument under way. If we were to describe the situation in slightly more sophisticated language, we could say that scholarly conclusions may not be under quite as much *epistemological pressure* as scholarly introductions.

Nevertheless, conclusions perform an important rhetorical function. As the writer's last chance to clarify his or her contribution to knowledge, conclusions represent what a reader is left with. Moreover, conclusions can do more than simply repeat or confirm knowledge. Sometimes, for example, writers in the humanities and social sciences choose not to present their overarching knowledge claim or thesis until the end of the paper, so that conclusions provide a *delayed thesis*. This strategy can contribute to the appearance of objectivity: evidence is considered before a position is sharply drawn. Other things can happen in scholarly conclusions, too. Readers may encounter *solutions to a problem*, a *call to action*, a *statement of relevance*, and *questions for further research*. Once again, academic writers can choose from a set of rhetorical features — in this case, rhetorical features that typically appear in the discourse of scholarly last words. Thus, just like introductions, conclusions merit close attention.

The remainder of this discussion identifies, more precisely, the particular rhetorical features commonly present in scholarly conclusions. As was the case with introductions, these features are not mutually exclusive; any given conclusion may incorporate one or more of the following gestures.

REPEATING OR INITIATING KNOWLEDGE CLAIMS

We already know that conclusions may repeat or initiate a thesis. In either case, the presentation of a thesis may also be accompanied by a review of main points in the core of the paper. Thus, conclusions can offer a brief summary of the knowledge that a writer has to offer. When this summary function occurs in a conclusion, scholars often pay particular attention to marking out the limits of their knowledge. Accordingly, we might expect to encounter a range of hedging or qualifying words, constructions that Janet Giltrow has identified as *limiting expressions*. Note the tables below, which have been adapted from Giltrow's book *Academic Writing* (2002, pp. 290–1):

Limiting Adverbs and Auxiliaries	
allegedly	apparently
roughly	generally
ostensibly	approximately
particularly	evidently
presumably	probably

rarely	possibly
hardly	perhaps
sometimes	usually
most	some
partly	often
typically	somewhat
could	might
ought to	appears
seems	may

Limiting Metadiscursive Verbs

I believe	I think
I sense	I feel
I attempt	I claim
I infer	I speculate
I suppose	

Limiting Prepositional Phrases

in part	to a lesser extent
at least	in one case/in this case/ in some cases
in the sense that	in one sense
for me	to me

The frequency of limiting expressions in academic writing defies the standard advice that is often given to students in basic composition courses: make bold and forceful claims. Conventional wisdom says that to waffle is bad! However, here are some real examples of scholars hedging their bets. Limiting expressions are italicized.

The first sample is taken from biology:

David Hamer

Forest Fire's Influence on Yellow Hedysarum Habitat and Its Use by Grizzly Bears in Banff National Park, Alberta

The high density of hedysarum shoots in the 2 burns *may* have no biological significance given that typically only a small fraction of available plants are dug by grizzly bears. Mattson (1997) found that biscuitroot density contributed little to distinguishing dug from undug biscuitroot sites in the Yellowstone ecosystem. However, *it is possible that* greater hedysarum density increases the *likelihood* of hedysarum growing or being abundant in specific microhabitat preferentially dug by bears, owing to a greater ease of digging or other factors. In addition, high hedysarum density *could* result in bears exposing more than one taproot per excavation. This *could be* important in late autumn when bears *appear to have* difficulty digging frozen ground. At this time bears *sometimes* enlarge a single excavation rather than break into the frozen topsoil of a new digging site, and can be observed enlarging the same excavation for > 1 h (Hamer and Herrero 1983, p. 138). [italics added]

The next sample comes from cultural studies in the humanities:

Arild Fetveit
Reality TV in the Digital Era: A Paradox in Visual Culture?

I have *suggested* that reality TV, itself, *might be* read partly as a symptom of unsettled issues in this transmutation. More precisely, it *might* express a longing for a lost touch with reality, prompted by the undermining and problematizing of indexicality. Not only does reality TV powerfully reclaim the evidential quality of photography said to be lost after digitalization, it also *seems to be* obsessed with conveying a sense of connectedness, of contact with the world—a trait that also, albeit on a less tangible psychological level, *might seem to be* lost in an era where silicon has replaced the silver of Daguerre and Talbot. [italics added]

Alternatively, scholars may be equally concerned about expressing their sense of certainty. Thus, depending on the degree of a writer's sureness, we might also expect to encounter *markers of obviousness*. Note the table below, which, once again, has been adapted from Janet Giltrow's work (2002, pp. 292–4):

Markers of Obviousness

certainly	it is evident that
surely	obviously
undoubtedly	of course
without question	overwhelmingly
decidedly	clearly

The following example is from art studies. The emphasis here is on certainty, but do you see any examples of hedging?

Ann Davis
A Study in Modernism: The Group of Seven
as an Unexpectedly Typical Case

The Group of Seven were *clearly* conservative modernists, skeptical of the artistic modes of the past, dedicated to creating a new, autonomous Canadian aesthetic. While trumpeting stylistic autonomy in their painting, the group usually retained enough forms and colours to allow the viewer a representational reading. At the same time their ideology was *thoroughly* objective and intuitive, based on mystical principles. These traits *firmly* link the Group of Seven to European modernism. [italics added]

In the next example, from history, we see a more evenly distributed mix of hedging and certainty.

David Peterson del Mar
Pimping and Courtship: A 1940 Court Case
from Northern British Columbia

If one does not expect to find prostitutes and pimps in love, one does not expect to find them in small towns. British Columbians have *usually* associated rural areas with innocence and virtue, not vice and immorality. The court case explored here *suggests* that prostitution, pimping, and

> courtship violence has a history in urban and rural North America alike,
> although locale has *certainly* shaped the nature of that history. [italics
> added]

Exploring Solutions to a Problem

On occasion, conclusions will explore solutions to a problem that
has been identified and demonstrated in the core of the paper.

Heather Castleden
The Silent North: A Case Study on
Deafness in a Dene Community

During formal and informal interviews with participants, the [Dene]
community revealed a desire to reestablish relationships, remove
communication and cultural barriers, and create an accessible
environment for all community members. All the participants, regardless
of their professional or personal relationship with [a young Dene boy
who is deaf], were emphatic about the need for better resources, supports,
and services in their community and across the territory. The family and
the community also commented on the importance of conducting this
study to serve the interests of other northern parents of deaf children in
isolated communities. The need was clearly expressed for improved
resources, services, and supports in their community and across the
territory, not only for deafness in children, but also hearing loss in young
adults and Elders. Further, during the course of the study, several
suggestions from the community were offered that would operationalize
coverage of the gaps in service. These recommendations indicate that
there are viable local solutions to local problems, and in this case the
community has concrete ideas for creating culturally specific and relevant
supports and resources for deafness.

Call to Action

Conclusions may also present a call for action, encouraging readers
to address a problem. At times, a call to action may be closely related
to exploring solutions to a problem, but we suggest that the former
tends to make a direct appeal to the reader. The following example is
from Native studies.

Marie Battiste, Lynne Bell, and L.M. Findlay
Decolonizing Education in Canadian Universities:
An Interdisciplinary, International Indigenous Research Project

Indigenous experience of education and its outcomes can be transformed only through the appropriate recognition and teaching of Indigenous knowledge. We can and must make this happen, speedily and effectively, for the benefit of all Canadians. Otherwise, we will have disappointed not only . . . ourselves, but also every child and adult learner in every instructional venue across this land.

The next example is from counselling psychology:

June Slakov and Mary Leslie
A Creative Model for a Post-Treatment
Group for Women with Cancer

We cannot take away the uncertainty or fear that characterizes this time after treatment [of women with cancer], but we can support the process of confronting the fear and facing one's mortality. We can introduce skills and a perspective to help anchor the participants in present reality and to hold uncertainty in a transformed way. While the experience of cancer is different for each woman, "borderland" will be part of the rest of their lives, as the possibility of recurrence is always with them.

Providing a Statement of Relevance

As previously noted, statements of relevance may occur in introductions, but they are perhaps most at home in conclusions. If introductions often lead *into* a topic by providing contextual information that functions as background, conclusions frequently lead *out* by providing contextual information that tells us why we should care about the author's research.

Thus, we could say that statements of relevance recontextualize topic and thesis by pointing toward a bigger, *moral* picture that lies beyond the immediate research domain (Giltrow, 2002, pp. 15, 314).

In this sense, statements of relevance tend to reveal a concern for the collective welfare. Such gestures seem to bridge the gap between highly focused or specialized scholarly activity and the lives of people beyond the academy.

The following example is from political science:

Michael Orsini
The Politics of Naming, Blaming, and Claiming:
HIV, Hepatitis C and the Emergence of Blood Activism in Canada

This article views the emergence of blood-tainted blood activism in Canada, especially among victims of Hepatitis C, through the lens of social movement theory. While blood-tainted victims were a difficult constituency to mobilize, they did so successfully and in a short time, securing not only compensation victories for victims but influencing the decision to overhaul Canada's blood system. This article sought to expand our understanding of public inquiries as sites for contestation over meaning. Inquiries not only provide a forum for groups to express their interest, but as Jane Jensen has explained, they also contribute to the ways in which these interests are re-articulated. . . . While victims were "successful" in securing compensation — a "textbook" outcome — they also succeeded in creating a collective identity for tainted-blood victims and altering public notions of the proper role of "sick" people in society.

The next example is from composition studies:

Wendy Bishop
Suddenly Sexy: Creative Non-Fiction Rear-Ends Composition

I believe the recent and continuing discussions taking place between composition and creative writing at, on, and about [the issue of creative non-fiction] have the possibility of infusing our classrooms with needed energy and offer a chance for teachers and students, together, to sideshadow the future in a manner that will allow them to discover what they don't yet know, to clarify what they don't yet understand, to preserve what they value, and to share their discoveries with others while writing essays that matter.

Presenting Opportunities for Further Research

The emphasis in some conclusions is on suggestions for further research. In this sense, papers may end as they begin, by identifying a *knowledge deficit*. For example, in "Ecological Classification, Status, and Management of the Gray Wolf, *Canis lupus*, in Canada," John Theberge identifies a number of further studies that need to be undertaken in order to assess Canadian wolf populations. In this sample, we again dip into the sciences:

John Theberge
Ecological Classification, Status, and Management of the Gray Wolf, *Canis lupus*, in Canada

Relevant conservation questions that come out of the foregoing review are: (1) whether the small extent of protection described here as existing for the wolf in Canada is adequate given developmental and exploitative pressures and Canada's place internationally; (2) whether more area-specific kill regulations are warranted wherever kill levels approach the danger threshold as explained, and especially for the Hardwood-Boreal Wolf whose range is under considerable pressure, as well as ecotypes on the southern periphery of the species' range; (3) whether existing protected areas need buffer wolf protection zones around them to ensure they accomplish their purposes; (4) what are research priorities, what constitutes ethically acceptable research, and who should fund it?

The following example comes from counseling psychology:

Shann R. Ferch and Marleen I. Ramsey
Sacred Conversation: A Spiritual Response to Unavoidable Suffering

Although clients have consistently reported experiencing a greater sense of personal development and relief from their suffering, we re-emphasize that empirical studies are needed to investigate the effectiveness of empathy, intentional forgiveness, and Sacred Conversation in relieving unavoidable suffering. Systematic, quantitative, and qualitative studies investigating the role of Sacred Conversation will bring greater understanding to how the approach enhances an individual's ability to create transcendent meaning from suffering and bring relief to physical and psychological pain. Survey research delineating the nature of this approach, along with experimental research measuring outcomes of the approach with regard to curative effects in anxiety, depression, stress, anger, and immunodeficiency levels are warranted. Phenomenological studies revealing the meaning of the approach for individuals and families are also warranted. Such studies will provide an important bridge toward clinical discernment with regard to suffering, emotion, and transcendent meaning.

IDEAS FOR FURTHER STUDY

1. Think about the precise way in which you might wish to recap the argument in your paper, especially with regard to limiting expressions and markers of obviousness. Also think about employing other rhetorical features typically found in academic conclusions, such as exploring solutions to a problem, statements of relevance, and questions for further research.

2. Identify the rhetorical features in the conclusion to the article that follows.

CHAPTER REFERENCES

Bishop, W. (2003). Suddenly sexy: Creative non-fiction rear-ends composition. *College English, 65*(3), 257–275.

Castleden, H. (2002). The silent north: A case study on deafness in a Dene community. *Canadian Journal of Native Education, 26*(2), 152–168.

Davis, A. (1998). A study in modernism: The Group of Seven as an unexpectedly typical case. *Journal of Canadian Studies, 33*(1), 108–121.

Del Mar, D.P. (1998). Pimping and courtship: A 1940 court case from northern British Columbia. In R. Sandwell (Ed.), *Beyond city limits: Rural history in British Columbia* (pp. 212–224). Vancouver, BC: UBC Press.

Ferch, S.R., & Ramsey, M.I. (2003). Sacred conversation: A spiritual response to unavoidable suffering. *Canadian Journal of Counselling, 37*(1), 16–27.

Fetveit, A. (1999). Reality TV in the digital era: A paradox in visual culture? *Media, Culture & Society, 21,* 787–804.

Giltrow, J. (2002). *Academic writing: Writing and reading in the disciplines.* 3rd ed. Peterborough: Broadview Press.

Orsini, M. (2002). The politics of naming, blaming and claiming: HIV, Hepatitis C and the emergence of blood activism in Canada. *Canadian Journal of Political Science, 35*(3), 475–498.

Theberge, J.B. (1991). Ecological classification, status, and management of the Gray Wolf, *Canis lupus,* in Canada. *The Canadian Field-Naturalist, 105*(4), 1–5.

INTRODUCTION TO THE READINGS

The paper by Laurie Dressler presents another outstanding example of student research, involving work in the archives of a local museum.

LAURIE DRESSLER

Harnessing the Peace: Economic and Environmental Themes Amid Public Responses to the Construction of the Bennett Dam, 1957–1968

If there is one thing that is of basic importance to the development of British Columbia, it is the development of the rich resources of the northern and central regions of the Province. The Peace River particularly is one of the areas in Canada most ripe for development ...

— W.A.C. Bennett[1]

1   The W.A.C. Bennett Dam (Bennett Dam) is located on the Peace River near Hudson's Hope, B.C. Construction of the dam commenced in April 1962 and was completed by December 1967; however, planning for the hydro-electric project began in the 1950s. In 1954, then Premier of B.C., W.A.C. Bennett, who held office from 1952 to 1972, first described his "Northern Vision."[2] At this time, Premier Bennett announced his plans for a $400 million hydro-electric project in the Rocky Mountain Trench, which would produce enough power to fulfill future demands in southern B.C. This project was to "bring untold wealth and prosperity to the region."[3] Behind the dam would lie an enormous reservoir, which would flood more than 177,300 hectares of wilderness land.[4]

2   This essay examines economic and environmental themes amid public responses to the building of the Bennett Dam, near Hudson's Hope, during the period 1957 to 1968. First, I will describe public responses from 1957 to 1963, when the project was announced and construction of the dam began. Second, I will address public responses from 1964 to 1968, when the construction phase neared completion and operation began. I will show that initial public responses to the building of the Bennett Dam emphasized a desire for industrial and financial growth; however, as the dam neared completion, public responses became focused on long-term economic and environmental issues.

Methods
3   The information gathered to describe public responses to the building of the Bennett Dam is taken from articles and editorial comments in the *Alaska Highway News*, Fort St. John, from 1957 to 1968. The North Peace Museum maintains a catalogued archive of the newspapers from March 16, 1944 to December 24, 1975. Articles pertaining to the dam are recorded in the catalogue; however, editorial comments and Letters to the Editor are not. Thus, in order to ensure the thoroughness of my own research, it was necessary to review each of the *Alaska Highway News* weekly publications, page by page, between 1957 and 1968. The back issues of the newspapers have been kept in very good condition in cardboard boxes, one year per box, and shelved according to the year of publication. Further responses by local residents are taken from Earl K. Pollon and Shirlee Smith Matheson's *This Was Our Valley*, a historical account of the people, environment, and economics of the area affected by the dam and its reservoir. I will also be drawing information from the *Fort Chipewyan Way of Life Study*, which addresses the impact on economic and environmental issues downstream of the dam on the Peace-Athabasca Delta, once the waterflow of the Peace River was reduced.

Public Responses to the Bennett Dam (1957–1963)
4   In 1957, Premier Bennett described to a Vancouver audience his plans for a hydro-electric dam on the Peace River, making B.C. the greatest manufacturing province because of its cheap and abundant power supply. The dam would create a reservoir that would provide opportunity for recreation, improve navigation on the Mackenzie water

routes, and would possibly change the northern B.C. climate.[5] When Premier Bennett spoke to a large audience in Fort St. John nearly a year later, he stated that the development of the dam would "bring untold wealth and prosperity to this region."[6] In a recent interview, Mary Humphries, long-time resident of the Hudson's Hope and Fort St. John areas, recalls an affirmative response to the Premier's message. According to Humphries, the people of the area looked to industry to provide security for their businesses and livelihoods, hoping that new industry in the area would diversify the economy and secure future development. However, Humphries also suggests that while people looked for immediate growth in their communities, they were not looking beyond the completion of the dam.[7]

5 Nevertheless, public responses in the *Alaska Highway News* did indicate some long-term environmental concerns. H.L. Briggs, manager of the B.C. Power Commission, issued public statements regarding the Premier's handling of the province's affairs. Mr. Briggs denounced the government's stewardship of the province and attacked Mr. Bennett's integrity.[8] Furthermore, Briggs commented on the signing of a pact between Premier Bennett and Wenner-Gren, a Swedish financier, to conduct surveys and begin planning for the hydro-electric project on the Peace River. Briggs accused the Premier of "robbing the generations unborn"[9] by signing the pact with the Wenner-Gren group. He suggested that the government had committed natural resources in the area to be flooded by the reservoir before the public had a chance to realize the value of such a commitment. Mr. Briggs wanted to reach out to the people who would be directly affected by the proposed dam, those who were not able to follow the developing controversy in the provincial capital, except through news media.[10] Similarly, mineral economist Desmond Kidd suggested that developing the energy, timber, and mineral resources of the north was not as important as developing power and selling it to southern B.C. Kidd was critical of the Wenner-Gren pact because he feared that the province might commit an error that would be regretted for many years to come. Kidd doubted that any industry would be brought to the north based on the available resources. Furthermore, he believed that the flooding of the reservoir would ultimately sacrifice these resources.[11]

6   While the Premier stressed industrial and financial opportunities, local residents questioned other aspects of the proposal. In her column, "The Other Side," Vera Loucks wrote about the Peace River development propaganda, which gave an impression of extensive industrialization in the area. Loucks claimed the real objective was to sell the power to southern B.C. and the United States. Indeed, Loucks indicated that the amount of power generated by the dam would exceed the demands in the north. Supporting Loucks' concerns, a September 1959 press release by Gordon Shrum, chairman of the B.C. Energy Board, suggested that B.C. should develop all of its power resources and quickly build an export market.[12]

7   However, in 1960, as final confirmation of the project approached, a widespread anticipation of immediate economic development in Hudson's Hope became apparent. According to a January 11, 1960 article in the *Alaska Highway News,* landowners were receiving regular purchase offers from those who wanted to establish businesses; the Hudson's Bay Company store was rumoured to be reopening; and sawmills were busy and expanding. A former business owner in Hudson's Hope, Art Anderson, reopened his hardware store, stating, "It's now at the dawn of a new era. No town in B.C. has a better future than Hudson's Hope . . ."[13]

8   Indeed, by 1960, all around the village of Hudson's Hope, residents were preparing for immediate industrial and financial growth. While there was some resistance to the tearing up of paths to widen street allowances and to the tearing down of fences, residents realized that this reconfiguring of their village was a prelude to the biggest development project in the province. Dan Murray of the *Alaska Highway News* reported that "big silver Canadian dollars took the place of those hostile beady eyes."[14] Murray noted that a new hotel was being built; plywood was being stockpiled, awaiting new builders; a new grocery store was opening; and an old cafe site had been purchased by Victoria businesspeople.[15] Other developments included the move of the Canadian Bank of Commerce, from a trailer to a permanent establishment. In addition, real estate prices had risen, and a gas station and taxi service were established. Travel options to and from Hudson's Hope were also improving with the start of Canadian Coachways daily bus run, an airstrip, and a new road south to the Hart Highway.[16]

9   However, despite the emphasis on financial and economic opportunities, public responses were becoming negative. The building of the Bennett Dam was attracting the attention of the public far outside the area of Hudson's Hope and northern B.C. The influx of people coming to Hudson's Hope to work on the dam was putting a strain on school facilities, forcing children to be bused to other schools out of their district, and away from their homes. An angry parent wrote "that B.C. Hydro [should] be willing to build schools in lieu of [paying] taxes, if the government is unable to find money for education."[17] As well, concerns were reported over water and sewer difficulties, due to the increase in the population. Without the construction of a sewer system, the village water wells could be in danger of contamination from sewage.[18] With the building of the dam under way, Hudson's Hope was in the early stages of a boom, which was affecting the lives of the residents of this once-quiet community. According to Harry Hazlett, "Progress is good in many ways, and we all like to see it, but it brings changes, takes away things that we dislike to lose, and brings some things with it that are not good."[19] In the following years, this resistance would mount.

Public Responses to the Bennett Dam (1964–1968)
10   By 1964, the general public response to the building of the Bennett Dam was clearly less enthusiastic. Mary Humphries wrote about the frustration of the local people who felt pushed aside to accommodate the dam, suggesting that the old ways were colliding with the new ways.[20] Further frustration appears in public responses from residents who were taxed for services and schools needed for the laborers working on the dam. For years, locals had survived by looking out for one another, by making a living to meet their needs, and by enjoying a quiet community; but the building of the dam disrupted their lifestyle. Dennis Geddes, the district administrator from 1963 to 1974, stated: "I never felt the powers-to-be intended that Hudson's Hope would benefit to any degree from the construction of the dam."[21] Residents of Hudson's Hope also expressed the need for a permanent hospital in their community. In February 1966, a chamber of commerce meeting was held in Hudson's Hope to address this concern. Reeve Mr. Gething, a district official, felt that because of the workforce at the dam site, the population warranted a hospital. The District of Hudson's Hope was attempting to acquire the Red Cross outpost

hospital property and building, and was looking into financing.[22] However, despite the chamber of commerce efforts, on June 29, 1967, the *Alaska Highway News* headline read, "No hospital for Hudson's Hope." The hospital, which had been promised by B.C. Hydro, would not materialize. The hydro commission was willing to finance the hospital, but was told that it would be for overnight and emergency cases only; normal confinement cases would not be allowed because funds could not be provided to ensure adequate facilities.General treatment cases would to go to Dawson Creek and Fort St. John.[23]

11 In 1963, Earl Pollon, a long-time resident of Hudson's Hope, described his personal frustration with the building of the dam, citing difficulties that the local people had getting employment at the dam site, the rush to build the dam, and the lack of respect for the acquisition of local property. Initially, Pollon supported the dam and the promise of prosperity, but he wrote a poem indicating his changing viewpoint:

> God How I hate It! Yes, I hate it!
> I wish this dam project in hell!
> With all the rumble and racket
> I'd sooner hear harness and bell!
> . . . .
> I'm afraid . . . I shake like a child.
> I long for a silence to last.
> My body's arrived at this epoch,
> My soul has remained in the past.[24]

Pollon eulogizes the quiet lifestyle he had enjoyed for many years, a lifestyle that would soon be gone.

12 In keeping with Pollon's sentiments, public responses to the new reservoir, later to be named Williston Lake, showed a heightened concern for the environment. By 1965, the dam was drawing thousands of tourists, and development of a recreation industry on the reservoir was being considered. Officials of the Bank of Montreal, who visited the site, suggested that once the reservoir had been filled, hunting, fishing, and other recreational activities would further support tourism.[25] However, according to Mary Humphries' editorial, the world's biggest human-made lake wasn't going to do anyone any good. She foresaw it as a menace to wildlife, and shipping on it would be nearly impossible. Humphries suggested that studies were needed to establish the lake's effects on area wildlife and climate. Additionally, surveys to determine maximum water levels were necessary to ensure adequate clearing of the shoreline and to avoid floating debris and dead trees, which would lessen the lake's tourism potential.[26]

13 Environmental concerns are described in a June 19, 1968 article, in which a boom holding back debris behind the dam gave way, freeing up hundreds of acres of debris to float down and jam up behind the dam. The boom was holding the debris until it could be burned. The amount of debris in the lake would take years to clean up, with tugboats working steadily between freeze-ups. Burning of the debris, once collected, was causing environmental concerns because of the amount of smoke created.[27]

14 Earl Pollon ultimately became a major spokesperson for environmental issues. In *This Was Our Valley*, Pollon reflects on his concerns about the sudden burst of activity in the area. Pollon speculates about the future of the river and valley. Graves of trappers, miners, Klondikers, prospectors, and Natives would be flooded by the reservoir. For Pollon, the past would be lost, buried twice over.[28] Moreover, he, too, was concerned about the effect the reservoir would have on the environment and animals in the valley. He expressed particular concern about the moose and their ability to find new habitat. Pollon also pointed out that Stone sheep would become more accessible to hunters as the water rose, even though it was illegal to hunt from a boat.[29]

15 By 1968, the dam had been completed and the boom-town situation in Hudson's Hope was subsiding. An editorial in the *Alaska Highway News* suggested that if Hudson's Hope could come up with an industry, commercial venture, or service, there was someone with a million dollars to invest. The article further noted that the chamber of commerce had received an inquiry and sent an invitation to the investor to come and look around. The editorial concluded that it would be hopeless to wait for Mr. Bennett and B.C. Hydro to address the future of Hudson's Hope: "They've got what they came for. The

future is up to us."[30] The large school, which had been built to support
the population explosion of the dam-building years, would now have
to be maintained through local taxes, since the Peace River Power
Project had been removed from the school tax rolls. "We've been cast
into Bennett-dammed water to sink or swim... leaving us with nothing
but a village and a large unorganized territory with a lot of overbuilt
services.[31] Moreover, the medical doctors who were brought by
Northern Powerplant Builders to work in Hudson's Hope announced
that they would leave toward the end of 1968, closing the mobile
clinic. Thus, Hudson's Hope would have no medical personnel in the
community.[32] Public responses at this time showed that the people of
Hudson's Hope realized that long-term economic growth would not
materialize, and that their community would be left to its own devices,
to develop and maintain industry.

16 As the construction era ended, intensified concerns for the
environment are represented in public responses. Residents, some of
whom were pioneers of the upper Peace River, faced displacement by
the flooding of the reservoir. The Beattie family, in particular, who
settled in the area in 1913, had to leave their ranch because the waters
of the reservoir would completely cover it. Mrs. Beattie visited the
ranch for the last time just before Hydro burned it to prevent debris
from floating to the surface once flooding began. On August 29, 1963,
the *Alaska Highway News* reported: "Mrs. Beattie loved and cared for
the land with dedication and devotion, and the mist won't only be
laying on the Peace River, some of it will be in her eyes."[33] Moreover,
Ross Darnall, Sr., brought a court case against B.C. Hydro over
compensation for his land, which was also to be flooded by the
reservoir. Mr. Darnall presented his points to the judge, stating: "What
is the value of a good fishing stream, the view of majestic mountains,
the stillness of the afternoon, as well as the value of timber on a 250
acre ranch, all soon to be lost to a watery grave[?]"[34]

17 Environmentally-based public responses from residents 1200
kilometers downstream of the Bennett Dam began once the Peace
River's flow had been reduced by the filling of the reservoir. The
Peace-Athabasca Delta and the hamlet of Fort Chipewyan were for
the first time seeing the impact of the dam. Athabascan Chipewyan,
Mikisew Cree, and Chipewyan Métis who inhabited the Fort

Chipewyan region had not been previously informed about the potential impact of the dam on their area. Charlie Voyageur, of the Athabasca Fort Chipewyan First Nation, worked as a driller on the dam site and could not recall thinking about or having it brought to his attention that the dam might have an impact on the people of the delta and Fort Chipewyan. Legislation to protect the environment and human communities was weak in the 1960s, and neither the Alberta nor B.C. government took measures to fully assess downstream effects. Low water levels on the delta, caused by the Peace River being held back to fill the reservoir, affected the existing vegetation supply for mammals, thus reducing species populations. This, in turn, affected the lifestyle of the residents by reducing their hunting, trapping, and fishing opportunities. The people of Fort Chipewyan and the Peace-Athabasca Delta not only worried that their livelihood would not recover if the water level didn't increase, but also that their recreational pleasure and spiritual inspiration would be lost as well. Moreover, the residents worried about possible permanent diminishment of their land and waterways. In 1970, the residents of Fort Chipewyan filed a lawsuit against B.C. Hydro, citing the effects that the Bennett Dam had on the Peace-Athabasca Delta.[35] To date, the court case has not been settled.

Conclusion

18 The building of the Bennett Dam on the Peace River inspired a desire for immediate industrial and financial growth. Responses from residents of Hudson's Hope and the upper Peace River initially showed optimism about new industry and wealth for the region. However, once the dam neared completion and the economy of the community began to slow down, responses showed concern for the long-term effects that the dam and its reservoir would have on human lives, economic security, and the natural environment. The people of the Peace-Athabasca Delta, who were unaware of the development on the Peace River until the dam was complete, also voiced concerns about the long-term economic and environmental effects on their region. In 1993, the Peace-Athabasca Delta Technical Studies were established to develop an ecosystem management plan. The goal of the program was to understand and select strategies for restoring the role of water in the delta.[36]

19 In retrospect, regional responses to the construction of the Bennett Dam can be situated in the larger context of a global environmental movement that expresses moral concern about the relationship between humans and the environment. Indeed, as the finishing touches were being put on the Bennett Dam, Greenpeace, Earth First, and other organizations began to speak out against activities such as nuclear testing, whaling, and the construction of dams elsewhere in North America. Furthermore, a heightened regard for the environment has since become evident within the Peace region itself. In the 1970s, when B.C. Hydro proposed to build yet another dam on the Peace River (at Site C), opposition to the dam mounted quickly.

20 Leo Rutledge, a long-time Hudson's Hope resident who was involved in several wilderness organizations and was a member of the Peace Valley Environmental Association, spoke out against the Site C Dam. Rutledge argued that a hearing needed to be held to inform the people of the effect the dam would have on the area.[37] Meanwhile, the people of the area remembered the long-term economic and environmental impact of the Bennett Dam and were less ready to be swayed by optimistic economic forecasts. Public responses showed a concern for the environment, for the animal habitats that would be lost, and for the farmland that would be flooded by the new reservoir.[38] Despite these concerns for the environment, some Fort St. John business people spoke out in favor of the Site C project, envisioning the building of another dam in the area as a way to provide jobs and improve the economy.[39] However, in 1980, the B.C. *Utilities Act* was passed, compelling B.C. Hydro to produce demand and supply forecasts, and to conduct social and environmental impact assessments.[40] In 1983, the B.C. Utilities Commission rejected the Site C proposal because the demand for power did not warrant another dam, and impact studies were not completed.[41] Today, twenty years later, B.C. Hydro has expressed renewed interest in Site C. Thus, citizens may again debate the desirability of another mega-project on the Peace River.

NOTES

1.   *Fort Chipewyan Way of Life Study* (Vancouver: Stuart Adams & Associates Planning Limited, 1998), p. 6.

2. Ibid.
3. "It'll Be the World's Largest," *Alaska Highway News*, 09 October 1958, p. 1.
4. "Welcome to the WAC Bennett Dam" Retrieved September 30, 1999 from http://www.hhcn.prn.bc.ca/district/bc_hydro/bchydro.html
5. "400 M P.R. Power Project," *Alaska Highway News*, 09 October 1958, p. 1.
6. "It'll Be the World's Largest," *Alaska Highway News*, 09 October 1958, p. 1.
7. Interview with Mary Humphries, 21 February 2000.
8. David J. Mitchell, *W.A.C. Bennett and the Rise of British Columbia*, (Vancouver: Douglas and McIntyre, 1983), p. 25.
9. H.L. Briggs, "Canada's Biggest Give-Away Show in Your Own Backyard," *Alaska Highway News*, 27 November 1958, p. 1.
10. "It'll Be the World's Largest," *Alaska Highway News*, 27 November 1958, p. 1.
11. Desmond Kidd, "Wenner-Gren Hydro Project Overrated," *Alaska Highway News*, 27 November 1958, p. 15.
12. Vera Loucks, "The Other Side," *Alaska Highway News*, 05 December 1959, p. 2.
13. "Hudson's Hope Begins to Stir as Zero Hour Nears," *Alaska Highway News*, 04 January 1960, pp. 1, 8.
14. Dan Murray, "Hudson's Hope . . . The Best Town by a Damsite!" *Alaska Highway News*, 07 September 1961, p. 10.
15. Ibid.
16. "Quiet Backwater Looks for Bigger Things," *Alaska Highway News*, 11 January 1962, pp. 1, 8.
17. "Our Readers Write," *Alaska Highway News*, 18 October 1962, p. 3.
18. "Quiet Backwater Looks for Bigger Things," *Alaska Highway News*, 11 January 1962, p. 8.
19. "Hudson's Hope, The Old and the New," *Alaska Highway News*, 10 October 1963, sec. 2, p. 3.
20. Mary Humphries, "White Water," *Alaska Highway News*, 14 November 1964, sec. 3, p. 2.
21. "Hudson's Hope 1965," *Alaska Highway News*, 13 January 1966, sec. 2, p. 4.
22. "Plans Go Ahead for Hospital Here," *Alaska Highway News*, 17 February 1966, sec. 2, p. 3.
23. "No Hospital for Hudson's Hope," *Alaska Highway News*, 29 June 1967, p. 1.
24. Earl K. Pollon and Shirlee Smith Matheson, *This Was Our Valley* (Calgary: Detselig, 1989), p. 183.
25. The Bank of Montreal Visits the Peace River," *Alaska Highway News*, 19 May 1966, sec. 3, p. 4.
26. "We Need Help," *Alaska Highway News*, 05 June 1968, sec. 3, p. 2.
27. "Dam Boom Breaks, Debris Lets Loose," *Alaska Highway News*, 10 July 1968, sec. 3, p. 6.
28. Earl K. Pollon and Shirlee Smith Matheson, *supra* 24, p. 131.
29. Ibid., p. 132.
30. "Editorial," *Alaska Highway News*, 24 January 1968, sec. 3, p. 6.
31. "Editorial," "Cast Aside?" *Alaska Highway News*, 08 May 1968, p. 1.

32. "Editorial," *Alaska Highway News,* 05 June 1968, sec. 3, p. 2.
33. "The River Gave," *Alaska Highway News,* 29 August 1963, pp. 4–6.
34. "Court Action Result of Hydro Land Grab," *Alaska Highway News,* 17 January 1968, p. 1.
35. *Fort Chipewyan Way of Life Study, supra* 1, p. 10.
36. *Peace-Athabasca Delta Technical Studies,* 1996, (WordPicture Communications), pp. 1, 2.
37. Earl K. Pollon and Shirlee Smith Matheson, *This Was Our Valley, supra* 24, p. 317.
38. Ibid., p. 310.
39. Ibid., p. 314.
40. Ibid., p. 310.
41. Ibid., p. 319.

Writing in the Sciences

Every great advance in science has issued from a new audacity of imagination.

— John Dewey

Scientific discourse has a reputation for being one of the more challenging forms of academic writing. It often involves highly technical language, numbers, graphs, equations, and tables that are unintelligible to the layperson. Some of us may feel as though scientists speak another language. Nevertheless, on the whole, we tend to tolerate and even respect such difficulty because we sense that something important is at stake. The goal of much science writing, after all, is to reveal patterns in nature, and that activity can have real and immediate significance in our lives. Further, scientific reports present data and interpretation in an effort to persuade others to accept or reject the hypotheses under consideration. Thus, while the humanities often struggle to justify their existence, science and technology are firmly entrenched as funding priorities among university and governmental administrators.

> Whereas the goal of writing in the humanities may be to speculate philosophically on the human condition, the goal of much science writing is to reveal patterns in nature. Scientists want to let nature speak for itself.

Given their search for an unmediated version of reality, scientists place a particularly high value on objectivity or empiricism (the pursuit of knowledge by observation and experimentation), and try to place careful controls on how knowledge is generated. Scientists want to say, with reasonable certainty, that something—some pattern, or relationship, or fact—exists "out there," on its own, and their language reveals this desire. More than any other form of academic discourse, science writing tries to eliminate subjectivity. Thus, while self-disclosure may be an increasingly popular rhetorical gesture in the humanities and social sciences, it is not a part of the rhetoric of the natural sciences. In research articles, biologists, for example, will not write about their personal background; instead, they will explain their methods—methods that others may, hypothetically at least, test and repeat.

In recent years, the rhetoric of science has received considerable attention. Ground-breaking books such as *Laboratory Life: The Construction of Scientific Facts* (Latour & Woolgar, 1986) and *Opening Pandora's Box: A Sociological Analysis of Scientists' Discourse* (Gilbert & Mulkay, 1984) demonstrate that academic knowledge-making, even in the core sciences, is a form of storytelling. Gilbert and Mulkay (1984), for example, contend that the cultural values of the sciences result in an "empiricist's repertoire" that involves an array of textual or *stylistic* practices. Superficially, perhaps, these practices downplay the role of the researching self, yet, at a deeper level, they also suggest that knowledge-making is a social phenomenon, a rhetorical activity that hinges, in part, on language use. Such studies show that the researcher is a highly socialized being who constructs knowledge claims according to disciplinary customs and expectations.

Until this point, most of the articles that we have looked at belong to the humanities and social sciences. These articles have consisted of introductions, cores, and conclusions, but despite these broad similarities, the authors have exercised a lot of narrative freedom. They have told their stories in different ways, using different methods of development, varying degrees of self-disclosure, and so on. In the natural sciences, however, where academic writers often want to describe some kind of controlled investigation or empirical study, a more rigidly structured kind of storytelling is evident. Scientists who want to explain the results of an experiment adhere to what is called the "report format," which has a predetermined narrative structure.

The APA *Publication Manual* (2001) actually recognizes the report format as a distinct *type* of scholarly article, one that "typically consists of distinct sections that reflect the stages in the research process" (p. 7). Indeed, scientific reports give unprecedented attention to a detailed, step-by-step account of how knowledge was generated. Perhaps the most noticeable sign of the report genre is a series of subheadings following a sequence something like this:

1. Abstract
2. Introduction
3. Methods (may be called Materials and Methods)
4. Results
5. Discussion
6. References

In the remaining portions of this discussion, we would simply like to touch on a few of the rhetorical structures that are evident in scientific reports.

FRONT MATTER

Title and Title Page

Unlike many titles in the humanities and social sciences, titles in scientific reports tend to reflect the factual content of the report in a straightforward manner, often in fewer than a dozen words. Such titles contain keywords that other researchers and Internet search engines recognize. Note the directness of the following examples:

- Climate change in the North Pacific region over the past three centuries
- Green tea inhibits vascular endothelial growth factor (VEGF) induction in human breast cancer cells
- Lead in grain size fractions of road deposited sediment
- Mercury, zinc, and copper accumulation in mangrove sediments surrounding a large landfill in southeast Brazil
- Properties of a fetal multipotent neural stem cell (NEP cell)
- Changes in soil physical characteristics during transition from intensive tillage to direct seeding

- Residential segregation of visible minorities in Canada's gateway cities
- Songbird community composition versus forest rotation age in Saskatchewan boreal mixed-wood forest
- Bioavailability of heavy metals in soils amended with sewage sludge
- Reviving central Brandon in the early twenty-first century

In these titles, the topic formula discussed in previous chapters (Abstraction + Research Site = Topic) may not be as evident. What we seem to be getting, in the titles above, are clearly foregrounded research sites that sometimes lack explicitly stated abstractions; in the sciences, where disciplinary problems are often agreed-on, prestige abstractions, which identify Big Issues, may be implicit. Note some possible abstractions that hover around a few of the research sites listed above.

- Mercury, zinc, and copper accumulation in mangrove sediments surrounding a large landfill in southeast Brazil [*environmental pollution*]
- Changes in soil physical characteristics during transition from intensive tillage to direct seeding [*agricultural ecology*]
- Reviving central Brandon in the early twenty-first century [*urban renewal*]

See the CBE Manual (1999, p. 580) for detailed instructions on title pages. Students should check with their instructor for further guidelines.

Running Head

The running head is a shortened form of the complete title. It is identified as such on the title page, and reappears at the top right of each page of the paper. The following examples show the reduction of the complete title to a running head.

Title: Winter severity, survival, and cause-specific mortality of female white-tailed deer in north-central Minnesota

---

Running Head: Survival of white-tailed deer

Title: Effect of fall-applied manure practices on runoff, sediment, and nutrient surface transport from silage corn in south coastal British Columbia

Running head: Manure effects on runoff, sediment, and nutrient transport

Title: Breeding bird response to midstory hardwood reduction in Florida sandhill longleaf pine forests

Running head: Bird response to midstory hardwood reduction

Abstract

The abstract, placed after the title page and before the first page of text, provides readers and other researchers with a summary of the purpose of the report, the data presented, and the major conclusions. In presenting the abstract clearly and concisely (about 200 words), researchers generally use the past tense to describe actions related to the carrying out of the experiment or research (for example, we developed, I investigated, we compared, we estimated, I included, we recorded, I identified, we gathered, we classified, I documented, and so on) and the present tense to describe results, conclusions, or the activity of the paper itself (for example, we detail, we review, we propose, we support, and so on). Although published scholarship contains abstracts using the personal pronouns "I" or "we" to refer to the researchers themselves (but not in the more general editorial sense), and abstracts that adopt a less personal approach (for example, the data suggest, these results indicate, this study shows, and so on), individual instructors may prefer abstracts without the use of "I" or "we" (see Passive Voice, below).

Note the various features in the following abstract for an article entitled "Abundance and Distribution of Breeding Waterfowl in the Great Clay Belt of Northern Ontario," which appeared in *The Canadian Field-Naturalist*, Jan.–March 2002. Although key words are not part of the abstract, in journal articles they are usually listed right after the abstract and before the start of the introduction.

Abstract

The abundance and distribution of breeding waterfowl in the Great Clay Belt of northern Ontario was determined through helicopter surveys of 177 fixed plots (2 x 2 km each) during the nest initiation periods from 1988 to 1990. This area has higher fertility, flat topography, high water table and better access than the surrounding Boreal Forest, and therefore has greater potential for increased waterfowl production through habitat management. Overall breeding density averaged 112.5 indicated breeding pairs per 100 km^2, 68% being of the four most common species [Mallard (*Anas platyrhynchos*), Ring-necked Duck (*Aythya collaris*), American Black Duck (*Anas rubripes*), and common Goldeneye (*Bucephala clangula*)]; 13 other species were encountered. The average total of breeding waterfowl for the region was estimated at 59,330 pairs. Distributions of the species were related to ecodistrict and to surficial geology. The more northerly of the two main ecodistricts had higher densities of American Black Ducks, Ring-necked Ducks, Common Goldeneyes, and Canada Geese (*Branta canadensis*). Mallard and Hooded Merganser (*Lophodytes cucullatus*) distributions correlated with presence of surficial clay and moraines, respectively. Less common species including Green-winged Teal (*Anas crecca*) and American Wigeon (*Anas Americana*) appeared to be concentrated in smaller-scaled habitat features (beaver pond sequences and estuarine marshes, respectively). Results generally agreed with those of earlier Clay Belt surveys. Total breeding density of waterfowl is slightly higher than that of surrounding regions.

Key Words: ducks, populations, habitat, boreal, forest, Ontario.

INTRODUCTION

Introductions in scientific reports serve similar purposes to introductions in reports in the humanities and social sciences: they set the stage for what follows, define the subject of the report, and answer the question "Why was this study performed?"

Setting the Stage

The opening sentences of Stephen Herrero and Andrew Higgins' "Human Injuries Inflicted by Bears in British Columbia: 1960–97" (1999) sound very much like an opening we might encounter in the humanities or social sciences, which sets the stage for what follows: "In 1967, 2 young women were killed during a 24-hour period by different grizzly bears in Glacier National Park, Montana. These were the first fatal grizzly bear–inflicted attacks in the park" (p. 288, this volume). In fact, these first two sentences could easily launch an essay about the psychology of fear, the sociology of outdoor recreation, or even a personal essay about surviving a bear attack.

In science writing, however, the introduction quickly focuses on the problem under investigation, often by providing a condensed history of pertinent research in the same or similar area of study through a *tradition of inquiry* (see Chapter 6 and below). As in the humanities and social sciences, researchers may go on to identify a *knowledge deficit* or *gap* (see Chapter 6) that will signal the importance of their own study.

Traditions of Inquiry

As we have already seen in the discussion on traditions of inquiry in Chapter 6, researchers are under an obligation to acknowledge what has previously been published relating to their study. The tradition of inquiry is, in a sense, a very brief literature review that contextualizes the study undertaken by acknowledging foundational work on which the present study is built. This part of the introduction may be densely packed with citations, as in the following example. In science writing, there is a convention, perhaps for purposes of economy, to present a tradition of inquiry through paraphrase and indirect reference. Note that the results of research, and not the researchers themselves, are foregrounded through the use of indirect reference:

> Composts normally contain all of the essential trace elements required by plants, plus substantial amounts of N, P, and K (e.g., Dalzell et al. 1987). Compost can also improve important soil physical properties, such as permeability, plant available water capacity, and air-filled porosity (Keener et al 2000; Stratfon and Rechcigl 1998). Consequently, positive crop yield responses to compost additions are frequently reported (Dick and McCoy 1993; McSorley and Gallaher 1996; Mamo et al. 1998).

On the other hand, for example, in the article by Stephen Herrero and Andrew Higgins (at the end of this chapter), note how, through direct reference in the third paragraph, the reader's attention is focused on the researcher and not merely on the results of the investigation. A glance at the Literature Cited list at the end of the article shows that Stephen Herrero has been publishing articles on this topic (human injuries inflicted by bears) since at least 1970. Furthermore, in the first paragraph of the Methods section of the article, we are told that he was instrumental in setting up and maintaining a North American database on bear–human interactions. In fact, he is referred to as "the senior author." So given the extent of the research and length of time Herrero has been publishing on bear–human interactions, it is not surprising that the authors, in this instance, have chosen to use direct reference (see Chapter 7).

Digressing for a moment, we might reconceive traditions of inquiry as a way of showing the "pedigree" of the knowledge about a certain area of study. Susan Peck MacDonald (1994) argues that scientific knowledge, in particular, tends to build on established points of consensus, foundational laws, or agreed-on problems to be solved (pp. 21–24). In this sense, scientific knowledge is more linear than knowledge in the humanities, which may demonstrate little, if any, progression, but instead, seems to be "recursive and reiterative" (Becher, as cited in MacDonald, 1994, p. 24), or "diffuse" (p. 22). In English studies, for example, there will never, in all probability, be an agreed-on meaning for Milton's *Paradise Lost*. Hence, literary scholars are destined to discuss forever, without any foundational consensus on which to build. Scientific knowledge, on the other hand, hinges on established laws and agreed-on problems that provide starting points for new studies. For this reason, the introductions that one encounters in scientific report format often place special emphasis on a tradition of inquiry. Scientists, in particular, place a high value on citing their predecessors and showing how knowledge in the current study is descended from previous work. In addition to the "pedigree" of the knowledge a researcher is using, other things may be at stake. Especially in cases where there are immediate practical applications for scientific research, such as patentable processes or products, the chronology of published research becomes even more important.

MacDonald's concept of a "diffuse" knowledge-making model in the humanities may be one reason why humanities students sometimes advance to the upper levels of an undergraduate degree without developing a sense that previous studies on their topic are important to their own work. If we return to English studies, first- and second-year students are not always required to use the library for research, but may be encouraged instead to rely on their own close reading of a text, without referring to previous studies. In essence, meaning is generated and presented in a vacuum. And while "the library" is supposed to become more important at the senior-undergraduate levels, in third and fourth year, the initial disregard for traditions of inquiry may be hard to reverse. Looking for analogies, one might point to the different emphases placed on prerequisites in the humanities and sciences. In the humanities, where MacDonald (1994) says diffusion prevails, prerequisites may not always be as vital as they are in the sciences.

Knowledge Deficit
As in the humanities and social sciences, a tradition of inquiry is sometimes followed by a knowledge gap. Here are some examples of how scientists express a knowledge deficit:

- We are not aware of any other publication where such a comparison has been made.
- No other study of . . . has been conducted.
- This study is one of the first attempts to demonstrate . . .
- Limited information exists on . . . Hence, the objective of this study was . . .

Topic
We have already touched on some of the rhetorical configurations of topic in the sciences. It is also worth noting that in the sciences, topic is often flagged as a statement of purpose or as an announcement of an objective somewhere toward the end of the introduction. Here are some examples:

- The objectives of this study were . . .
- The primary objectives of this study were to . . .
- The objective of this research was . . .
- Hence, the objective of this study was to examine . . .
- Therefore, we focus our research on . . . but we also present some evidence about . . .

- • . . . is the focus of this study
- • This paper reports on . . .
- • In this paper, we summarize . . .

In the examples above, topic may again sound like general forecasting (see Chapter 6).

Hypothesis

At the simplest level, a hypothesis is a premise or an assumption that will be tested; it is a statement that is deemed plausible and that will be tested in the course of an experiment. In effect, a hypothesis in the sciences takes the place of a thesis in the humanities. A hypothesis represents a kind of sophisticated guess. The "hypo" prefix in "hypothesis" means "under" or "below." So a hypothesis is "below the surface," serving as a foundation or basis for investigation. Sometimes, the hypothesis is implied in the objective or statement of purpose (topic). A hypothesis can never be "proven," but the results of the investigation can either support or negate the hypothesis.

The presence of a hypothesis in scientific writing implies a cautious approach to the generation of knowledge. Rather than beginning with a claim, scientific writing begins with a plausibility or a tentative assumption, which is then tested. When the same results are obtained with many repeated testings, a hypothesis may become accepted knowledge. Like thesis claims in the humanities and social sciences, hypotheses are usually stated in the final paragraph or sentence of the introduction.

Here is an example in which the researcher presents an objective followed by two hypotheses:

> The objective of this study was to determine changes in stream channel morphology in response to 2 seasons (wet and dry) and 3 intensities (no grazing, moderate, and concentrated) of grazing. Our first hypothesis was that grazing induced bank erosion along the bedrock limited intermittent streams at the San Joaquin Experimental Range would increase stream channel width at bank full compared to that measured in the baseline year or in the ungrazed channel reaches. Our second hypothesis was that bedload deposition was dynamic and would result in yearly fluctuations in stream channel depth.

Alternatively, science writers might express something called a null hypothesis. Whereas a hypothesis anticipates a particular result, a null hypothesis rejects that anticipated result. It may be useful, in thinking about the purpose of an experiment, to suggest a hypothesis and the countering null hypothesis as exploratory steps in arriving at a statement of purpose. In the example below, at the outset of the experiment, the results are unknown. However, it is suspected that the application of herbicide will damage seed production and viability. Alternatively, analysis of the experimental data may show that there was no effect. The hypothesis and null hypothesis represent the "on the one hand" and "on the other hand" possibilities for the outcome of the experiment.

As a Statement of Purpose: The objective of this study was to determine if herbicide treatments damage seed production or seed viability.

As a Hypothesis: The hypothesis was that herbicide treatments would damage seed production and seed viability.

As a Null Hypothesis: The null hypothesis was that herbicide treatments would not damage seed production and seed viability.

Another way of thinking about all this is to say that in a null hypothesis, scientists state that what they *really* think is going to happen, isn't going to happen. In this sense, a null hypothesis is a fictitious prediction, a form of make-believe. Rhetorically, at least, the null hypothesis is a way of pre-empting assumptions. In effect, scientists play the devil's advocate with themselves. Nowhere, perhaps, is the production of scientific knowledge more openly "constructed" than in the articulation of a null hypothesis. The null hypothesis is a rhetorical artifice.

Methods

While we have encountered Methods sections in our reading so far, such sections become even more important as we deal with report format in the sciences. In fact, Methods sections (also called Materials and Methods) sometimes comprise a large part of scientific reports, taking several pages. Perhaps more than any other discursive feature in the sciences, Methods sections reveal a concern for objectivity. The function of a Methods section is to demonstrate properly controlled observation through the use of instruments, measurements, and so on. Thus, Methods sections describe scientific procedure in an effort to ensure reliability (see Chapter 6 for Methods in the social sciences).

The Methods section lists materials used, describes any special pieces of equipment needed, tells how they were used, and explains where and when the work was done. This last point is especially important in field studies, where the particular locale or season in which the experiment or investigation was carried out can be a crucial factor in the results. This section is often divided further by subheadings such as site description, experimental design, data collection, sampling procedure, and data analysis. Inclusion of various subheadings will, of course, depend on the specifics of the experiment undertaken or the phenomenon being studied.

In Chapter 6, we noted that Methods sections often defy standard notions of good writing, presenting choppy sentences and agentless or passive-voice constructions. Moreover, Swales (1990) notes that in some Methods sections, particularly in the natural sciences, "an enormous amount is taken for granted ... [and] this belies the common belief that the purpose of Methods sections is to permit replication" (pp. 120–121). In fact, some would "deny that replication is really possible" (Swales, 1990, p. 121). The peculiarities and complications that Swales notes should remind us that Methods sections, like every other feature of academic writing, are highly mediated forms of expression.

Results

The Results section answers the question, What did the researcher find? It presents data, measured values (quantitative results), and observations, but no interpretation, implications, or conclusions. In the text, researchers usually summarize the data from the experiments as opposed to discussing every individual result. Tables, graphs, and other illustrative material (for example, photographs, maps, drawings), which should always be referred to in the text of the report, can be used to illuminate or supplement the text. Data in a table should not be duplicated in a graph or figure, and readers should be alerted as to what information to look for in a table or figure. For example, "Bats responded most to light intensity and colour treatments used during experimental tours (Table 1). In general, all responses were highest during full-white light level and lowest during the no-light level (Fig. 1)." Figures and tables are referred to in the text by their number, for example, "Figure 1 shows that the activity . . ." or "The activity decreases after five minutes (Fig. 1)."

Discussion

Discussion and Conclusion sections in scientific reports present many of the rhetorical gestures that we have already discussed in relation to conclusions in the humanities and social sciences (see Chapter 8). In the Discussion section, researchers interpret the data that they gathered during the experiment or the field research. They may relate the results to existing theory and knowledge, and explain the logic that allows them to accept or reject the original hypothesis. The discussion may also include suggestions for improving experimental technique, explain some influence that may have unexpectedly affected results, or clarify areas for additional research (thus identifying a further *knowledge deficit*).

In the following example, the research team draws attention to the weaknesses of the tactical model used in the experiment:

> The utility of a tactical model is determined by the extent to which it can be used to analyze the problem for which it was developed and the extent to which it can be generalized to others. . . . There are 3 major areas where the model we used may have been oversimplified. The first, and most important is the mechanism by which . . . The second oversimplification in the model concerns the way in which control measures were implemented. . . . The third oversimplification relates to habitat.

In the next example, note how the researchers point out possible limitations to their study on near-death experiences (NDE):

One limitation of our study is that our study group were all Dutch cardiac patients, who were generally older than groups in other studies. Therefore, our frequency of NDE might not be representative of all cases — e.g., a higher frequency could be expected with younger samples, or rates might vary in other populations. Also, the rates for NDE could differ in people who survive near-death episodes that come about by different causes, such as near drowning, near fatal car crashes with cerebral trauma, and electrocution. However, rigorous prospective studies would be almost impossible in many such cases.

In the following example, the first part of the Discussion section of a study of the survival of white-tailed deer centres on assumptions outlined in a previously published study. Note how the researchers contextualize their study by relating their findings to that earlier work. Here, then, a *tradition of inquiry* emerges relatively late in the paper.

Discussion
Survival Analysis

Assumptions: Tsai et al. (1999) discuss 7 assumptions for statistical inference based on survival data from radiotagged animals. They include (1) animals in the study cohort constitute a representative sample of the target population, (2) survival times of individuals are uncorrelated, (3) radiocollars do not affect survival, (4) animals recruited at different calendar times and ages have the same underlying survival function, (5) death times are exact, (6) censoring is random (noninformative), and (7) the underlying hazard is constant or at least piece wise exponential. We consider each of these as they relate to our study.

Assumption 1. We standardized all aspects of Clover trapping (e.g., trap size, door height, trap locations) in this study to preclude a trapping bias for any age class of does. . . .

Assumption 2. The deer in our study were competing for the same progressively declining winter resources; thus, the clustering of >80% of the death times in winter strongly suggests correlation. . . .

Assumption 3. We excluded from our analysis 12 deer that died within 7 days of capture because their deaths may have been capture-related. The remaining deer gave no evidence of any adverse effects.

In the Discussion section, researchers may also address connections to other phenomena or the significance of their experimental results, gestures that are akin to a *statement of relevance*. In the article on near-death experience, for example, the authors say that "NDE pushes at the limits of medical ideas about the range of human consciousness and the mind–brain relation."

Furthermore, science writers may also speculate about the meaning of the experimental results. In the near-death article, the researchers speculate about why people have near-death experiences — they consider neurophysiology and changing states of consciousness, but clearly state that their experiments did not show that psychological, neurophysiological, or physiological factors caused the experiences. If speculation is part of the discussion, it should be clearly identified as such.

Conclusion

The Conclusion section gives researchers a final chance to summarize the particular data and discussion, and draw conclusions about the experiment or research they have conducted. Often, metadiscursive "flags" explicitly signal the summary function of conclusions. In the examples below, the metadiscursive verbs point to the emergence of a *thesis* or *knowledge claim* at the end of the study:

- The results of this study showed . . .
- This study showed that . . .
- Our data from four experiments . . . indicate that . . .
- This study provides evidence of . . .

As in the humanities and social sciences, we should not be surprised to encounter *limiting expressions* in the articulation of knowledge claims (see Chapter 6).

In the following examples, note how the Conclusion contains a rejection of the hypothesis.

In conclusion, we detected no significant streambank erosion, thus we must reject our hypothesis that grazing increases width in these bedrock limited stream channels. We detected a significant increase in depth in the control treatments. Additionally, we found significant year effect on morphological parameters that included depth in their measurement or calculation, supporting our hypothesis that annual stream flow dynamics have a large effect on depth of the stream channels we studied. The large year effect and weaker year x grazing effect on stream morphology confirms the need for long-term studies to separate natural variation in stream morphological parameters from those caused by land management activities.

The assumption that the soil chemical properties in the Cg horizon would remain stable during the study period did not hold.

Areas for additional research may also be identified in a Conclusion. We've seen this in other disciplines, where at the end of a paper, scholars present *opportunities for further research*. See the following example:

Also, further research should be directed towards practices that reduce the amount of runoff and contaminant loads during the crucial runoff period in the fall immediately following manure application.

Further research is required to elucidate the major mechanisms of liquid swine manure N losses in these soils under the Saskatchewan climatic conditions.

A brief review of journal articles in various disciplines, however, shows that not all published articles have a Conclusion section. Sometimes, conclusions are incorporated into the Discussion section. Depending on the discipline and the topic, a variety of other subheadings may be used instead of "Conclusion":

- Intended Applications
- Implications

- Management Implications
- Modification and Future Development
- Recommendations

Acknowledgements

Scientists often receive help from various sources. In a short paragraph at the end of the written report of their studies, often just before the Literature Cited, researchers acknowledge the help they receive from assistants, funding agencies, university libraries and facilities, and other agencies or individuals:

> We thank observers . . . for assisting in field trials. We gratefully acknowledge the University of Washington's Friday Harbor Laboratories for providing boat dockage and office support. We appreciate the helpful reviews by . . . of earlier drafts of this manuscript. This work was funded by . . .

References

This section presents an alphabetized list of references cited in the paper, and not a general bibliography of works consulted on the topic. Individual instructors may request a particular style of documentation, for example, APA or CBE, and student researchers should diligently observe formatting requirements. Our suggestion is that unless otherwise advised by their instructor, students should follow the official style manual for the documentation style that they choose for their papers, and not one of the many variations that individual journals adopt as their "house" style. Following is a sample References page, showing some of the most often used kinds of references, formatted first according to APA style, and then according to CBE style. Students should check the most recent editions of the *Publication Manual of the American Psychological Association* and *Scientific Style and Format: The CBE Manual for Authors, Editors, and Publishers* for complete details on formatting citations and references.

APA Style

References

Evans, R.A., & Love, R.M. (1957). The step-point method of sampling: A practical tool of range research. *Journal of Range Management, 10,* 208–212.

Hosmer, D.W., & Lemeshow, S. (2000). *Applied logistic regression.* 2nd ed. New York: John Wiley & Sons.

Morgan, K.A., & Gates, J.E. (1983). Use of forest edge and strip vegetation by eastern cottontails. *Journal of Wildlife Management, 47,* 259–264.

National Oceanic and Atmospheric Administration. (2001). National Climatic Data Center Climate Data Online. Retrieved January 21, 2001 from http://cdo.ncdc.noaa.gov/plclimprod/plsql/poemain.poe

Worton, B.J. (1989). Kernel methods for estimating the utilization distribution in home-range studies. *Ecology, 70,* 164–168.

CBE Style

References

Evans RA, Love RM. 1957. The step-point method of sampling: A practical tool of range research. Journal of Range Management 10:208–12.

Hosmer DW, Lemeshow S. 2000. Applied logistic regression. 2nd ed. New York: J Wiley. 373 p.

Morgan KA, Gates JE. 1983. Use of forest edge and strip vegetation by eastern cottontails. Journal of Wildlife Management 47:259–264.

Worton BJ. 1989. Kernel methods for estimating the utilization distribution in home-range studies. Ecology 70:164–168.

SENTENCE-LEVEL CONSIDERATIONS

There is much that could be said about how sentence patterns in the natural sciences differ from sentence patterns in other disciplines. In this chapter, we will limit the scope of our discussion to the passive voice and nominalization, stylistic features also observable in the humanities and social sciences. In the natural sciences, however, these tendencies are even more apparent. Indeed, among scientists, the passive voice may sometimes be preferred over the active voice, and bulky noun phrases are especially common.

Active Voice and Passive Voice

In English grammar, "voice" shows the relationship between the subject and the verb of the sentence. We can construct sentences in the active voice or the passive voice. In the active voice, the doer of the action is the subject of the sentence; for example, "Mary ate the apple." The active voice shines a spotlight on the subject of the sentence as the doer of the action. On the other hand, the passive voice presents the subject of the sentence as the receiver of the action, often leaving the doer of the action unstated and implied. The passive voice uses a grammatical construction that consists of a form of the verb "to be" (*is, are, was, were, has been*) plus the past participle of another verb. Basic composition instructors usually frown on the passive voice because it often sounds wordy and can be a form of agentless expression that disguises or downplays the doer of an activity. For instance, we could simply say, "The apple was eaten." In this case, the doer of the action has not been named.

Yet in certain sections of scientific reports, the passive voice is useful. Note how the doers of the action — that is, the researchers — are relatively unimportant in the following examples:

- The study was established in 1993 at Lacombe, Alberta, Canada . . .
- Seeding was followed by harrowing.
- All paddocks were hand weeded during the summer.
- Baseline data was collected in 1994.
- The preliminary study was followed by four years of treatment application and data collection.

The above examples are from Methods and Materials sections, parts of scientific reports often written in the passive voice. Other sections of research papers may also employ the passive voice. Note, for instance, how often it is used in the introduction to John Theberge's "Ecological Classification, Status, and Management of the Gray Wolf, *Canis lupus*, in Canada":

> The Gray Wolf *is listed* as a furbearer in all jurisdictions. None provide quotas for trappers. It *is listed* as a game species in all jurisdictions except Alberta and Labrador. Only in British Columbia *is* it actually *managed*, with area-specific bag limits. Wolves *are killed* to protect livestock in most jurisdictions (Table 1). [italics added]

Note, however, that the following examples, also drawn from Methods and Materials sections, use the active voice:

- We identified three vegetation associations within the study area based on field reconnaissance and following Hernandez (1998).
- We followed Lehr (1978) for plant nomenclature.
- We determined diets of desert bighorn sheep based on fecal pellets collected two times each season.
- We systematically travelled the area on foot across washes, ridgetops, and cliffs and observed sheep with a pair of 10 x 50 binoculars and a 30 x 16 spotting scope.
- We avoided disturbing the animals.

In sum, we advise students to check with their instructors for preferences concerning active and passive voice, as well as for use of the personal pronouns "I" and "we" to refer to the researchers themselves.

Nominalization

The word "nominalization" comes from the Latin "nomen," meaning name. Thus, in the most basic sense, "nominalization" simply refers to the act of naming. We can see this Latin root in terms such as "nominate," "nomenclature," and *"nom de plume."* In studies of academic writing, however, nominalization has acquired a more specialized meaning. It refers to instances in which noun phrases replace subject-predicate constructions, thereby turning actions into "things" (Giltrow, 2002, pp. 213–218). This kind of nominalization is often what's at stake when readers complain that academic writing is hard to read, or that it is jargon-ridden.

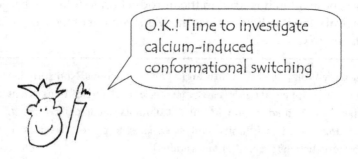

The words that tend to trouble people the most are the nouns or noun phrases that "absorb" subjects, verbs, and prepositions. Like the passive voice, nominalization is not limited to scientific writing, but it has a familiar home there. The following examples of nominalization are drawn from published scientific articles:

- Rent-appropriation opportunities
- Accessibility research
- State energy program outputs
- Methodology of energy demand forecasting
- Corporate competence building
- Energy-efficient procurement practices
- Economic optimal stocking rates
- Cricket paralysis virus internal ribosomal entry site
- Calcium-induced conformational switching
- First-principles molecular dynamics investigation
- Anaerobic ammonium-oxidizing micro-organisms
- Microbial secondary metabolite formation
- Penicillin-susceptible target proteins
- Microbial cellulose utilization
- Osmotic stress signaling
- Quantization
- Plant-associated symbiotic growth states

Nominalization can be a good thing. It can be used to accomplish the following:

- Stabilize phenomena, permitting cause/effect analysis
- Economically reinstate high-level concepts
- Precisely identify specific concepts
- Replicate the kind of language that academics are used to

On the other hand, as previously noted, nominalization can also make prose difficult to read. When readers complain that writing is wordy, nominalization is frequently the grammatical culprit causing the problem. Too much nominalization can obscure meaning: noun phrases may make some sentences nearly unintelligible. Accordingly, academic writers should make informed judgements about the use of such "freight-train phrases" (*Scientific Style and Format*, 1999, p. 119), weighing the advantages with the disadvantages. Remember that your reader seeks meaning and clarity.

IDEAS FOR FURTHER STUDY

1. As you read the reports at the end of this chapter, and others that you may access through the library or databases, pay special attention to rhetorical features such as the title, abstract, introduction, materials and methods, results, statistical data, charts, discussion, and conclusion. Also look for metadiscursive "flags" that signal the function of various sections. Focusing on particular examples, discuss whether these aspects of scientific style cloud or clarify meaning.

2. Find your own examples of the passive voice and nominalization in scientific sources. A good method is simply to browse the titles of articles in databases such as the General Sciences Index. Sooner or later, nominalization will appear under virtually any subject.

3. Using the sample titles given earlier in this chapter (see Title), write appropriate running heads.

4. Still working with these titles, see if you can supply abstractions for a few more of the research sites.

5. Look back at the examples of nominalization earlier in this chapter. Rewrite each as a simpler phrase that restores subjects, verbs, and/or prepositions.

6. In a video entitled *Science, Culture, and the Modern World* (Ideas Channel, 1993), two scientists, Michael Rose and Gregory Benford, claim that the humanities and sciences are "piling up against each other in some gigantic academic football game." Do you see any signs of competition between the humanities and sciences at your college or university? On a related point, do you think that different stereotypes accompany popular conceptions of people in the humanities and people in the sciences?

CHAPTER REFERENCES

APA *publication manual*. (2001). *Publication manual of the American Psychological Association*. 5ᵗʰ ed. Washington, D.C.: American Psychological Association.

Frye, N. (1971). *The bush garden: Essays on the Canadian imagination*. Toronto: Anansi.

Gilbert, G.N., & Mulkay, M. (1984). *Opening Pandora's box: A sociological analysis of scientists' discourse*. Cambridge: Cambridge University Press.

The Harbrace Handbook for Canadians, 5ᵗʰ ed. (1999). (Eds.) John C. Hodges, et al. Toronto: Harcourt Brace.

Herrero, S., & Higgins, A. (1999). Bear-inflicted injuries in British Columbia, 1960–97. *Ursus, 11*, 209–218.

Latour, B., & Woolgar, S. (1986). *Laboratory life: The construction of scientific facts*. Princeton: Princeton University Press.

MacDonald, S.P. (1994). *Professional academic writing in the humanities and social sciences*. Carbondale: Southern Illinois University Press.

Martin, E. (1991), The egg and the sperm: How science has constructed a romance based on stereotypical male-female roles. *Signs, 16*(3), 485–501.

Science, culture, and the modern world. (1993). Videotape. Discussion between Michael Rose & Gregory Benford. Ideas Channel.

Scientific style and format: The CBE manual for authors, editors, and publishers. (1999). Cambridge: University of Cambridge.

Theberge, J.B. (1991). Ecological classification, status, and management of the gray wolf, *Canis lupus*, in Canada. *The Canadian Field-Naturalist, 105*(4), 1–5.

INTRODUCTION TO THE READINGS

The following report by Stephen Herrero and Andrew Higgins is relatively accessible and deals with a subject that has broad popular interest. Documentation follows an in-house journal style, presenting a variation of CBE style. The laboratory report, written for this text by David Hamer, a biology instructor, was constructed as a model for science students.

STEPHEN HERRERO AND ANDREW HIGGINS

Human Injuries Inflicted by Bears in British Columbia: 1960–97

Abstract: There is controversy in British Columbia regarding how dangerous bears are. Grizzly bear *(Ursus arctos)* population estimates range from 10,000–13,000; black bears *(U. americanus)*, 120,000–160,000. From 1960–97, significantly fewer grizzly bears inflicted about 3 times as many serious injuries (N = 41 versus 14) but the same number of fatal injuries (N = 8) as black bears. The trend in terms of average number of bear-inflicted injuries/year increased each decade from the 1960s through the 1990s, as did the human population in British Columbia. It is likely that more people in bear habitat affected this increase in the number of injuries. In 88% of serious or fatal grizzly bear attacks, those injured were engaged in hunting, hiking, or working, typically in back-country areas. In 77% of black bear attacks, those injured were either hiking, watching the bear, working, or recreating, typically in front-country areas. Eighty-one percent of parties injured by grizzly bears and 69% of parties injured by black bears were composed of 1 or 2 people. Bear access to human food or garbage was associated with a relatively small number of incidents for each species. In grizzly bear incidents where the age and sex class were known, adult females were identified in 79% of incidents. All incidents where the gender of an attacking black bear was known involved males. These incidents were equally divided between adults and subadults. Poor health of the bear was identified in 16% of black bear and 7% of grizzly bear incidents. Sixty-two percent of the serious or fatal grizzly bear incidents, where the bear's motivation could be inferred, were categorized as involving a bear being startled at close range (<50 m) and 19% involved ungulate carcasses. For black bear incidents, where the bear's motivation could be inferred, 83% involved possible predation. None involved ungulate carcasses and none involved the bear being startled. Risk of bear attack can be managed through individual responsibility and communication targeted at individuals and groups such as ungulate hunters, hikers and campers, and persons working in bear habitat.

1   In 1967, 2 young women were killed during a 24-hour period by different grizzly bears in Glacier National Park, Montana. These were the first fatal grizzly bear-inflicted attacks in the park. In an article in *BioScience,* one biologist wrote that grizzly bears in Glacier and Yellowstone national parks were too dangerous and they should be extirpated (Moment 1968, 1969). This opinion spurred the first scientific assessment of bear-inflicted injuries and their circumstances (Herrero 1970a). One of these circumstances was the potential danger of grizzly bears that have become food-conditioned by eating people's food or garbage and thus have become habituated to the presence of people. These behavioral changes seemed the most probable explanation for

the bears' behavior in Glacier National Park and in subsequent incidents in which grizzly bears attacked and killed sleeping tourists camped in tents or in the open in Glacier and Yellowstone national parks (Herrero 1985, 1989). These were offensive attacks, not defensive actions, such as a sow grizzly with cubs might make when encountering a person at close range (Herrero 1985).

2   Within a few years of the 1967 fatalities, Glacier and Yellowstone national parks responded by implementing some of the best food and garbage management practices in North America. The Rocky Mountain national parks (Banff, Jasper, Kootenay, Waterton, and Yoho) in Canada followed suit, but only after a food-conditioned and human-habituated grizzly bear killed 1 person and seriously injured 3 others near Banff in 1980 (Herrero 1985). As a result of improved food and garbage management techniques, Glacier and Yellowstone national parks in the United States have dramatically reduced injury rates by both grizzly and black bears. At the same time they have handled, killed, or translocated dramatically fewer bears (Gunther 1994, Gniadek and Kendall 1998). While never as high as their U.S. counterparts, injury rates in the Canadian Rocky Mountain national parks also have decreased with better food and garbage management techniques (Herrero unpublished data).

3   Herrero (1985) also identified and evaluated other circumstances associated with grizzly bear attacks such as sudden surprise and harassment, and for black bears, rare instances of predatory attacks (Herrero 1985, Herrero and Higgins 1995). Herrero and Fleck (1990) showed that bear-inflicted injuries (grizzly and black bear combined) in North American national parks were few between 1980–85. Total number of park visitors/bear-inflicted injury varied between 317,700 for Kluane to 6,693,859 for Yoho. Back-country overnight users had significantly greater chances of injury. Here, rates varied from 5,691 visitors/injury for Waterton to 118,297 for Denali. Many national parks had no injuries during 1980–85.

4   With an estimated 120,000–160,000 black bears and 10,000–13,000 grizzly bears, British Columbia (B.C.) supports some of the highest numbers of bears of any jurisdiction in North America (BC Bear Facts, undated publication, Ministry of Environment, Lands and Parks, Victoria, British Columbia, Canada). Most bears exist outside of

national parks or other protected areas and they are hunted. B.C. covers 948,000 km^2, and has a human population of approximately 3,941,500. During the mid- to late-1990s, about 450 grizzly bears and 5,885 black bears were known or estimated to have been killed by people each year in B.C. through a combination of legal hunting, poaching, and as a result of bear-people conflicts (BC Bear Facts, undated publication, Ministry of Environment, Lands, and Parks, Victoria, B.C., Canada). At least 1 prominent outdoorsman is of the opinion that current management policies combined with large numbers of bears creates danger that is unacceptable to the point that "To ensure public safety . . . bear populations [should be reduced] by about 25% in parks and places where people and bears must co-exist" (Shelton 1994:209). One of the objectives of our paper is to provide data on the extent and nature of bear-inflicted injuries in B.C. so that management policies regarding human safety around bears in B.C. can be objectively evaluated.

5   Injuries from bears have been little studied in areas where they are hunted outside of national parks and other protected areas. The few existing studies are primarily from a medical perspective, in Alberta (Tough and Butt 1993) and B.C. (Thommasen et al. 1994). Somewhat more in-depth studies have been done in Alaska, but these have relied primarily on newspaper accounts of incidents as Alaska does not officially investigate bear attacks (Middaugh 1987, Miller and Tutterow 1999). Hunting, hiking, and, recently, camping were identified as primary activities associated with bear-inflicted injuries in Alaska (Middaugh 1987). Miller and Tutterow (1999) reported that between 1986 and 1996, brown bear attacks resulted in 2.75 injuries and 0.42 deaths/year in Alaska, whereas black bear attacks resulted in 0.33 human injuries/year and only 1 fatality during this 11-year period. Alaska has approximately half of the brown (grizzly) bears in North America, with an estimated population of 31,700; at least as many black bears are thought to be in Alaska (Miller and Tutterow 1999). In the Bob Marshall Wilderness of Montana, grizzly bear–inflicted injury rates were estimated to be 1 injury/4.5 million recreational visitor use days, 1956–94 (U.S. Fish and Wildlife Service 1997).

6   People's acceptance of injury rates is fundamental to bear conservation. Despite what appear to be relatively low injury rates in

national parks and in Alaska and elsewhere, to some people any chance of injury by a wild animal may be unacceptable. For this reason, as well as the general obligations of wildlife managers, we need to understand circumstances associated with bear-inflicted injury so as to better manage bears and risk of injury and to advise the public regarding risk of injury and what individuals can do to decrease that risk. This research was formulated partly to address these questions in the Province of British Columbia.

Methods

7 We gathered data for 1980–93 by contacting all management agencies within B.C. with jurisdiction over bears and requesting copies of investigation reports and other such information on bear attacks. This was part of a larger effort to systematically update a North American database on bear–human interactions that was begun by the senior author in 1967. Data for 1960–79 were from the original database as described in Herrero (1985). Data from 1994–97, inclusive, were based on annual summaries and detailed case reports gathered by the Wildlife Branch of the B.C. Ministry of Environment, Lands, and Parks, and by contacting national parks within B.C. Other sources for data included the B.C. Division of Vital Statistics, coroners' reports, and other published accounts (e.g., Thommasen et al. 1994).

8 The methods used to compile incidents in national parks were an extension of those reported by Herrero and Fleck (1990) for 1980–85. We collected injury data from the national parks through 1997. However, because visitor use data were available only prior to 1994, we calculated injury rates only for 1986–93. These data represent *all* bear-inflicted injuries in the national parks in B.C., including minor injuries. In all other sections of this paper, only serious injuries or fatalities are analyzed.

9 We entered individual incidents into a database and analyzed the aggregate data. We classified data according to methods described by Herrero and Higgins (1995). We believe the data for B.C. represent all fatal and serious injuries (requiring 24 hours or more of hospitalization) inflicted by bears during 1960–97, although a few incidents may be missing from the early decades. Because the data represent the population of such incidents, and not a sample of them, all differences are significant. Some details regarding certain incidents

were lacking. In these cases, we had a sample of data, and we used the *G* test with Williams correction factor to test for differences between frequencies (Zar 1984). We did not analyze incidents of minor injury because of inconsistent recording, except in national parks in B.C. from 1980–93. Because some incidents resulted in injury to >1 person, the total number of serious and fatal injuries was greater than the total number of incidents.

10 We obtained visitor use data for the national parks from Parks Canada and bear harvest data from the Wildlife Branch of the B.C. Ministry of Environment, Lands, and Parks. Human population data were downloaded from the homepage of B.C. Stats, B.C. Ministry of Finance and Corporate Relations. We sometimes found correlations between different data sets. Only when several converging and independent lines of evidence suggested the same conclusion was correlation assumed to have a reasonable probability of indicating causation.

Results
11 Grizzly bears inflicted most (68%, 49 of 72) serious or fatal injuries (Table 1). Grizzly and black bears were responsible for equal numbers of fatal injuries. The number of serious and fatal injuries inflicted by bears increased each decade from the 1960s to the 1990s (Fig. 1). While the number of serious injuries and fatalities varied from year to year, the overall trend for 1960–97 was up, as shown by a 3-year running average (Fig. 2). The injury rate from both species of bears combined (the mean number of residents of B.C./bear inflicted injury) increased during the 1980s and 1990s (Table 2). The rate of increase in injuries significantly exceeded the rate of human population increase during the 1990s (Fig. 2). All differences are significant because we are describing populations of events, not samples.

12 Serious injuries and fatalities were clustered from May–October, with the peak in August (Fig. 3). There were no serious injuries or fatalities recorded in the months of February, March, April, or December.

13 For incidents where the time of the attack was known, 85% (33 of 39; $G_1 = 20.3$, $P = 0.000$) that involved grizzly bears, and 94% (17 of 18;

Table 1. Number of serious or fatal injuries and incidents inflicted by grizzly bears and black bears, 1960–97, British Columbia, Canada

Species	Number of incidents resulting in serious injury or fatality	Number of serious injuries	Number of fatalities	Total number of serious injuries and fatalities[a]
Grizzly	44	41	8	49
Black	19	14	8	22
Unknown	1	0	1	1
Total	64	55	17	72

[a] A single incident may include multiple serious injuries or fatalities; therefore, the total number of serious injuries and fatalities exceeds the total number of incidents.

Figure 1. Annual average of bear-inflicted serious injuries and fatalities by decade, 1960–97, British Columbia, Canada

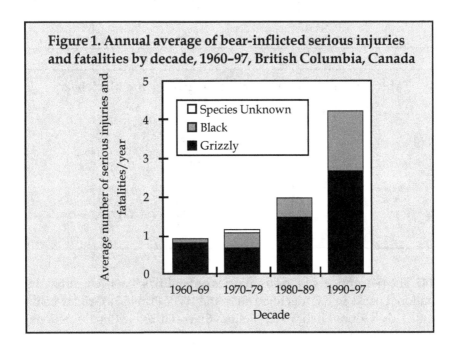

G_1 = 16.8, P = 0.000) that involved black bears, occurred during the daytime (between 0600 and 1800). One grizzly bear and no black bear incidents occurred between midnight and 0600.

Figure 2. Bear-inflicted serious injuries and fatalities and human population, 1960-97, British Columbia, Canada

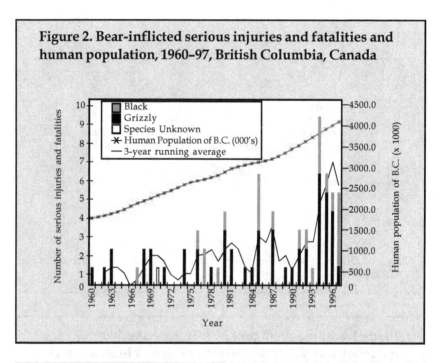

Table 2. Combined injury rates for grizzly and black bears, 1960-97, British Columbia, Canada

Decade	Number of serious or fatal injuries	Averaqge human population	Annual injury rate (per person)
1960s	9	1,855,470	1/2,061,630
1970s	11	2,452,250	1/2,229,320
1980s	19	2,977,090	1/1,566,890
1990s	33	3,620,440	1/877,680

14 The percentage of serious injuries or fatalities that occurred in the national parks in B.C. declined since the 1970s (Table 3). Grizzly bears inflicted all serious injuries or fatalities that occurred within the national parks from 1960-97.

15 Consistent with the 1980-85 rates (Herrero and Fleck 1990), the injury rates for front or back-country visitors to the national parks in B.C. from 1986-93 were low (Tables 4 and 5). While the back-country injury rate for Yoho National Park increased 1986-93 compared to

Figure 3. Monthly distribution of serious injuries and
fatalities inflicted by bears, 1960–97, British Columbia,
Canada

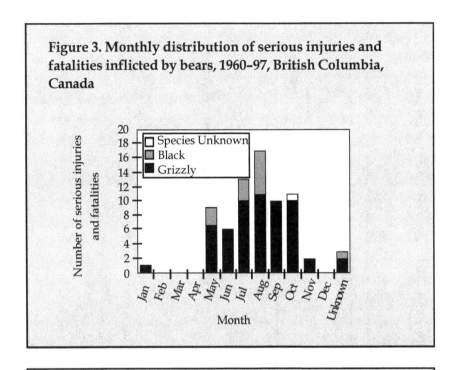

Table 3. Bear-inflicted serious injuries and fatalities by
decade, for national parks and areas outside national parks,
1960–97, British Columbia, Canada

Decade	Total number of serious injuries and fatalities	Number of serious injuries and fatalities outside national parks	Number of serious injuries and fatalities in national parks (%)
1960–69	9	8	1 (11)
1970–79	11	8	3 (27)
1980–89	19	18	1 (5)
1990–97	33	31	2 (6)
Total	72	65	7 (10)

1980–85, the injury rate for front-country visitors declined for the
same periods. The small number of injuries for any individual park
can make the injury rates quite variable, reducing the validity of trends
in these rates. Back-country visitors were significantly more likely to
be injured by a bear than were front-country visitors.

Table 4. Rate of injurious interactions between park visitors and black or grizzly bears for national parks in British Columbia, Canada, 1980–93

Park	Mean Number visitors/year		Mean number of visitors per injury from					
			Black bear		Grizzly bear[a]		Total bears	
	1980–85	1986–93	1980–85	1986–93	1980–85	1986–93	1980–85	1986–93
Kootenay	1,913,773 [b]	1,572,003 [c]	–[d]	–	–	12,576,024	–	12,576,024
Mt. Revelstoke-Glacier	3,899,154	4,783,819 [e]	–	–	–	–	–	–
Pacific Rim[f]	677,247	790,313	–	–	*	*	–	–
Yoho	1,137,956	2,624,375 [g]	–	20,995,000	6,693,859	20,995,000	6,693,859	10,497,500

a * Species does not occur in park.
b Total visitation for Kootenay is for 1980–83 inclusive.
c Mean number of visitors excludes 1986 (no data available)
d – Indicates no injuries or deaths by this species for the period noted.
e Mean number of visitors excludes 1986 and portions of 1987–89 (no data available)
f Pacific Rim total visitation is for Long Beach Unit only.
g Mean number of visitors excludes 1986, 1987, and portions of 1988 and 1993 (no data available).

Table 5. Rate of injurious interactions between humans and black or grizzly bears in back-country areas of national parks in British Columbia, Canada, 1980–93

Park	Mean Number back-country user nights/year		Mean number of back-country user nights per back-country injury from					
			Black bear		Grizzly bear		Total bears	
	1980–85	1986–93	1980–85	1986–93	1980–85	1986–93	1980–85	1986–93
Kootenay	3,146 [b]	3,383 [b]	–[c]	–	–	27,064	–	27,064
Mt. Revelstoke- Glacier	1,351	no data	–	–	*	*	–	–
Pacific Rim	22,791	33,346 [d]	–	–	*	22,288	–	–
Yoho	2,703	2,786	–	22,288	15,900	22,288	15,900	11,144

a * Species does not occur in park.
b Average back-country visitation for Kootenay excludes 1985, 1986, 1991 (no data available)
c – No injuries or deaths by this species for the period.
d – Average back-country visitation results for Pacific Rim excludes 1980 (no data available). All Pacific Rim back-country use results are for the West Coast Trail Unit.

16   Gwaii Haanas National Park, a new park in the Queen Charlotte
Islands off the northwest coast of B.C., was established in early 1996.
Prior to this it had varying degrees of protection from resource
extraction and hunting. Only black bears occur in this area, and no
serious or fatal bear-inflicted injuries were reported during 1985–97.
Visitation was low, averaging less than 5,000 people/year.

17   *Bear Harvest Numbers*: Grizzly bear harvest numbers declined from
the 1960s to 1990s, and this declining trend seemed inversely related
to the grizzly bear–inflicted injury rate, although there was year-to-
year variability (Fig. 4). The black bear harvest increased during the
1960s and 1970s and leveled off during the 1980s and 1990s (Fig. 4).
The number of injuries inflicted by black bears was not strongly
correlated with harvest.

People and Parties Injured
18   In 81% (35 of 43) of incidents involving grizzly bears, the injured
groups consisted of 1 or 2 people. These small groups were more

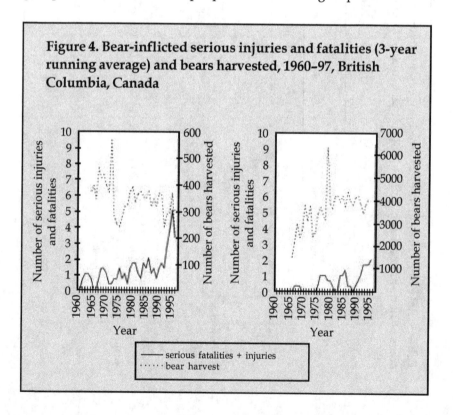

Figure 4. Bear-inflicted serious injuries and fatalities (3-year running average) and bears harvested, 1960–97, British Columbia, Canada

likely to be injured by a grizzly bear than larger groups (G_1 = 18.1, P = 0.000), but we do not know the relative proportions of different group sizes for the hiking population as a whole. In 69% (11 of 16) of incidents involving black bears where the size of the group was known, the groups consisted of 1 or 2 people (G_1 = 2.2, P = 0.135). There were no recorded injuries inflicted by a bear to groups of 6 or more people.

19 Seventy-seven percent (17 of 22) of persons injured by black bears were hiking, watching the bear, working, or recreating (Table 6). Eighty-eight percent (43 of 49) of persons injured by grizzly bears were hunting, hiking, or involved in work (Table 6). Eight percent of grizzly bear-inflicted injuries (4 of 49) occurred while the person was in camp.

20 Eighty-one percent (58 of 72) of victims of serious or fatal injuries were male. The ratio of male to female victims was larger for grizzly bear than for black bear-inflicted injuries (5:1 and 2.7:1, respectively).

21 Twelve of the 18 (67%) victims of potentially predatory black bear attacks were adults, 5 (28%) were youths (age 10–19) and 1 (6%) was a child (<10 years old). Three of the 5 victims of potentially predatory grizzly bear attacks were adults and 2 were youths.

Bears that Inflicted Injury
22 In all but 1 of the 64 incidents studied, only 1 bear was actively involved in the attack. In the incident in which 2 bears were involved, a grizzly bear sow was the most aggressive bear, but her cub participated by biting the person's arm and dragging him.

23 In incidents involving grizzly bears (N = 44), the bear was identified as female in 74% (23 of 31) of the incidents where the sex of the bear was known (G_1 = 7.4, P = 0.006; Table 7). The bear was an adult in 88% (28 of 32) of the incidents where the age class of the bear was known (G_1 = 19.9, P = 0.000). The adult female cohort was responsible for 79% (22 of 28) of the incidents where the age and sex class of the bear were known (G_1 = 9.5, P = 0.002).

24 In incidents involving black bears (N = 19), the bear was male in all (13 of 13) of the incidents where the sex of the bear was known

Table 6. Activities of victims prior to injury by bears in British Columbia, Canada, 1960–97

	Hunting	Hiking	Working	Camping	Other or unknown	Total
Grizzly bear victims	Hunting (14) Cleaning animals (3)	Walking (5) Hiking, noise level unknown (4) Hiking, quietly (4) Hiking, noisily (2) Hiking, with a dog (1)	Forestry (7) Geological exploration (3)	Back-country (2) Front-country (1) In a tent (1)	2	
Grizzly bear total	17	16	10	4	2	49
Black bear victims	Fishing 1 Cycling 1 Playing 1	Walking (2) Hiking, noise level unknown (1)	Forestry (2) Geological exploration (1)	Back-country (1)	Watching bear (4) Other (3) Unknown (1)	
Black bear total	3	7	3	1	8	22

Activity (number of incidents)

Table 7. Sex and age classes of grizzly and black bears involved in serious injury or fatal incidents in British Columbia, Canada, 1960–97

Sex	Age class	Grizzly bear	Black bear
Male	Adult	5	5
	Subadult	0	6
	Cub	0	0
	Unknown	3	2
Female	Adult	22	0
	Subadult	0	0
	Cub	1	0
	Unknown	0	0
Unknown	Adult	1	2
	Subadult	3	1
	Cub	0	0
	Unknown	9	3
Total		44	19

(Table 7). The bear was an adult in 50% (7 of 14) of the incidents and subadult in another 50% (7 of 14) where the age class of a black bear was known. Five of the 15 black bears involved in potentially predatory attacks were adult males, 5 were subadult males, 2 were males of an unknown age class, 2 were adults of unknown sex, and 1 was an unknown sex and age class (Table 7).

25   In 3 of the 19 incidents involving black bears, the bear was judged to have had low body weight by inspecting B.C. Conservation Officers. Possible predation was the inferred motivation of all 3 bears. These 3 incidents represented 6 serious or fatal injuries. In 1 case, the B.C. wildlife officers who necropsied the bear observed "almost no body fat."

26   In 3 of 44 incidents involving grizzly bears, poor physical condition of the bear was identified by inspecting B.C. Conservation Officers. Body weights of 2 bears were judged to be low. These bears were reported to have had little fat and generally poor body condition. The inferred motivation in 1 of the attacks was a female acting in defense of her cubs. The second incident involved a male bear, and

the inferred motivation was a bear attempting to claim a hunter's kill. The third case involved an adult male bear who, when autopsied, had apparently normal fat reserves but infected teeth. The bear was not in hibernation in January at the time of the attack. The inferred motivation of this incident was possible predation.

Bear Attacks: Associated Variables
27 In 16 of 22 (73%) grizzly bear attacks where the duration of attack was known, the attack lasted <2 minutes, (G_I = 4.6, P = 0.032). For 5 black bear attacks the duration was: <2 min (1), 10–30 min (3), and 1–2 hours (1).

28 In 2 of the 19 incidents involving black bears, human food or garbage was noted within 100 m of the attack site; a known history of feeding on human food or garbage was noted in 3 incidents, the bear was judged to be "searching for food and garbage" in 2 incidents, and we judged the trigger for aggression to be food odors in 1 incident. In 3 of 44 incidents involving grizzly bears, human food or garbage was noted within 100 m of the attack site; the bear had a known history of feeding on human food or garbage in 3 incidents; the bear was "searching for food and garbage" in 2 incidents; and the trigger for the aggression was judged to be food odors in 1 incident. Five incidents (resulting in 5 injuries) involved grizzly bears defending animal carcasses. Three other incidents (resulting in 3 fatalities and 1 serious injury) involved grizzly bears attempting to claim hunters' kills as the hunters were cleaning or carrying their kills.

29 In 23 of 37 (62%) incidents involving grizzly bears, where the bear's motivation could be inferred, the motivation was "startled" (G_1 = 2.1, P = 0.140). In 76% (16 of 21) of these incidents where the bear's motivation was "startled," the initial encounter distance was <50 m in 76% (16 of 21) (G_1 = 5.9, P = 0.015); in 2 incidents the distance was >100 m. Only 11% (4 of 37) of the grizzly bear incidents were attributed to "possible predation" (G_1 = 25.6, P = 0.000), whereas 83% (15 of 18) of black bear incidents were judged to be predatory (G_1 = 8.5, P = 0.004).

30 There were no incidents involving black bears where the inferred motivation was "startled."

31 Twenty-seven of 34 (79%) incidents involving grizzly bears, where the location with respect to development was known, occurred in back-country locations, while 7 of 34 (21%) occurred in front-country (G_1 = 12.4, P = 0.000). In 16 incidents involving black bears where proximity to development was known, 38% (6 of 16) occurred in back-country locations and 62% (10 of 16) occurred in front-country (G_1= 1.0, P = 0.322).

Discussion

32 Even though there were an estimated 12 times as many black as grizzly bears in B.C. during 1960–97 (BC Bear Facts, undated publication, Ministry of Environment, Lands and Parks, Victoria, British Columbia, Canada), grizzly bears inflicted about 3 times as many serious injuries and the same number of fatalities as black bears. This is consistent with, but more quantitative than, previous findings regarding the relative aggressiveness of the 2 species (Herrero 1972, 1985; Middaugh 1987; Miller and Tutterow 1999).

33 The average number of serious and fatal injuries inflicted by bears each year increased significantly per decade from the 1960s and 1990s. The rate of increase exceeded the rate of increase in the total population of B.C. during the 1990s. The causes for the increases in number of injuries and rate of injury are not apparent from available data, but may be explained by people's increased use of bear habitat, an increase in the bear population, changes in bear behavior, or a complex interaction of some or all factors.

34 While bear populations probably increased in a few areas, they decreased in others. Increases in recreational and occupational uses of bear habitat seem likely to account for most of the increase in injuries, although one type of recreation, ungulate hunting, declined (M. Austin, Wildlife Division, Government of B.C., Victoria, Canada, personal communication, 1998). The decline in ungulate hunting paralleled a decreasing trend in grizzly bear harvest. The black bear harvest, which rose during the 1970s, has remained stable since the 1980s. While grizzly bear harvest was inversely related to the number of grizzly bear–inflicted injuries, changing black bear harvest was not correlated with changes in average number of injuries/year/decade.

35 We do not have data to directly evaluate whether the rising number of injuries by grizzly bears was due to less hunting of grizzlies or to increased use of bear habitat. In B.C., relatively few injuries occurred in national parks where bears were not hunted. In Yellowstone National Park, Wyoming, even with back-country use, grizzly bear-inflicted injuries are now few (Gunther 1994). We found peaks in the average number of bear-inflicted injuries during July and August, when outdoor recreation is greatest in B.C. This supports the idea that bear-inflicted injuries are related to levels of human use, a finding previously reported in Glacier National Park, Montana (Martinka 1982, Gniadek and Kendall 1998).

36 Bears that were accustomed to feeding on people's food or garbage were associated with about 10–15% of injuries. This contrasts with the situation in national parks during the 1950s through the mid-1980s, when food-conditioned and habituated grizzly bears were responsible for most serious and fatal injuries (Herrero 1970a, b, 1985, 1989; Gunther 1994; Gniadek and Kendall 1998). Food-conditioned bears inflicted few injuries in B.C. despite extensive feeding at dumps by both bear species as recently as the 1990s. The low number of injuries in this context may be explained by hunting, management removals, and, perhaps, poaching, all activities that select against bears that approach people or campsites. Even the relatively few injuries by food-conditioned bears of both species could have been avoided with better garbage management.

37 Consistent with previous findings (Herrero 1970a, b, 1985), most injuries occurred to people in groups of 1 or 2. Although we do not know the frequency of different sizes of groups active in bear habitat in B.C., small groups may be at higher risk of attack because we believe they tend to be quieter and appear less intimidating to bears than larger groups.

38 Attacks by grizzly bears and black bears occurred primarily during daytime hours and were preceded by a variety of outdoor activities. In 88% of grizzly bear-inflicted injuries, the victim was actively hunting, hiking, or working.

39 Hunting was the activity most commonly associated with grizzly bear attacks ($N = 17$), which suggests the potential for competition between hunters (especially ungulate hunters) and grizzly bears. There were 5 serious or fatal injuries involving a grizzly bear defending a carcass and 3 other incidents involving a grizzly bear apparently attempting to claim a hunter's kill as the hunter was cleaning or carrying it. None of the black bear-inflicted injuries were preceded by hunting or involved carcasses, which confirms previous findings (Herrero 1985) and further highlights behavioral differences between the species.

40 Most grizzly bear-inflicted injuries occurred in back-country areas, whereas most injuries inflicted by black bears occurred in front-country areas nearer to developments. These data are consistent with the notion that grizzly bears avoid developed areas more than black bears do (Herrero 1985). They also suggest that persons traveling in the back-country are probably in greater danger of surprising a grizzly bear.

41 There were dramatic differences between grizzly and black bears regarding the nature of injurious incidents and the gender of bears involved in incidents. As reported in earlier studies (Herrero 1985, Herrero and Higgins 1995), almost all serious or fatal injuries inflicted by black bears involved possible or actual predatory attacks by males. Although data were limited, predatory incidents tended to last 10–30 minutes, further suggesting the intent and persistence of the bear (Herrero 1985, Herrero and Higgins 1995). Female black bears rarely attack when startled and in defense of young (Herrero 1985), as confirmed by the total absence of such incidents in the B.C. database. Males have a different adaptive strategy than females, perhaps taking more chances to acquire the resources needed to fatten and compete with other males (Herrero 1985). People were rarely chosen as prey. In most areas of B.C., large numbers of black bears have co-existed with people without serious or fatal injuries.

42 Adult females with dependent young inflicted most injuries by grizzly bears. These incidents were usually of short duration and occurred when the attacking bear appeared to be startled at close range. This agrees with previous findings regarding the sometimes aggressive defensive behavior of grizzly bear females with young (Herrero 1970a, 1972, 1985). Since grizzly bear hunting in B.C. is structured so that about 2 males are killed for each female, reducing the risk of grizzly bear-inflicted injury through hunting would require increased female harvest, which would probably put populations into decline. While we recorded only 4 serious injuries or fatalities in which a grizzly bear's behavior was thought to be predatory on people, we cannot conclude that predation is more likely in black bears because B.C. has approximately 12 times as many black bears as grizzly bears. In the 1 predatory grizzly bear incident where the bear's gender was known, it was male.

43 Given the number of people and bears in B.C., the number of injuries is a very small fraction of the total number of times bears and people interact in B.C.

Management Implications
44 Current management policies and actions regarding bear hunting in B.C. do not appear to be responsible for increasing numbers of injuries inflicted by bears; however, this possibility cannot be completely rejected, especially with regard to grizzly bear-inflicted injuries. We suggest more in-depth studies to better understand the complex relationships between grizzly bear and human densities, human food attractant management, and hunting intensity.

45 Assuming that increases in injuries are primarily related to increases in various human activities in grizzly bear habitat, management of bear attack risk should focus on people's behavior in bear habitat. Improved food and garbage management practices decrease the risk of bear-inflicted injuries and should be encouraged, using laws and their enforcement if necessary (Herrero 1985, Gunther 1994). There are science-based strategies for decreasing the risk of surprise encounters with grizzly bears and deterring potentially predatory attacks by either bear species (Herrero 1985, Herrero and Higgins 1995).

46 In a few incidents involving both species of bears, the bear was starving or diseased. This suggests that food stress or disease occasionally may predispose a few bears to attacks on people. This is not typical, however, because years of bear-food crop failure often result in bear depredation problems, especially for black bears, but only seldom in human injury (Herrero 1985). Managers may want to consider removing bears that have significantly less than normal fat reserves or diseased animals should they be captured as a result of displaying unusual aggression toward people. However, in most incidents, including predatory ones, the attacking bear appeared to be healthy and of normal body weight.

47 Educational and interpretive efforts aimed at decreasing risk of bear attack should focus on individuals and groups at risk, particularly ungulate hunters, hikers, campers, forest industry workers, geologists, and oil and gas industry employees. Worker's compensation regulations in B.C. require bear safety training for persons working in bear habitat. Such programs could be expanded to include other risk groups. B.C. Forest Service and other government divisions have produced good-quality videos and pamphlets explaining safety in bear country. There is understanding of how people's behavior can avoid or deter most potential bear attacks (Herrero 1985). Red pepper spray (with capsaicin as the active ingredient) appears to be an effective deterrent for most aggressive grizzly bears (Herrero and Higgins 1998). For people trained in using firearms to shoot erratically moving targets and where firearms are legal and feasible to carry, they can offer a significant, but not complete, degree of safety. Trails and public facilities can be located to minimize the risk of sudden confrontations between people and grizzly bears (Herrero et al. 1986). This approach has been used extensively in B.C. provincial parks (McCrory et al. 1989). The final responsibility for safety in bear country should come from a partnership between land and wildlife management agencies and individuals.

Acknowledgements
Our sincere thanks to the many conservation officers and other B.C. Fish and Wildlife and Provincial Parks employees who assisted in data collection. Special thanks to M. Austin of B.C. Fish and Wildlife for extraordinary help in data collection. Thanks to D. Poll and M. Brunell of Parks Canada, Calgary, for assisting us with injury and visitor use data in B.C.'s national parks.

308   DESIGNS FOR DISCIPLINES

LITERATURE CITED

Gniadek, S.J., and K.C. Kendall. 1998. A summary of bear management in Glacier
National Park, 1960-1994. Ursus 10:155-159.

Gunther, K.A. 1994. Bear management in Yellowstone National Park, 1960-93.
International Conference on Bear Research and Management 9:549-560.

Herrero, S. 1970a. Human injury inflicted by grizzly bears. Science 170:593-598.

———. 1970b. Grizzly bear and man: Past, present, but future? BioScience 20:1148-
1153.

———. 1972. Aspects of evolution and adaptation in American black bears (Ursus
americanus Pallas) and brown and grizzly bears (U arctos Linne) of North
America. Pages 221-231 in S. Herrero, editor. Bears: their biology and
management. International Union for the Conservation of Nature, Morges,
Switzerland.

———. 1985. Bear attacks: their causes and avoidance. Nick Lyons Books, New
York, New York, USA.

———. 1989. The role of learning in some fatal grizzly bear attacks on people.
Pages 9-14 in M. Bronley, ed. Bear-people conflicts. Proceedings of a
Symposium on Management Strategies, Yellowknife, Northwest Territories,
Canada.

———, and S. Fleck. 1990. Injury to people inflicted by black, grizzly or polar bears:
Recent trends and new insights. International Conference on Bear Research
and Management 8: 25-32.

———, and A. Higgins. 1995. Fatal injuries inflicted to people by black bear. Pages
75-82 in J. Auger and H.L. Black, eds. Proceedings of the Fifth Western Black
Bear Workshop, Brigham Young University Press, Provo, Utah, USA.

———, and ———. 1998. Field use of capsicum spray as a bear deterrent. Ursus
10:533-537.

———, W. McCrory, and B. Pelchat. 1986. Using grizzly bear habitat evaluations to
locate trails and campsites in Kananaskis Provincial Park. International
Conference on Bear Research and Management 6:187-193.

Martinka, C.J. 1982. Rationale and options for management in grizzly bear
sanctuaries. Transactions of the North American Wildlife and Natural
Resources Conference 47:470-475.

McCrory, W., S. Herrero, and G. Jones. 1989. A program to minimize conflicts
between grizzly bears and people in British Columbia's provincial parks.
Page 93-98 in M. Bromley, editor. Bear-people conflicts—Proceedings of a
Symposium on Management Strategies. Northwest Territories Department
of Renewable Resources, Yellowknife, Northwest Territories, Canada.

Middaugh, J.P. 1987. Human injury from bear attacks in Alaska, 1900-1985. Alaska
Medicine 29:121-126.

Miller, S., and V.L. Tutterow. 1999. Characteristics of nonsport mortalities to brown
and black bears and human injuries from bears in Alaska. Ursus 11:239-252.

Moment, G.B. 1968. Bears: The need for a new sanity in wildlife conservation. BioScience 18:1105–1108.

_____. 1969. Bears and conservation: Realities and recommendations. BioScience 19:1019–1020.

Shelton, J.G. 1994. Bear encounter survival guide. James Gary Shelton, Hagensborg, British Columbia, Canada.

Thommasen, H.V., G. Shelton, and A.W. Trites. 1994. Bear maulings in British Columbia. British Columbia Medical Journal 36:745–748.

Tough, S.C., and J.C. Butt. 1993. A review of fatal bear maulings in Alberta, Canada. American Journal of Forensic Medicine and Pathology 14:22–27.

U.S. Fish and Wildlife Service. 1997. Grizzly bear recovery in the Bitterroot Ecosystem. Draft Environmental Impact Statement, U.S. Fish and Wildlife Service, Missoula, Montana, USA.

Zar, J.H. 1984. Biostatistical analysis. Second edition. Prentice-Hall Inc., Englewood Cliffs, New Jersey, USA.

DAVID HAMER

The Effect of Light Intensity, Heat, and Herbicide on Photosynthesis

Abstract: Spinach chloroplasts were extracted to determine the effect of light intensity, heat, and herbicide on photosynthesis. The rate of disappearance of the blue dye, DCPIP, which is transformed to a colourless form during the process of photosynthesis, was used to measure the rate of photosynthesis. Photosynthesis initially increased with increasing light intensity, but eventually approached a plateau, suggesting saturation. Placing chloroplast suspension in a boiling-water bath for 10 minutes prior to the experiment did not have a conclusive effect, whereas the herbicide DCMU effectively stopped photosynthesis.

Introduction

1   Photosynthesis is the process whereby living things convert solar energy into high-energy sugar. With the exception of those relatively uncommon bacteria that carry out chemosynthesis, it is the green plants and other photosynthetic organisms that produce the energy-rich molecules (the food) that directly or indirectly support the remaining forms of life on earth.

2   Studies have shown that photosynthesis can occur under very low light conditions. For instance, phytoplankton photosynthesize under snow and ice, where light intensity is as little as 0.5% of incident radiation (Wetzel 1983, p. 371). As light intensity increases, the rate of photosynthesis increases proportionately, but only to a point: an upper limit is expected if the enzymes of the chloroplast become saturated with light, electrons, or substrate molecules in the manner shown by enzymes generally when they become saturated with substrate (Campbell and Reece 2002, p. 99).

3   Studies also indicate that photosynthesis should be impaired or stopped if placing chloroplasts in a boiling water bath denatures the enzymes or other proteins of the chloroplast (Campbell and Reece 2002, p. 78). Similarly, an herbicide such as 3-(3,4-dichlorophenyl)-1,1-dimethylurea (DCMU) is expected to impair photosynthesis.

4   The primary objective of this study was to determine the effect of light intensity on the rate of photosynthesis in spinach chloroplasts. I hypothesized that photosynthesis would increase with increasing light intensity, but that this increase would begin to level off at higher light intensities. A secondary objective was to measure the effects of heat and the herbicide DCMU on this activity. I hypothesized that heat and DCMU would prevent photosynthesis from occurring.

Methods

Extraction of Chloroplasts
5   Spinach leaf blades (60 g) were homogenized with 100 mL cold buffer (tris pH 7.8 in 0.4 M sucrose) in a chilled blender at top speed for 30 s. The resulting slurry was filtered through cheesecloth, and the filtrate was centrifuged for 7 min. The supernatant was discarded and the pellet, containing the chloroplasts, was resuspended in 100 mL cold buffer and stored in an ice bath. The chloroplast suspension was diluted with additional buffer to an absorbance of 0.8 using a Spectronic 20 spectrophotometer at 620 nm with buffer as the reference solution.

Measuring Photosynthesis
6   The blue dye 2,6-dichlorophenol indophenol (DCPIP) was used to measure the rate of photosynthesis. This blue dye becomes

colourless when exposed to the chemical reactions of photosynthesis (Harrison 1989). Thus, I used a spectrophotometer to determine the rate at which the blue dye was transformed to its colourless form, and assumed that the rate of loss of blue colour would be proportional to, and thus a valid index of, the rate of photosynthesis.

7   Four beakers were placed 15, 30, 60 and 120 cm from a 100 W incandescent bulb such that they did not shade each other. The overhead lights were turned off while the experiments were in progress. Nine test tubes were prepared by pipetting 4.0 mL of buffer and 2.0 mL chloroplast suspension to all tubes except control tube #1 ("DCPIP only") which contained 2 extra mL of buffer and no chloroplast, and experimental tube #8 ("boiled"), which contained 2 mL of chloroplast suspension previously placed in a boiling water bath for 10 minutes.

8   The tubes were run in three sets. Set one consisted of control tubes #1 (DCPIP, no chloroplast) and #2 (chloroplast, no DCPIP). The spectrophotometer was calibrated to zero absorbance with tube #2 (to control for the opacity of the chloroplast suspension). At time zero, two drops of DCPIP were added to tube #1, and the tube was carefully inverted twice to ensure thorough mixing of the DCPIP with the tube contents. The absorbance was read at 620 nm, and the tube then was placed 30 cm from the light. The absorbance of tube #2 was read at time=30 s, and then tube #2 also was placed 30 cm from the light. Absorbance subsequently was read at one-minute intervals for five minutes (thus, tube #1 was read on each full-minute, and tube #2 was read on each half-minute). Between readings the tubes were kept in the beaker 30 cm from the light.

9   Set two consisted of tubes #3–#6 placed 15, 30, 60, and 120 cm from the light, respectively. At 15-second intervals, DCPIP was added to each tube as above, and absorbance was read at 1-minute intervals for 5 minutes (i.e., tube #3 was read on each full-minute; tube #4, 15 s after each full-minute; tube #5, on each half-minute; and tube #6, 45 s after each full-minute).

10   Set three consisted of tubes #7–#9 handled in the same manner (readings at 20-s intervals), except that tube #7 was placed in an

aluminum-foil sheath with foil lid and kept 30 cm from the light (removed from the foil only for absorbance readings), tube #8 contained the "boiled" chloroplast suspension, and tube #9 contained 2 drops of DCMU.

Data Analysis

11 Absorbance was plotted over time for each tube, and the slope of each graph was calculated. If the data were not linear, the slope at the steepest part of the curve was calculated (i.e., the tangent at time zero, or instantaneous initial rate). The absolute values of the slopes were used (the graphs had zero or negative slopes because the blue dye becomes colourless, and thus absorbance falls, as photosynthesis continues). These positive values, representing the rate of disappearance of blue dye, were used as my index of the rate of photosynthesis. An index of light intensity was calculated as $1/D^2$ ($1/m^2$) where D = distance of the tube from the light source.

12 No replicates were run, but results from other class members were shared to ensure that data conformed to class averages. My results for tube #7 were inconsistent with class data, and were replaced with data obtained by Student Lab Group A2.

Results

13 Table 1 presents the absolute values of the slopes of the graphs of absorbance over time (Figure 1) for tubes #1–#9. Control tubes #1 and #2 both showed no change in absorbance over time, supporting the validity of the experimental procedure. The rate of photosynthesis initially increased rapidly with increasing light intensity, but then levelled off at higher light intensities, suggesting a plateau in the response (Figure 2).

14 Heating the chloroplast suspension prior to the 5-minute run with DCPIP (tube #8) reduced photosynthesis by 21% compared to tube #4 which contained normal chloroplast and was placed the same 30 cm from the light source (Table 1). The herbicide DCMU almost completely inhibited photosynthesis (Table 1).

Table 1. Rate of DCPIP dye reduction in test tubes #1–#9. Values are the absolute values of the slopes of the absorbance versus time graphs of Figure 1.

Test tube	Distance from light source (cm)	Light intensity $(1/m^2)$	Rate of loss of blue colour (change in absorbance/min)
#1 DCPIP only	30	11	0.00
#2 chloroplast, no DCPIP	30	11	0.00 [1]
#3	15	44	0.36
#4	30	11	0.22
#5	60	2.8	0.09
#6	120	0.7	0.03
#7 foil sheath	30	(foil)	0.01 [2]
#8 "boiled"	30	11	0.15
#9 DCMU	30	11	0.02

1 Test #2 was the reference tube used to calibrate the spectrophotometer to zero absorbance
2 Data from Student Lab Group A2.

Figure 1. Absorbance versus time graphs for tubes #1–#9. The graph of test tube #2 lies on the x-axis.

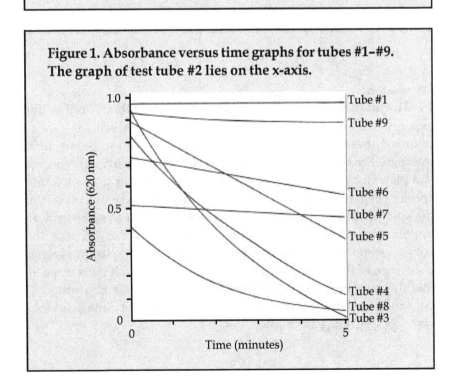

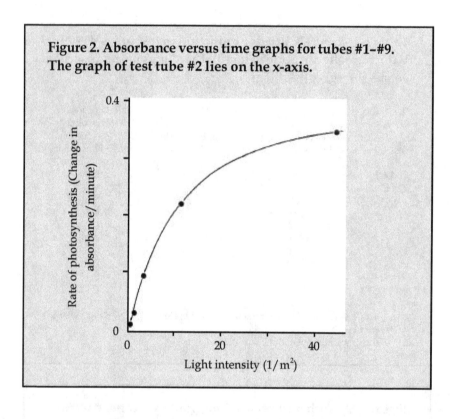

Figure 2. Absorbance versus time graphs for tubes #1–#9.
The graph of test tube #2 lies on the x-axis.

Discussion

15 The rate of photosynthesis did not increase without limit in this
experiment. Figure 2 suggests a plateau above which the rate of
photosynthesis would not increase regardless of increasing light
intensity. The rate of photosynthesis rises to a plateau in many species;
this plateau can occur at very low light intensities in shade-tolerant
species (Begon et al. 1990, p. 82). Evidently, the enzyme systems in
the spinach chloroplasts were becoming saturated at some critical,
limiting step. A rate-determining step could possibly occur at the
enzyme responsible for the splitting of water, or in the electron-carrier
molecules of the electron-transfer chain. Alternatively, it is possible
that the pigments of the chloroplast, responsible for absorption of
light and transfer of this energy to the next reactions of photosynthesis,
were approaching saturation.

16 Excess heat from the incandescent light source could be an alternative explanation for the plateau in my rate of photosynthesis. The 100-W lamp was located only 15 cm from tube #3, and the heat from this incandescent bulb could have inhibited photosynthesis. However, this explanation seems unlikely, given that the rate of photosynthesis was essentially set in the first minute of the experiment (see Figure 1), and given that one minute seems too short for significant heating of the test tube contents to occur. Nevertheless, replacement of the incandescent bulb with a cooler light source could improve the experimental procedure.

17 The tube placed in the aluminium-foil sheath showed a photosynthetic rate slightly greater than zero. This result is not unexpected given that the tube was removed from the foil six times (at one-minute intervals) in order to obtain its absorbance readings. In other words, this procedure approaches, but certainly does not achieve, zero-light conditions.

18 The placement of tube #8's chloroplast suspension in a boiling water bath prior to the experiment did not appear to effectively inhibit photosynthesis. A comparable result was found by some, but not all, student groups. It is possible that 10 minutes was insufficient time for the contents of tube #8 to reach a temperature that would cause much denaturation. This could explain the variable results within the class. Because some students likely left their tubes in the bath longer than others, this may have led to varying degrees of denaturation.

19 Two drops of the herbicide DCMU effectively inhibited photosynthesis. Because the concentration of the DCMU was unknown, the effectiveness of this herbicide is only qualitatively suggested by the experiment. An experiment using a range of known concentrations of DCMU could provide more information on the effect of this chemical on photosynthesis.

20 Results for tube #7 were obtained from another student. In my results, the absorbance of tube #7 showed first a rise and then, after 3 min, a drop in absorbance. This was attributed to experimental error: because DCPIP was added in the blue form, the dye could be transformed into its *less-blue* form (hence, lower absorbance), but it is unreasonable to expect that it could be changed to a *more-blue* product with higher absorbance. Most likely, I incompletely mixed the DCPIP with test-tube contents at time zero, resulting in a falsely low absorbance until the dye eventually spread through the tube, causing the absorbance to rise midway through the 5-minute run.

REFERENCES

Begon M, Harper JL, Townsend CR. 1990. Ecology: individuals, populations and communities, 2nd ed. Oxford: Blackwell Scientific Publications. 945 p.

Campbell NA, Reece JB. 2002. Biology, 6th ed. San Francisco: Benjamin Cummings. 1247 p.

Harrison RP. 1989. Electron flow in photosynthesis. In: Peifer RW, editor. Tested studies for laboratory teaching, Volume 10: proceedings; 10th Workshop/ Conference of the Association for Biology Laboratory Education. p. 43–58.

Wetzel RG. 1983. Limnology, 2nd ed. Philadelphia: Saunders College Publishing. 767 p.

Revising and Proofreading

I see but one rule: to be clear. If I am not clear, all my world crumbles to nothing.

—Stendhal

One of the clichés in the field of composition is that good papers are not written, they are rewritten. Like a number of other clichés, this one is reliable. However carefully you may have worked throughout the term to develop a first-rate paper, your work will benefit from revision and correction. This means that it is advantageous to complete a draft well before the paper is due. With a completed draft in hand, you can begin to reconsider your work and look for ways in which it might be improved. In actuality, of course, completing a draft ahead of time is not easy: it is a feat that calls for organization and commitment throughout the term. In order to foster a situation in which revising and proofreading are possible, we advise instructors and students to plan ahead and set aside time from the beginning of term. One way for instructors to do this is to incorporate revising and proofreading into their course syllabus, devoting entire classes to these activities near the end of a semester.

In the discussion that follows, we frame revising and proofreading as peer activities, but students should also consider these practices on their own and enlist the help of instructors or tutors where permissible. Indeed, the peer approach is simply one facet of a larger process of rewriting. Granted, peer evaluation sometimes makes students feel uncomfortable. You may not like the idea of commenting on another student's work and be even less comfortable about having another student comment on yours. Nevertheless, the peer approach can turn revising and proofreading into mutually rewarding exercises, presenting opportunities to improve both your paper and someone else's. If your class adopts the peer model, be prepared to offer and receive *constructive* criticism, and remember that this kind of exchange exemplifies the critical thinking skills that colleges and universities are supposed to promote. Moreover, comments can take the form of questions rather than brisk or forceful demands. In such cases, readers and writers can learn together.

The guidelines presented here involve a minimum of two sessions, each consisting of approximately one and a half hours. Thus, if your class meets for a three-hour block once a week, the entire block could be devoted to peer evaluation. If your class meets for two one-and-a-half hour blocks per week, the two proofreading sessions could be held on separate days. The entire process should be initiated by an exchange of papers, so that all students have someone else's paper in front of them. Try to ensure that you are handing over a *complete* draft, including the References or Works Cited; otherwise, you will compromise the help that your partner will be able to provide.

SESSION ONE: REVISING

People who are unfamiliar with rewriting tend to focus on small, local details—on spelling, sentence structure, the fine points of documentation, and so on. All of these considerations are important, but we're not there yet. Genuine *revision* involves a reconsideration of even more important elements that relate to the overall structure of a paper. This macrostructure involves such things as the ongoing use of a particular prestige abstraction, the wording of a thesis claim, the order of sections within the core of a paper, and paragraph structure. *The Allyn & Bacon Handbook* (1994) has this to say about revision:

> Accomplished writers expect to revise. They know that good revision reaches deep; that it is not, for the most part, about cosmetic changes (a word scratched out here, another added there) but about fundamental changes and redirections that help you discover meaning. Above all, readers expect *clarity* of ideas in your writing. When you revise, you rethink and you clarify; you will serve your own interests and your reader's by committing yourself to meaningful revision. (p. 99)

In the first session, try to avoid tinkering. Think big. The steps we've outlined correspond to the introduction–core–conclusion pattern often found in the humanities and social sciences. If you are reading a scientific report, you will need to reconceptualize the steps.

Step One: Reviewing the Introduction

❑ Highlight the border between the introduction and the core.

❑ Identify the rhetorical gestures in the introduction and comment on their placement and effectiveness. Pay special attention to the placement and clarity of the thesis claim. (Use the margins to make your comments.)

Step Two: Reviewing the Core

❑ As you proceed through the core of the essay, highlight borders between main points or main sections. Are the borders clear? Are there clear subheadings? If not, should there be?

❑ In light of the thesis, comment on the relevance of each main section.

❑ Consider paragraph structure within each of the main sections – do paragraphs have adequate guiding sentences and low-level detail? (Once again, use the margins to make your comments.)

Step Three: Reviewing the Conclusion

❑ Does the conclusion clearly recap the argument? If not, should it? What other typical concluding features does it contain?

Step Four: Discussion

❑ Gathering in groups of two or three, allow about ten minutes to discuss each paper. Where there is uncertainty about the merit of some suggestions, instructors might offer their opinion.

SESSION TWO: PROOFREADING

In this second session, pairings can remain the same or be changed. Whether or not you have the same paper in front of you, now is the time to dwell on details. If revising involves significant structural adjustments, proofreading descends more to the level of microstructure. The recommended procedure is relatively simple: once again, we will read papers from beginning to end, but this time watch for the following:

❑ Are sentences clear and grammatically correct? Are there spelling errors?

❑ Is the level of discourse appropriate for a college- or university-level research paper? (Is the language too colloquial? Do you see effective or ineffective examples of nominalization?)

❑ Does the paper provide adequate documentation? (Is it using an effective mix of direct reference, indirect reference, paraphrase, and quotation? Do you see effective examples of the envelope technique? Do the citations in the essay clearly correspond to a list of references at the end of the paper? Does the paper consistently and correctly employ a particular style of documentation?)

❑ Gathering in groups of two or three, again allow about ten minutes to discuss each paper. Remember that instructors might be willing to offer suggestions.

IDEA FOR FURTHER STUDY

1. To prepare for peer proofreading, it might be helpful for all members of the class to review a sample draft paper. Instructors will likely have material that could be used for this purpose.

CHAPTER REFERENCE

The Allyn and Bacon handbook, 2nd ed. (1994). L.J. Rosen, & L. Behrens (Eds.). Boston: Allyn & Bacon.

Index